The French Revolution and the English Novel

The French Revolution and the English Novel

By

Allene Gregory, Ph.D.

KENNIKAT PRESS, INC./PORT WASHINGTON, N. Y.

THE FRENCH REVOLUTION AND THE ENGLISH NOVEL

Copyright 1915 by Allene Gregory
Reissued in 1965 by Kennikat Press

Library of Congress Catalog Card No: 65-27134

PREFACE

THIS study in the *tendenz* novel was begun with the idea of paralleling Dr. Hancock's book, *The French Revolution and the English Poets*,[1] in furnishing detailed consideration of a literary form which Professor Dowden's general treatment of the period necessarily presents in outline merely.[2]

It is evident, however, that the Revolutionary poets and the Revolutionary novelists must rest their claims to our interest on different grounds. A discussion of Wordsworth, Coleridge, Byron, and Shelley needs no justification. But it must be confessed that the novelists we are about to consider can not escape the condemnation of mediocrity. There is scarcely one of them whose work has lived through the intervening century. What, then, shall be our apology for invading their well-merited obscurity?

There are two distinct uses of the historical methods in the study of literature. The first, admirably exemplified in Dr. Hancock's book, resorts to a study of the age and its antecedents

[1] Albert Elmer Hancock, *The French Revolution and the English Poets*, Henry Holt and Company, New York, 1899.

[2] Edward Dowden, *The French Revolution and English Literature*, New York, 1897.

for the purpose of gaining a truer appreciation of the work of authors whose greatness unquestionably warrants such effort. But there is a second use of the historical method with a somewhat different end in view. Some special phase of literature may be studied as a means of gaining insight into the intellectual and (in a broad sense) spiritual life of a historical period.

Considered with the second purpose in mind, there was perhaps no literary form in Revolutionary England so significant as these same obscure novels. The poets of the time were for the most part only temporarily in sympathy with the Revolution. They were carried away by the tide of popular enthusiasm, rather than expressing their own mature convictions. The drama, in some respects the most social of literary forms, was perhaps the least adapted to express so complex and reflective a philosophy. Moreover, censorship, official and popular, during the reaction served to eliminate from the drama the later developments of Revolutionism.

All this might seem to indicate that the proper field for a study of political philosophy is in the distinctively doctrinary and propaganda writings of the time rather than in any form of imaginative literature. But Revolutionism was more than an academic philosophy. It was a social religion, in the sense that it was to many men their "serious reaction to life as a whole."

Perhaps every faith by which men have lived

Preface

is better than it seems from a mere analytical statement of its doctrines. Such formulations have often much the same relation to reality that an architect's plans and specifications have to the house they represent. The plans afford a general view and valuable information as to the soundness of construction; one would certainly wish to see them before making the house one's own. But the architect's plans do not tell the whole story. Those who have lived in the house may know that certain rooms that appear dark and ill ventilated are really little used; that tortuous passages have been made easy by custom; and that the main rooms afford scope for a life of dignity and service.

The real value of the novels we are about to consider lies not in their intrinsic merit, but in the illustrations they offer of the practise of Revolutionary ethics, as conceived by its sympathizers and its opponents. They are a frank give-and-take criticism disguised as fiction; and in the course of them many values are made plain which the metaphysical treatises somewhat obscured. After reading *Political Justice* one wonders how any man whose sense of fact was not entirely atrophied could have taken Revolutionism seriously. In the novels one sees how sensible and kindly men like Holcroft and Bage made of it an eminently livable philosophy.

I wish to express here my gratitude to Professor Chester N. Greenough of Harvard University, under whose scholarly guidance it was my good fortune to pursue this subject in post graduate study, and who at every stage of the work has given me most generous assistance. My thanks are due also to Professor William Allan Neilson and Professor Irving Babbitt, to whose kindness I am indebted for much valuable suggestion and criticism.

A. G.

ROCKFORD COLLEGE,
    September, 1914.

CONTENTS

	PAGE
INTRODUCTION—ON THE ECONOMIC INTERPRETATION OF LITERATURE	1

CHAPTER I

BACKGROUNDS	15
Section 1. Background of Events	15
Section 2. The Background of Ideas	30

CHAPTER II

A REPRESENTATIVE REVOLUTIONIST	49
Thomas Holcroft	49

CHAPTER III

REVOLUTIONARY PHILOSOPHERS	86
Section 1. William Godwin	86
Section 2. The Young Shelley	120

CHAPTER IV

SOME OPPONENTS OF THE REVOLUTIONARY PHILOSOPHERS	134

CHAPTER V

REVOLUTIONISTS AND RADICALS OF VARIOUS DEGREES 161

    Section 1. The Novels of Robert Bage . 161

    Section 2. Novels Representing Miscellaneous Novelists 180

CHAPTER VI

SOME TYPICAL LADY NOVELISTS OF THE REVOLUTION 191

    Section 1. Mrs. Elizabeth Inchbald . 191

    Section 2. Mrs. Amelia Alderson Opie . 203

    Section 3. Mrs. Charlotte Smith . . 213

    Section 4. Some Other Lady Novelists . 222

CHAPTER VII

THE FRENCH REVOLUTION AND THE RIGHTS OF WOMAN 231

    Section 1. Introduction and Background 231

    Section 2. Mary Wollstonecraft . . 239

    Section 3. Some other "Rights of Women" Novels 259

CHAPTER VIII

SOME OTHER FORMS OF LITERATURE AFFECTED BY THE FRENCH REVOLUTION . . . 270

    Section 1. The Poets 270

    Section 2. The Drama 283

CHAPTER IX

CONCLUSIONS 293

APPENDIX TO CHAPTER VIII, SECTION 2 . 309
    Lists of Plays Showing Tendencies Influenced by the French Revolution . . 309

BIBLIOGRAPHY 321

INDEX 333

The French Revolution and the English Novel

INTRODUCTION

ON THE ECONOMIC INTERPRETATION OF LITERATURE

PREFACED to Dr. Hancock's discussion of *The French Revolution and the English Poets* there is a very suggestive "Note" by Professor Gates urging the extension of the historical method in criticism. Under this term he includes not merely an observation of the continuous development of literary forms from age to age, but also a study of the historical events in any given period as an aid to the appreciation of its literature. This conception of the relation of historical fact to literary form and content is so sound that it will bear a fuller development.

Our own time has seen a remarkable change of emphasis in the writing and teaching of history. The lists of battles, treaties, coronations, and other epoch marking events which formerly constituted the historian's stock in trade are now relegated to the background as secondary causes. The modern basis for the study of a historical period is its economic and social conditions.

According to this depersonalized method even the Great Man theory of progress, beloved of literary historians for its dramatic value, has been consigned to oblivion as unscientific. Carlyle has been vanquished by Dry-as-dust.

When we have fairly made up our minds, however, to accept the Dismal Science in lieu of Hero Worship, our sacrifice to intellectual honesty is more than rewarded. The Dismal Science is not unlike that Loathly Ladie whom Gawain submitted to wed and found a princess in disguise. The sociological and economic method proves a revealer of new values and unguessed relationships whereby both the complexity and the significance of human events are enormously enhanced.

If history has been so incalculably the gainer through the adoption of this method, the question naturally occurs whether literature may not share in the results of this new accession of fact? One would fancy this suggestion a matter of course, requiring no comment or justification, but for the fact that it is so seldom acted upon except in the most superficial manner.

It may be objected that all this is included in the accepted historical interpretation of literature. That is not altogether true. Economic changes and the resulting social conditions do undoubtedly affect literature through the medium of the general events which they cause. But they also affect literature in a more direct way, without the intervention of those political occurrences which determine the chronology of historical epochs.

Indeed, this chronological vagueness forms one of the chief difficulties in the economic interpretation of literature. Industrial developments and the shifting of the balance of power from one economic class to another take place so gradually as a rule that the fixing of dates becomes a matter, not of "when" but of "how much." This prevents the obvious coincidences of dates that are so satisfying and convincing to an order-loving mind, and makes the whole matter of determining the limits of periods distressingly uncertain. All this is very salutary, however. The student of literature can never be too fully aware that he is dealing with infinitely complex reality. Chronological generalizations made in a pigeon-holing spirit are valueless. They are merely matters of convenience, like the imaginary figures one traces among the stars to aid in distinguishing constellations. If they are made a fetish and allowed to destroy the sense of continuity they may become positively harmful.

If one accepts the economic factor as a basis for generalization tempered by discretion, however, certain periodic coincidences become apparent. An examination of almost any one of the generally recognized movements in literature will show that it was immediately preceded by some economic or industrial change of a significant nature, involving a change in the relative power of the economic groups in the state.

For example, in the fourteenth century the general aristocratic and ecclesiastical tone of literature was broken by a curious little strain of pure democracy. This finds expression in the writings of Langland (especially the *Vision of Piers Plowman*, 1376–1393), and in the records of Wycliffe and his "pore prestes," whose chief contributions to the time were a Bible translation and some very well-organized trades-unions. The historical interpretation of literature contents itself with pointing to the Great Plague (1348), the consequent wage legislation, the preaching of John Ball (1360–1380), and the rebellion under Wat Tyler (1381) as the culminating event. The economic interpreter insists on going back to the common cause behind both events and ideas. During the early part of the fourteenth century there had been a steady rise of the yeoman class, as the villeins were emancipated into a free tenantry. The lords of the manor, frequently in want of cash, were gradually accepting a rent paid in money for their ancient claims to service. It was primarily an ill-advised attempt on the part of the landlords to revive a rent paid in labour that brought about the Peasants' Revolt. The attempt to extort labour rents was the result of the Great Plague and the consequent shortage of labour. But it is to be observed that the event alone would have had little effect but for the gradual class development that preceded it.

Here we have a situation not unlike that in England at the time of the French Revolution: a class is gradually gaining in power and importance when some event occurs (the Plague in one case, and the invention of the power loom in the other), which precipitates a sharp clash of interests. There is a corresponding conflict of ideas, and a sudden prominence given to revolutionary concepts in literature. But in both cases it was a minority report; a side current in literature, and a political movement of revolt that proved abortive.

Again, the history of a social form of literature like the drama offers excellent material for economic discussion. The growth of the market towns and the rise and fall of the Guilds have a very direct bearing upon the development of the miracle and morality plays. As the drama was taken up by a wealthier class, and became the concern of men of leisure and learning, it assumed a different form altogether. The closing of the theatres was brought about by a social crisis directly traceable to economic changes. Restoration Comedy and the heroic plays were class drama; so were Sentimental Comedy and Domestic Tragedy. The transition between them coincides with a decided increase in the power of the merchant and manufacturing classes at the expense of the land-owning aristocracy. This was fundamentally an economic change, although it found expression in a political Revolution

All these observations are superficial and commonplace. But the method which they are intended to suggest is not one of facile generalization, but of careful study of the economic conditions and the intellectual temper of a given period with a view to ascertaining causal relationships.

It would be easy to reduce this method to absurdity by pushing it too far. But no method of literary interpretation is proof against a student without discretion. It is easy to recognize in the literature of any given period certain prevailing ideas and ideals, in spite of individual variations. It is also easy to perceive periodic changes in economic conditions, resulting in changes in the social structure. In order to establish a causal relation it is not necessary to assume that economic situation actually created the idea. We may say that various ideas being present in the national mind, the economic condition is a prime factor in determining which ones shall be emphasized. An age, like an individual, takes up the problems it is ready for; understands what it is capable of understanding; and believes, in general, what it finds to its own advantage to believe. The interests of different economic classes are not the same, however. Consequently there frequently occur sharp conflicts of ideas, reflecting the conflicting interests. It is the ethical and aesthetic standards of the dominant class that prevail, as a rule.

Perhaps at this point it may be well to cite the popular theory known as economic determinism. This is our "economic interpretation" carried to an extreme. We may quote an early and authoritative statement of this conception, by a political and economic thinker the stimulating value of whose writings is in no wise affected by their frequent misinterpretation at the hands of over-enthusiastic followers.

At a certain stage of their development, the material forces of production in society come in conflict with the existing relations in production, or—what is but a legal expression of the same thing—with the property relations within which they had been at work before. From forms of development of the forces of production these relations turn into their fetters. Then comes the period of social revolution. With the change of the economic foundation the entire immense superstructure is more or less rapidly transformed. In considering such transformations the distinction should always be made between the material transformation of the economic conditions of production and distribution which can be determined with the precision of a natural science, and the legal, political, religious, aesthetic, and philosophic—in short, the ideological forms in which men become conscious of the conflict and fight it out. Just as our opinion of an individual is not based on what he thinks of himself, so we cannot judge of such a period of transformation by its own consciousness; on the contrary, this consciousness must rather be explained from the contradictions of material life, from the existing forces of production and the relations of production. No social order ever disappears before all the productive forces for which there are room in it have been developed; and new higher relations of production never appear before the material conditions of their existence have matured in the womb of the old society. Therefore mankind always takes up only such problems as it can solve; since, looking at the matter more closely, we find that the problem itself arises only when the material conditions for its solution exist or are at least in the process of formation.[1]

Protests against the economic interpretation of literature are likely to come from two distinct points of view. The Romantic critic will say that all this is too materialistic; that it destroys the aesthetic and imaginative and spiritual values of literature. The humanist may object that it tends to substitute an over-pragmatistic conception of the development of ideas for the abiding human values; that it makes for a sense of relativity so strong as to destroy certain fine intellectual disciplines.

The latter, as the more serious objection, we may consider first. If it can indeed be shown that an economic interpretation tends to diminish the

[1] Karl Marx, *A Contribution to the Critique of Political Economy*, translated from the German by I. N. Stone, pp. 12–13. Date of publication of the original, 1859.

humane dignity of literature, and place "Law for thing" above "Law for man,"[1] that objection must be conclusive. Certainly that would be true of any extreme or undiscriminating use of the method. In the hands of the humanist himself, however, a full recognition of the economic factor in the *Zeitgeist* may make for a clearer perception of the values that are permanent. After all, it requires an Aristotelian soundness of judgment to profit by a pragmatistic sense of fact.

The Romantic protest may receive a less qualified answer. Nothing that makes for a truer sense of the complexity of life and at the same time has a synthetic value can result otherwise than in an enrichment of the imagination. The imaginative and the spiritual values can be trusted to take care of themselves, to a far greater extent than their defenders are aware. Keats's dictum that "Beauty is truth, truth beauty," is neither "all we know on earth," nor "all we need to know." But if the Romantic critic is convinced of that (and from his fondness for the quotation one might naturally suppose that he endorses it), there is no conceivable reason why he should so carefully guard his cherished conception of "beauty" from the rude contact of facts and ideas. It is really a rather suspicious circumstance when beauty shrinks from honest analysis. This type of protest tends to produce in the critic who is

[1] *Cf.* the discussion of humanism in chapter i. of *Literature and the American College*, by Professor Irving Babbitt.

interested in ideas rather than emotions a not unnatural distrust of Romanticism. It is not fair, however, to misjudge the Romantic ideal because it is defended by Sentimentalists.

Often, however, the Romantic critic meets the economic interpreter half-way. Like the humourist who was so deeply interested in the Civil War that he was willing to sacrifice all his wife's relatives to preserve the Union, our defender of a sacrosanct and incomprehensible beauty cheerfully admits that "tendenz" literature may be interpreted in the light of economic conditions: but hands off from true poetry! Now this is a concession which we can in no wise accept. We must have all or nothing; for if we cannot exercise judgment and discrimination in applying the criticism of fact in really important matters, we had better let it alone altogether.

Moreover, this concession involves a fundamentally false distinction. In the reaction from didacticism and from reform propaganda disguised as literature the very phrase "literature with a purpose" has come to have a damnatory significance. This has its foundation in a very right feeling that the commonplaces of social and personal ethics and the questions of the day are not problems worthy the consideration of universal and abiding art. But in our time this half-truth has been somewhat over-emphasized. When we turn back to the literary criticism of ages artistically greater than our own, we find no such undiscriminating horror of "purpose." Aristotle was not afraid in his great doctrine of Catharsis to assign to the highest of art forms a purpose— to purify the soul. Milton, Dryden, and Pope were frankly didactic. Even Shakespeare, although the profoundness of his moral perception did not admit of expression in convenient aphorisms, was by no means so purposeless as the advocates of "art for art's sake" would have us believe.

The reconciliation of this apparent contradiction lies, of course, in the distinction between a higher and a lower "purpose," between a public spirited interest in such matters as housing reforms and workingmen's insurance laws, and the insight which pierces below the surface maladjustments of the age to the deeper issues involved which are to some extent true for all ages.

It follows from this perception that the Romanticist's condescending permission to interpret "tendenz" literature in the light of economic conditions lays open his very citadel to our attack. Shelley, *par excellence* the poet beloved of Romanticists, is among the writers whom we are about to discuss in his connection with the Industrial Revolution as well as the French Revolution.

In his preface to Francis Thompson's impressionistic *Essay on Shelley*, Mr. Wyndham expresses the idea that this is the sort of appreciation that Shelley himself would have enjoyed. Such a generalization cannot be refuted. But the writer has a private conviction that Francis Thompson's very beautiful little essay is precisely the sort of appreciation that Shelley would have felt as almost insulting. The Shelley that we know, not merely in the poems, but in his prefaces and prose works and in the records of his friends, was rather intensely in earnest about ideas as well as about beauty of form. He submitted quietly to hatred and abuse during his life rather than court success by writing poetry which did not express his unpopular social ideals. One fancies how he would have "enjoyed" being discussed as a perpetual child, no matter how aesthetically the conception was expressed! "Bold foot along the ledges of precipitous dream" is a fine phrase for Shelley; but his own phrase is finer, as well as more complete,

> A nerve o'er which do creep
> The else unfelt oppressions of this earth

Shelley was beyond all doubt a writer with a purpose. In the preface to *Prometheus Unbound*, which he himself considered the greatest of his works, he has left us a frank confession of his "passion for reforming the world," together with a masterly analysis of the very point which we have been discussing—the higher and lower "purpose" in literature.

We have endeavoured to indicate some ways in which the study of the history of literature might be enriched through a closer alliance with the study of economic and industrial conditions, not merely in so far as they are included in the general history of events, but considered as direct influences. We have cited for purposes of comparison an authoritative expression of the doctrine known as economic determinism, which is the extreme form of our suggestion. We have frankly admitted the need of sound judgment in the use of this method if it is to be made a valuable servant subject to the discipline of that true humanism to which the student of literature should unceasingly aspire. Finally, we have considered the Romantic objection that although it may do well enough in the case of an inferior form like "tendenz" literature, the economic interpretation is a profanation when applied to the higher imaginative forms, such as poetry. We have pointed out that the distinction between so-called "tendenz" and didactic literature and the literature of great ideals is not a distinction in kind, but in depth of insight and artistic skill in expression; and that even the most spiritual of Romantic poets submits to our so-called economic interpretation by virtue of his concern with the deeper social maladjustments of his age.

In the following discussion of the "tendenz" novels of Revolutionary England we shall endeavour to illustrate to some extent the practical application of the method here suggested. To a consideration of the English history of French Revolutionary philosophy, and of the stimulus given to English radicalism by the example of France, we shall add some observation of the social maladjustments arising from the Industrial Revolution and their influence on the thought of the time.

For this our treatment must extend somewhat beyond the period of actual Revolutionary events. We may begin our discussion as early as 1780 (the date of Holcroft's first novel) and continue it at least to include the year 1820, the date of the great dramatic poem in which the influences of the French Revolution and the Industrial Revolution converge, Shelley's *Prometheus Unbound*.

CHAPTER I

BACKGROUNDS

SECTION I: BACKGROUND OF EVENTS

ONE of the most striking characteristics of the literature reflecting the French Revolution in England is its apparent inconsistency. In 1789, poets, novelists, and statesmen are touched with a fine glow of enthusiasm for liberty and the sovereignty of the people. A few years pass, and these same ardent friends of the Revolution, all save a few stubborn or courageous souls, have recanted, and are busily engaged in exposing and denouncing the dangerous tendencies of their former doctrines.

It is not sufficient explanation to charge a whole nation with having been over ready to praise something which sober second thought could not approve. A closer analysis shows us that the term "French Revolution" is a misleading one. It should be, "French Revolutions"; for there was a series of them, as different as possible in character. Not merely the course of events but the principles themselves were changed. A man might well approve one without approving all. Perhaps then, it may be well to review briefly the chronology of this extremely complex movement.

France during the reigns of Louis XIV. and Louis XV. was apparently in a flourishing and orderly condition. It was the most brilliant of despotisms. English writers, forced to admit the critical supremacy of their ancient enemy, consoled themselves with complacent references to British liberty and the glories of a constitutional government. But they really accepted the feudalism and oppressions of France as one of the unalterable features of the universe; ordained, perhaps, to furnish Whig orators with perpetual material for eloquent antitheses. The Bourbon régime, however, was on an increasingly unsound basis. In the extreme centralization of the government the nobles had been deprived of their administrative functions, but not of their feudal privileges. These in no wise strengthened their power, and were a source of intense irritation to the nonprivileged classes of the bourgeoisie and the proletariat. Moreover, what was more important, the brilliant court of Versailles was financially unsound. In spite of the complex and oppressive machinery of taxation, extravagance and mismanagement had brought the French government to the verge of bankruptcy. Finally, the brilliant writers of the Enlightenment were furnishing eloquent interpretations of the doctrines of popular sovereignty and political rationalism borrowed largely from England, and calculated most effectively to undermine authority not based on reason.

A corrupt and frivolous court; a government needing money; an angry people; and a Revolutionary philosophy ready to hand: this was the situation that confronted the well-intentioned mediocrity of the young Louis XVI. on his accession to the throne in 1774. The first fifteen years of his reign were a series of blunders in the choice of ministers. After the dismissal of Turgot, sporadic attempts at reform under the sententious Necker alternated with periods of incredible mismanagement under the queen's favourites. By 1783 the *parlements* were growing refractory and demanding the summoning of the almost forgotten States General. The king was forced to submit; and in 1789, after considerable archæological research as to methods of election, the States General met for the first time since 1614.

Serious disagreements as to methods of voting caused the Representatives of the Third Estate to withdraw and declare themselves the Constituent Assembly. By this time the turbulent mobs of Paris were aroused. The Bastile, for centuries the symbol of oppression, was captured by a mob; and the Revolution began to assume a somewhat less academic aspect.

In the midst of increasing popular risings the Constituent Assembly continued serenely to quibble over political metaphysics, and in the course of time produced a Declaration of Rights and a Constitution. These documents, together with the Cahier presented by local assemblies at the opening of the States General, represent the constructive work of the Revolution up to 1791. These Cahiers offered interesting evidence as to the temper of the three Estates. The clergy were the most conservative. They are willing to make some gifts in return for their exemptions, but then expected a grateful nation to reimburse them at once. The nobility, somewhat more liberal, seemed genuinely ready to sacrifice their privileges and co-operate in reforms. The Third Estate (represented, as Burke observed, chiefly by lawyers and small property owners, and thoroughly bourgeoisie in character) sent in Cahiers full of the doctrines of the *Social Contract*, but also distinctly more specific than those of the other two orders in their demands for social and legislative changes.

As might be expected from such an Assembly, the *Declaration of Rights* is full of echoes of Rousseau and Locke. "Ignorance and forgetfulness or contempt of the Rights of Man," says the preamble, "are the sole causes of public miseries and of corruptions of government." But the Constitution itself is curiously conservative. The king is given full executive power and a suspensive veto, property rights are carefully secured, and a property qualification for the suffrage is insisted upon. On the whole, the machinery of government was awkwardly planned, although in the general conception there was much of permanent value. In September, 1791, the Constitution was accepted by the king. In the following month the National Legislative Assembly was elected, according to constitutional provisions.

This marked the first stage of the Revolution. So far, in spite of occasional outbreaks of mob rule, there had been little of which England could not approve. With the exception of a few thinkers of the type of Burke, popular opinion was strongly in favour of the Revolution. Englishmen condoned its faults, seeing in it a triumph of orthodox Whig principles. Even the abolition of titles of nobility (June 19, 1790) was viewed without serious alarm.

The Constituent Assembly had been almost entirely bourgeois. But with the year 1792 the forces which had hitherto been subordinate began to take the lead. The plotting of Louis and the court party, together with the menaces of foreign interference were rapidly making a constitutional monarchy impossible. The Jacobin clubs controlled the elections. The Girondins, who were the most extreme of the philosophic radicals, dominated the Assembly, subject only to the mob in the galleries. The proletariat was taking the Revolution out of the hands of the bourgeoisie.

In June, 1792, the First Coalition was formed against France. The repeated treachery of the king and queen lost them the last remnant of popular favour, and in August they were brought to Paris and imprisoned in the Temple. A demand for a new and more radical constitution brought about the election of a National Convention, which immediately declared France a Republic (September 21, 1792), and promised aid to all nations desiring to overthrow their kings.[1] The loss of trade monopolies through the opening of the Scheldt to unrestricted commerce had already aroused a spirit of hostility in England. This action of the Assembly put an end to all former sympathy with the Revolution. In January, 1793, when the king was tried and executed, Parliament was on the point of declaring war against France. The Assembly forestalled them. From this time until the battle of Waterloo, war between England and France was almost continuous. The treaties were little more than truces.

Events moved rapidly in France for the next three years. The foreign wars, the rebellion in the Vendée, continual fear of a counter revolution, and the even greater danger of mob law made the situation of the party in power a most difficult one. In March, 1793, the Revolutionary Tribunal and the Committee of Public Safety were established, The Terror was resorted to, not as a manifestation of lawlessness, but as a govern-

[1] In the earlier stages of the Revolution the idea of spreading the doctrines of Liberty, Equality, and Fraternity by example and precept took a firm hold of the French imagination. But when the foreign wars began, the propaganda of a general insurrection against kings became a threat, and an officially recognized part of the policy of the Republic.

ment measure necessary to secure authority over a lawless nation. But the guillotine became a general resource of the party in power; and parties changed with alarming rapidity. The Jacobins ousted the Girondins, and they in turn were succeeded by the Hebertists, the Dantonists, and Robespierre. After the execution of Robespierre (July 28, 1794), the Revolutionary Tribunal was reorganized, an amnesty offered the rebellious Vendée, and the Girondins readmitted to the Convention. The Terror was at an end. In the following year the Catholic religion (which had been replaced by the Worship of Reason in 1793, and by the Worship of the Supreme Being in 1794) was reinstated. By October, 1795, France was again under a Constitution. The period of the Revolution, as it is usually considered, was closed.

So far we have observed three distinct stages in the attitude of England towards the French Revolution: (1) 1789 to 1791, general approval of the fall of a despotism. A confident expectation that France would establish a constitutional monarchy on Whig principles. (2) 1792. Rapidly waning confidence in the Revolutionists, as the bourgeoisie lost control and the movement threatened to become genuinely democratic. England further antagonized by her economic interests. (3) 1793 and 1794. The reaction at its height. War was declared. National hatred and class hatred together reached fever heat. These were evil days for the Revolutionists in England.

During the ten years preceding the battle of Waterloo hatred of France and detestation of anything remotely suggesting Revolution or even reform continued unabated. As the power of Bonaparte increased an element of terror was added. England was fighting literally for national life as well as for the world market her increasing manufactures demanded. Never had the feeling of nationality run so high.

The war period from 1795 to 1815 may be said to constitute a fourth period in the history of English Revolutionism. The last stage, from the battle of Waterloo to 1820, was the worst of the reaction, when the stimuli of anger, fear, and patriotism had ceased and a heavy pall of disillusionment and conservatism without ideals seemed to have settled over the whole country.

Such were the five stages of the influence of the French Revolution on popular feeling in England. But a consideration of France alone cannot furnish a sufficient background of events for our discussion of so complex a movement as Revolutionism. Another and greater Revolution was nearing completion in England itself, and it is to this that we must look for the explanation of many elements in the thought of the time.

The eighteenth century found English manufactures under the domestic system; it left them under the factory system. Just what that signifies we can perhaps understand better by comparing any factory town of our own time with

Defoe's description of his trip through Yorkshire in 1724.

> The land [he says] was divided into small enclosures of from two acres to six or seven each, seldom more, every three or four pieces of land having a house belonging to them; hardly a house standing out of speaking distance with another. At every considerable house there was a manufactory. Every clothier keeps one horse at least to carry his manufactures to the market; and every one generally keeps a cow or two, or more, for his family. By this means the small pieces of enclosed land about each house are occupied, for they scarce sow corn enough to feed their poultry. The houses are full of lusty fellows, some at dye-vats, some at looms, others dressing the cloths, the women and children carding and spinning; all being employed, from the youngest to the oldest.[1]

The change in the industrial system came about slowly and inevitably through a succession of great inventions. In 1770 James Hargreave patented the spinning-jenny. In 1771 Arkwright employed a spinning-machine worked by water-power. In 1779 Crompton combined the two. In 1785 Cartwright added the power-loom. Most important of all, in 1769 James Watt took out a patent for his steam-engine, which was used in mining, and later introduced into factories. To these were added a host of minor inventions and

[1] Daniel Defoe, *A Tour Through the Whole Island of Great Britain*. 4 vols. London, 1724–27.

improvements; and by 1790 the great change was fairly complete.

Closely connected with the Industrial Revolution was a similar and practically contemporary change in the agricultural system. As the ownership of land was concentrated in the hands of a decreasing body of proprietors, many men were reduced to the status of wage-earning agricultural labourers and many were driven to seek other employment. Common lands were enclosed, to the great detriment of the cottager class. All this was caused partly by the fact that the small landowning manufacturers, whom Defoe describes, were driven into factories on wages that did not permit of their owning their homes, and partly by the tendency of the growing capitalist class to acquire land for profitable farming on a large scale. Also, in England the ownership of land carried with it a certain social distinction which made it particularly attractive to the social aspirations of the new aristocracy of wealth.

The significance of these profound changes in the economic and social structure of society is hard to estimate. The most obvious result was the enormous increase in wealth that sustained England through the Napoleonic wars (which were themselves brought about partly by the struggle for a world market). The growth of the great fortunes fired the popular imagination, encouraging an increasingly extravagant standard of living. All classes seemed more determined than usual to live just a little beyond their incomes. As a result, the debtors' prisons were full, and the literature of the time was pervaded with denunciations of senseless luxury.

Besides all this, there was real suffering among the dispossessed working-classes. These formed a discontented, unstable class, given to riots, and an easy prey to Revolutionary demagogues. If there was ever any real danger of the doctrines of the French Revolution gaining a following in England, it was through this class and not through the little group of writers and philosophers whose works we are to consider.

Theories of political economy of course adapted themselves to the dominant interests of the time. The *laissez-faire* system was in high favour in this age of individualism. Adam Smith's interpretation of this accommodating doctrine (in *The Wealth of Nations*, 1776) was religiously observed by the parties in power; the right of the individual child of four to sell his labour in open market according to the laws of supply and demand was in no wise interfered with. Consequently the accounts of factory conditions in the Blue Books of the period make somewhat ghastly reading. The prevalence of epidemics among factory populations finally convinced the dominant classes that in self-protection something must be done to remedy conditions. In 1802 the Tories overcame their terror of Revolutionism sufficiently to pass the First Factory Act. But many years passed before Parliament dared venture on anything else in the nature of social reform.

The most fundamental social change growing out of the Industrial Revolution is perhaps less obvious. A shifting of power that had been going on for over a century was suddenly completed; the capitalist, or the mercantile and manufacturing class had superseded the older land-owning aristocracy as the dominant class in the national life. And in every historical period it is the ideas and the ideals of the dominant class in that period that prevail.

Such changes are too subtle and complex to be indicated offhand. We talk glibly enough about the epoch-making changes wrought by the French Revolution in its eight or ten years crowded with the conflicts of parties and ideas. Its dramatic values appeal to the imagination. But who shall estimate the dramatic values of the great silent Revolution whose shadow is over us still?

The remaining topic in our discussion of the background of events brings us once more to the safer ground of definite political occurrences. The eve of the French Revolution found England apparently on the point of securing certain measures of much-needed parliamentary reform. The American war had just closed with the loss of the colonies. It was evident that there had been flagrant mismanagement from beginning to end. In 1783 the Shelburne Ministry was overthrown by an alliance between the Whigs under Fox and the Tory followers of Lord North.

Never [says Green], had the need of a representative reform been more clearly shown than by a coalition which proved how powerless was the force of public opinion to check even the most shameless faction in Parliament, how completely the lessening of the royal influence by the measures of Burke and Rockingham had tended to the profit, not of the people, but of the borough mongers who usurped its representation.[1]

In the same year Pitt proposed a reform in representation. But as the Whig majority had no notion of permitting any reforms to their own disadvantage the bill was thrown out. In 1788 Wilberforce brought in a bill for the abolition of the slave trade. This was promptly defeated by the Liverpool slave merchants. It was evident that there was a strong popular demand for reforms. It was also evident that Parliament was in the hands of those to whose interest it was to prevent reforms. But England had always before been able to bring refractory Parliaments to reason in the long run.

At this juncture, however, the Revolution began in France. Pitt, always liberal, regarded it with decided favour. Burke alone among the prominent Whigs opposed it. But Burke had lost his hold over the House and his eloquent warnings had no effect. His own party went over entirely to Fox, whose sympathies were with the Revolution. This led to the dramatic scene in the House

[1] Green, *Short History of the English People*, p. 421.

which ended the long personal friendship between the two Whig leaders. Events soon brought public opinion to Burke's side again, as we have seen; his *Reflections on the Revolution in France* became one of the most popular books of the time.

The reaction against Revolutionism was so violent that all chance of parliamentary reform was lost for several decades to come. In 1809 Sir Francis Burdett ventured to touch upon the forbidden question. Only fifteen members supported his bill. When a little later he published it in pamphlet form he was promptly committed to the Tower. This ended the discussion of representative reform by Parliament until the period of reaction was past.

Meanwhile, the nation as a whole was by no means so indifferent to the question of Representation as their representatives seemed to be. On the eve of the Revolution there had been started a Society for Constitutional Information,[1] which distributed pamphlets and drew up a program "which included such advanced demands as universal suffrage, equal electoral districts, abolition of property qualifications for members of the Commons, payment of members, and vote by ballot at parliamentary elections."[2] During the Revolutionary enthusiasm of 1790 innumerable

[1] To which, incidentally, most of our Revolutionary novelists belonged. This was the society against whom the Reflections of Burke was particularly directed.
[2] Ogg, *Social Progress in Contemporary Europe*, p. 126.

Jacobin clubs sprang up all over the country, which distributed literature, discussed the most radical reforms, and incidentally did all they could to prepare the country for a Revolution after the model of France. But in 1794 the government had a nervous attack resulting in a fit of persecution. All these noisy little clubs, together with some that were more worthy, were suppressed with a high hand. After this miniature conservative Reign of Terror we hear no more of the English Jacobins.[1]

During the Napoleonic wars the public mind was sufficiently occupied with the national danger; and agitation for parliamentary reform virtually ceased. After 1815, however, the popular demand for reforms broke out again in full force, and again the government began its campaign of suppression. "The *habeas corpus* act," says Dr. Ogg, "was suspended until it became almost a nullity." The climax was reached in the "Peterloo Massacre" of 1819, when a peaceable gathering assembled in St. Peter's Field, Manchester, to discuss questions of parliamentary reform, was attacked by a troop of cavalry and several persons were killed. This was followed in the same year by the infamous Six Acts, "Whereby public meetings for the considerations of grievances was prohibited."

This marked the turning point of the Reaction. After 1820 reform legislation began to be forced

---

[1] *Cf.* account of the trial of Holcroft, in Chapter III.

by public opinion. The nation took up the question of adapting its laws and government to changing conditions where it had been dropped in 1792. The influence of the French Revolution both as a stimulus and as a check to progress may be said to have come to an end.

SECTION 2: THE BACKGROUND OF IDEAS

To give anything like an adequate account of even one of the currents of thought that were stirring the public mind in England previous to the outbreak of the French Revolution would require a volume in itself. To cover the whole field even superficially is of course impossible. What is attempted here is in the nature of an enumeration of headings, indicating the basis for a few generalizations.

There is a tendency in most brief accounts of the literature of this period to speak of the group of ideas which we may include under the title Revolutionism, as having come into England with the writings of Rousseau and the Encyclopaedists, and gained a brief vogue through the popularity of the French Revolution in its early stages. This is not an altogether adequate statement of the case. To supplement it, however, we must go back some distance, to the political philosophies of the preceding century in England. It is Chesterton, I think, who observes that all accounts should begin: "In the beginning God created Heaven and Earth." That is particularly true of all accounts of the historical development of ideas. But we shall be making in all conscience a sufficient deviation from the usual chronology if we take for our genesis the Puritan Revolution instead of Rousseau.

Previous to the Reformation in England the world of political philosophy was a very simple and orderly one. State and Church alike were established upon a principle of unquestioned authority. From serf to emperor, from friar to pope, every one had his foreordained place in the scheme of things, and his recognized superior to whom he owed deference and from whom he received guidance and protection. The keystone of the whole social and ecclesiastical structure was a revealed religion which included the divine right of kings. The recognition of the subordination of the individual to an authority external to himself penetrated every branch of human thought and activity.

The Reformation did not change this conception fundamentally. It was at first merely an attempt to clear away certain deviations from the original revelation. This was especially true of the Anglican Church. So that we may consider the age of absolute authority in England as continuing to the time of the Stuarts.

The old order had made for discipline and

civilization in the ages of violence, but it was inelastic. As the middle classes, the merchants and producers, increased in power they began to find their subordinate place in the established system somewhat irksome. In the early part of the seventeenth century we find such writers as Buchanan, Althusius, and Mariana advancing antimonarchic theories. It was at this time that three significant doctrines appeared in English political controversies: a pre-political state of nature, the contractual origin of society, and the sovereignty of the people. These, it will be observed, involve a fundamentally different basis of thought; government derives its authority from man, instead of from God. Changes, then, even the most radical, may be inexpedient, but cannot be sacrilegious.

This changed concept gained wide acceptance, often where its full import was not perceived. Grotius was affected by it; his contribution to political thought was a formulation of the rights between nations no longer held together by the great bond of unity under the Church. His great work, *De Jure Belli et Pacis*, appeared in 1625, the year Charles I. came to the English throne; which brings us to the eve of the Puritan Revolution.

Under the Commonwealth there were two parties opposing the old doctrine of the divine right, representing two entirely distinct interpretations of the new doctrine of the sovereignty of the people.

(1) The prevailing conception, represented in Parliament chiefly by the Presbyterians, and later by Cromwell, recognized the people in their collective capacity as competent to choose the rulers to whom they will submit. (2) The extreme individualistic conception, represented by the Independents and Levellers, demanded universal suffrage, absolute freedom of speech and opinion, and a government perpetually subject to popular control. It is in this early democratic individualism that we have the true genesis of Revolutionism in England. A contemporary writes of this party in terms that suggest Burke on the French Revolution:

> Though the lawes and customes of the kingdom be never so plain and cleer against their wayes, yet they will not submit but cry out for naturall rights derived from Adam and right reason.[1]

The doctrines of the Levellers were embodied in the "Agreement of the People," framed by the council of the army in 1647. This provided for ratification by the signatures of every individual Englishman, and granted to the government only a delegated authority, subject always to popular recall. Parliament, however, fell into the hands of Cromwell, who had small regard for the Levellers and their doctrines. The Revolution was carried through by the Rump, under furious

[1] Dunning, *Political Theories*, p. 236.

protests from Lilburne and other Independent writers. Democratic individualism disappeared from among the doctrines of English practical politics for more than a century.

Among the political writers of the latter seventeenth century the issue is between authority by divine right and authority derived from the people, not, be it observed, between the principles of authority and individualism. "Milton never favoured universal suffrage and the rule of the numerical majority," says Dunning, " 'Liberty for all and authority for such as were capable' was his creed."[1] Harrington was even less radical; he would rest the supreme authority with those who own most of the property of the community. Algernon Sydney was essentially an aristocrat, modified by the republicanism of classical antiquity. He held that authority must rest upon consent, but his dislike for democracy was manifest.

The leading philosophical opponents to these so-called republicans were Filmer and Hobbes. Filmer's *Patriarchia*[2] takes the extreme stand for divine right, regarding the state as essentially a family, with the king in undisputed paternal supremacy over all subjects. Hobbes, on the

[1] Dunning, *Political Theories*, p. 247.

[2] The *Patriarchia* was not published until 1680. The exact date of writing is difficult to determine; but Filmer died in 1653 and this was probably written some years before the time of his death, so that it is safe to say that the *Patriarchia* antedates Hobbes's *Leviathan*.

other hand, is in the curious position of attempting to justify the old conception with arguments derived from the new. His rationalism was extreme. He begins with a state of nature, *bellum omnium contra omnes*, in which man is antisocial, governed entirely by passions and instincts, with no distinction of right and wrong. Natural right is the right of every man to do that which is necessary for the preservation of his existence. Natural laws are the rules determined by reason as being necessary to self-preservation. These are three: (1) to seek peace and preserve it, (2) to abandon natural liberty in order to secure peace, and (3) to keep covenants made. Hobbes thus arrives at the conclusion that in order to escape from the anarchic wars of the state of nature, men are forced to resign their liberty to a sovereign power. This is not a contract, for the sovereign promises nothing, the only agreement being among the subjects, who have surrendered their liberty by common consent. Starting with the individual bound only by self-interest, Hobbes leaves him with no rights whatever against the state which his self-interest has forced him to constitute.[1]

In the long run, however, Hobbes's philosophy worked against rather than for the absolute monarchy which he intended it to support. He had made too many dangerous admissions. Subsequent thinkers might accept his premises, but they drew their own conclusions.

[1] Hobbes, *Leviathan*, 1651.

In the Restoration the doctrine of divine right in its most extreme form enjoyed a brief triumph; one of the significant features of which was the firm alliance between Church and king. Every effort of the Whigs to liberalize existing institutions was met by the obstinate resistance of the churchmen. Even Hobbes's rationalization of the obscurantist doctrine was condemned. During this period the dissenting bodies among whom the doctrines of individualism had flourished were thoroughly subdued. Henceforth their only political endeavours lay along the lines of securing for themselves religious toleration.

In the Revolution of 1688 it was the doctrine of modified authority that triumphed. The opposition to the last two Stuart kings was led by men of rank and property, having no affinity whatever with the Levellers and Republicans of the earlier Rebellion. The Whig Revolution found its complete philosophical expression in the writings of John Locke (1632–1704). Locke began as Hobbes did, with a hypothetical state of nature. But he rejected Hobbes's conception of the state of universal war. His state of nature is social, though not political; equality, governed by reason and natural law. Even property rights were respected in such a state, as being based upon each man's right to his own labour, and consequently to those things to which he has added his labour. The state of nature is terminated by a social contract, by which men give up their right of executing laws and punishing offences in exchange for protection for life and property. But the power of the sovereign is limited still by the natural rights retained by the individual.

All this adds nothing to the discussion which was not involved in the conceptions of previous philosophers; it is merely a clear formulation of the position adopted by the leaders in the Whig Revolution. The Lockian ideas found popular expression in the writings of Bolingbroke and others.

The next philospher to make any real contribution to political theory was David Hume (1711–1776). Although a Whig himself, Hume did more perhaps than any other writer to undermine the comfortably complete philosophy of modified authority which Locke had made appear so reasonable and the Whigs had accepted so complacently for nearly half a century. Hume adopted Hobbes's view of human nature, and a consistently utilitarian system of ethics. He rejected absolutely the contract theory as a justification for government.

> If the reason be asked [says Hume], of that obedience which we are bound to pay to government, I readily answer, "Because society could not otherwise subsist:" And this answer is clear and intelligible to all mankind. Your answer is, "Because we should keep our word." But besides, that nobody, till trained in a philosophical system, can either comprehend or relish

this answer: Besides this, I say, you find yourself embarrassed, when it is asked, why we are bound to keep our word? Nor can you give any answer, but what would, immediately, without any circuit, have accounted for our obligation to allegiance.[1]

This brings our discussion of political theory down to the middle of the eighteenth century, to the beginning of the French influence. To sum up the situation so far: the old conception of an absolute authority of divine origin has given place to the conception of a modified authority derived from the people in their collective capacity, and rendered morally binding by a social contract. The doctrine of democratic individualism has appeared and been for a time supported by a considerable party among the dissenters; but since its defeat in 1647 it has ceased to be a factor in the dominant political philosophies of the eighteenth century. Finally, the accepted Whig basis of authority has already been attacked by the utilitarian scepticism of Hume.

Before we take up the French philosophers influencing Revolutionism, however, there remains another aspect of English thought which must be considered: the religious philosophies. We have observed how close was the connection between the doctrine of divine right in government and the Church of absolute authority. The

[1] Hume, *Essays, Moral, Political, and Literary* (1741–42). (Ed. London, 1882. Vol. i., p. 455–56.)

Established Church and the Whig government maintain a like similarity. The principle of authority remained, but it was a rationalized authority. Revelation was justified by reason.[1] But this common-sense faith did not succeed in dominating the religious thought of the time quite so completely as the common-sense government did the political thought. An increasing group of churchmen were dissatisfied with a faith in revelation made perfectly rational. What need, they began to ask, of any revelation at all? Natural religion and Deism, influenced by the empiricism of Locke, made rapid headway. In the hands of writers like Shaftesbury, Bolingbroke, Toland, Tindal, and a host of others the Deist controversy became a thing to be reckoned with by orthodox theologians.

Meanwhile, the Establishment, not rational enough to satisfy the Deists, had grown too rational, it seemed, for a very large group of people who demanded of religion something more than a system of ethics. The Wesleyan movement, begun as a reform within the Church, resulted in the establishment of a new sect of dissenters. Methodism was primarily a reaction against a narrow rationalism that was limiting and overdefining the religious life. But the ultimate philosophy of the movement involved a complete break with the principle of authority in the name of religious Individualism. Dr. M'Giffert says

[1] *Cf.*, for example, the sermons of Tillotson and Barrow.

of Methodism: "It meant a transfer of emphasis from the Church as an institution to the personal religious experience of the individual Christian."[1] That is, the cardinal fact in religion was taken to be, not a generally authoritative revelation embodied in an institution, but an emotional crisis in the life of each individual which he took to be a direct and personal revelation. This was an assertion of the rights of individual feeling, as Deism may be said to be an assertion of the right of individual judgment. Such were the main currents of thought during the first half of the eighteenth century. This brings us up to the beginning of the French influence, which is usually identified with the English philosophy of Revolutionism. But be it observed, not one element of importance came into English radical thought through Rousseau and the Encyclopaedists which was not there already. The main doctrines of the Revolution had been familiar to English philosophers since the time of Cromwell at least. But the issue between Authority and Individualism had become somewhat obscured. Authority, in Church and State, was rationalized, and Individualism, forced out of practical politics, was manifesting itself chiefly in the religious world, and in sceptical philosophies.[2]

[1] M'Giffert, *Protestant Thought Before Kant*, p. 163.

[2] The French philosophers whose writings gained the greatest vogue in England were Voltaire and the Encyclopaedists, Rousseau, Holbach, and Helvetius. As these are discussed in some detail by Dr. Hancock, we need do no more than mention them

All this is in no way intended to minimize the part the French philosophers had in stimulating English Revolutionism. If they introduced no new concepts into English thought, they restated the old ones with genius. Rousseau especially exerted an influence in England which it would be hard to overestimate. Never had the doctrines of Sentimental Individualism been so alluringly presented. The state of nature previous to the social contract, which was to Hobbes a state of war and misery, and to Locke a state of mere negative excellence, became in Rousseau's hands the earthly paradise. Deism, which not even the enthusiasm of Shaftesbury could make more than a somewhat chilly hypothesis, became a real faith as interpreted by the Savoyard Vicar. The belief that feeling in itself constitutes virtue was carried to its logical conclusion by this arch Sentimentalist. Julie, St. Preux, Émile, Sophie, and the Rousseau of the *Confessions* became living ideals in the minds of Englishmen who would never have thought of reading a metaphysical discussion of the philosophy of feeling.

But the true reason for connecting the movement in England, which we are discussing, with the French Revolution does not lie in the stimulus which it undoubtedly received from French writers. It was the events of the year 1789 that

---

here. But it may be added, if these influenced English thought, they had themselves been previously influenced by English thought.

removed Revolutionism from the realm of purely speculative philosophy to that of active political propaganda, for the first time since the Commonwealth.

In England there was, as we have seen, a growing social unrest due primarily to economic causes. Philosophies of change and revolution were already familiar to the English mind. The fall of the Bastille was symbolic. It was a tocsin call at whose sound the older democratic individualism, which had not appeared in practical politics since its defeat in 1647, awoke and became a force to be reckoned with by conservative statesmen.

The situation in England was, as we have observed, extremely complex. Issues were not so clear as those in France. A century of rationalizing and sentimentalizing on both sides had obscured the ancient conflict between Authority and Individualism. But, as in the days of Independents and Levellers, it was among the dissenting sects that individualism as a political principle found its readiest acceptance. The intellectual affinity between dissent and Revolutionism was perhaps emphasized by the discontent arising from the legal disabilities still attached to nonconformity. .

The Revolutionists in England were at no time a large or powerful group, although the example afforded them by France and the prevalence of social unrest gave the government some cause to fear that their doctrines might spread and ultimately result in the overthrow of the monarchy.

The most important among the Revolutionists, fortunately for our discussion, used the novel as a vehicle for their propaganda. There are a few, however, who wrote no novels, but whom we must mention for the sake of completeness. Dr. Price, a dissenting preacher, and Joseph Priestley, a philosophical writer of the school of Locke, were among the earliest if not the most radical of the Revolutionists. "In their writings," says Sir Leslie Stephen, "we catch for the first time the true Revolutionary tone."[1] They are, however, important chiefly as they influenced more prominent men.

Thomas Paine possessed the merit of popularizing the doctrines of more intellectual men than himself. It was Paine, not Godwin, nor even Rousseau, whose works were printed in cheap form and read by Jacobin clubs of discontented workingmen. The *Rights of Man* had hundreds of readers where *Political Justice* had one. In the type of audiences which Paine found, ideas linger. Curiously enough, Paine's crude but vigorous denunciations of priesthood and tyranny still find readers in certain circles.

Among the opponents of Revolutionism two deserve especial mention. Burke's writings are

[1] Leslie Stephen, *English Thought in the Eighteenth Century*, vol. ii., p. 252.

too well known to require discussion here. But perhaps the answer to Revolutionism which most influenced thought in the following century was not Burke's *Reflections*, but the theory of population advanced by Malthus. He perceived the absurdity of the theories on which Godwin's belief in the perfectibility of man and the speedy coming of an age of peace were founded. The objections which he raised, that in such an event the population would outgrow the food supply and civilization be overthrown by the mere struggle for existence, continued to trouble social idealists as late, certainly, as the date of Tennyson's second *Locksley Hall*, in spite of the floods of "answers" to Malthus which were written from almost every conceivable standpoint. Perhaps it was too sound Darwinism to be answered except by facts.

Perhaps before we turn to the novels, it may be well to quote in *extenso* a concise and admirably critical statement of the Revolutionary philosophy by a younger contemporary of the novelists whom we are considering. William Hazlitt was not only acquainted with that point of view as it appeared in books, but had the advantage of knowing the authors personally, and hearing their informal discussions of the questions involved. His own attitude is not unsympathetic, although he is writing during the last decade of the Reaction. This summary of the leading doctrines of Revolutionism may furnish a good point of departure for our discussion of its variations at the hands of individual writers.

The opinion of the power of truth to crush error had been gaining ground in this country ever since the Reformation; the immense improvements in natural and mechanical knowledge within the last century had made it appear nearly impossible to limit the discoveries of art and science; as great a revolution (and it was generally supposed as great improvements) had taken place in the theory of the human mind in consequence of Mr. Locke's Essay; and men's attention having been lately forcibly called to many of the evils and abuses existing in society, it seemed as if the present was the era of moral and political improvement, and that as bold discoveries and as large advances towards perfection would shortly be made in these, as had been made in other subjects. That this inference was profound or just, I do not affirm, but it was natural, and strengthened not only by the hopes of the good, but by the sentiments of the most thinking men.

As far as any practical experiment had been tried, the result was not discouraging. Of two revolutions that had taken place, one, that of America, had succeeded, and a more free and equal government had been established, without tumult, civil discord, animosity, or bloodshed, except what had arisen from the interference of the mother country. The other Revolution, that of France, was but begun: but it had at that time displayed none of those alarming features which it afterwards discovered. . . . The pillars of oppression and tyranny seemed to have been overthrown: man was about to shake off the fetters which had bound him in wretchedness and ignorance; and the blessings that were yet in store for him were unseen and incalculable. Hope smiled upon him, and pointed to futurity.

With these feelings and with these encouragements, from the state of the public mind, reasoning men began to inquire what would be the ruling principles of action in a state of society as perfect as we can suppose, or the general diffusion of which would soonest lead to such a state of improvement.

·   ·   ·   ·   ·

In such a state of things (men) believed that wars, bloodshed and national animosities would cease; that peace and good-will would reign among men; and that the feeling of patriotism, necessary as it now is to preserve the independence of states, would die away of itself with national jealousies and antipathies, with ambition, war and foreign conquest. Family attachments would also be weakened or lost in the general principle of benevolence, when every man would be a brother. Exclusive friendships could no longer be formed, because they would interfere with the true claims of justice and humanity, and because it would be no longer necessary to keep alive the stream of the affections by confining them to a particular channel, when they would be continually refreshed, invigorated, and would overflow with the diffusive soul of mutual philanthropy and generous, undivided sympathy with all men. Gratitude to benefactors would be forgotten; but not from a hateful, selfish spirit, or hardened insensibility to kind offices; but because all men would in fact be equally ready to promote one another's welfare, that is, equally benefactors and friends to each other without motives, either of gratitude or of self-interest. Promises, in like manner would be no longer binding or necessary. False honour, false shame, vanity, emulation, and so forth, would upon the same principle give way to other and better motives. It is evident that laws and punishments would cease with the cause that produces them, the commission of crimes. Neither would the distinctions of property subsist in a society where the interests and feelings of all would be more intimately blended than they are at present among members of the same family, or among the dearest friends. Neither the allurements of ease or wealth, nor the dread of punishment would be required to incite to industry, or to prevent fraud or violence, in a state where all would cheerfully labour for the good of all; and where the most refined reason and inflexible justice actuated the whole community. The labour, therefore, requisite to produce the necessaries of life, would be equally divided among the members of such a community, and the remainder of their time would be spent in the pursuit of science, in the cultivation of the noblest arts, and in the most refined and intellectual enjoyments.

However wild and visionary this scheme may appear, it is certain that its greatest fault is in expecting higher things of human nature than it seems at present capable of, and in exacting such a divine or angelic degree of virtue and wisdom, before it can be put in practice, as without a miracle in its favour must for ever prevent its becoming anything more than a harmless dream, a sport of the imagination, or an exercise of the schools.[1]

[1] Hazlitt, *Memoirs of Holcroft* (1816), vol. ii., pp. 123-33.

NOTE.—We shall have occasion to use the term Sentimentalism rather frequently in the course of our discussion. As this is one of the critical terms which each writer uses, apparently, with a slightly different shade of meaning, it may be well to define the sense in which we shall use it here. Sentimentalism is that view of life, and incidentally, that view of art, which regards feeling as an end in itself. Sentimentalism is not a matter of degree of emotion, or even of quality of emotion; it depends entirely upon one's attitude towards one's own emotional experiences. One may value feeling very highly as a stimulus to fine action, or for the powers of insight and imagination which intense emotion sometimes releases, without being in the least a Sentimentalist. The Sentimentalist is interested in his emotional reactions quite apart from their cause or their result. Feeling for him has ceased to be a means or a by-product, and becomes the central fact of his existence. When he feels virtuously, that for him constitutes virtue.

CHAPTER II

A REPRESENTATIVE REVOLUTIONIST

THOMAS HOLCROFT

THE fact that we are considering Revolutionism through the medium of the novel gives us one distinct advantage over more general treatments. We are entitled to give the first place in our discussion to the unfortunately little known Thomas Holcroft rather than to the usually somewhat overemphasized work of Godwin. This arrangement is the more satisfactory one, for several reasons. It is historically correct. Holcroft was the older man, and decidedly the more original and independent thinker of the two. Godwin himself admits this and acknowledged his indebtedness. *Anna St. Ives* was one of the earliest and fullest popular expressions of the Revolutionary philosophy in any form. Certainly it is the earliest and fullest in fiction.

But more important than chronological correctness, Holcroft is a truer representative of Revolutionary idealism. The new philosophy as it appears in his novels is saner, kindlier, and more comprehensible than are the doctrines of the ex-Calvinist Godwin. One can better understand the sudden fervour of devotion with which so many young poets greeted what seemed a new evangel. Since we are to listen in another chapter to the case against Revolutionism, it is well that we may see it first through the medium of a personality so winning as that of Thomas Holcroft.

One of the things which Holcroft always intended and always delayed was the writing of his autobiography. In the last year of his life he actually began the task, and in spite of intense physical suffering managed to dictate the first few chapters. The work was completed after his death, with the aid of his diary and letters, by the friendly hand of William Hazlitt. This is a book which tempts to quotation; it is one of the most vital of biographies. But it is enough for our purpose here to indicate in outline as brief as may be something of the life of this "acquitted felon" (as his opponents called him), this Revolutionary dreamer who was forced into exile for the faith a generation earlier than Shelley.

Holcroft came naturally by his lifelong financial incapacity; his father before him was one of the chronically unsuccessful. During Thomas Holcroft's childhood, he was successively a shoemaker, groom's helper, horse trader, and finally, wandering pedlar. But he was an affectionate father, and gave his son the best education in his power. Thomas was taught to read early; at the age of four his task was "eleven chapters a day in the Old Testament," which he supplemented on his own account with chapmen's books of adventure, borrowed from a friendly 'prentice lad. This was the extent of his father's ability in the way of "book learning." But he added other lessons which the boy never forgot: to endure hardship without complaining, to despise self-indulgence in all forms, to speak the truth, and to fear nothing but cowardice. Thomas had need of such lessons, for his childhood was not an easy one. As the family fortunes declined and both father and mother took to peddling, the little boy trudged after them through town and country, often faint with weariness and hunger. Before he was nine, he tells us, he was "trusted with business more like an adult than a child,"[1] and severely beaten for loitering on errands. The picture is not all dark, however. There were pleasant memories of sunny summer highways, and country fairs and market days where the future comedian listened in rapture to the rude jests of the merry-andrew. Nor was the passion for books quite lost. A stray ballad or so was a very treasure trove. But, he remarks, in naïve apology for his deficiencies: "I had little leisure or opportunity to acquire any knowledge by reading. I was too much pressed by fatigue, hunger, cold, and nakedness." He adds: "There was a single instance in which I travelled a-foot

[1] Hazlitt, *Memoirs of Holcroft*, vol. i., p. 46.

thirty miles in one day. I think this happened before I was ten years of age."[1] But there is no trace of self-pity in the telling. Holcroft never sentimentalizes over his forlorn childhood. He records it all in a matter-of-fact way, with evident pride in his childish powers of endurance, and loving respect for his ne'er-do-well father.

Soon after this, thanks to his indomitable courage and his stunted growth, young Holcroft attained to the summit of his ambitions, the position of stable-boy in a racing stable. Here he was entirely happy. He was not starved, not much overworked, and (after he had thrashed all his young companions) not molested in his eager pursuit of whatever chances of education might fall in his way. Stray copies of Addison and Swift opened new worlds to him. To these were added Bunyan, and Baxter's *Saints' Rest*. Even as a child Holcroft seems to have had a strong religious sense; but he was always singularly free from superstition or sentimentalism. Of this early fondness for devotional books he writes very sensibly: "I was truly well intentioned, but my zeal was too ardent and liable to become dangerous."[2] Holcroft also found time to learn something of music, and finally arranged to get a little desultory schooling in off hours.

At the age of sixteen he left the stables and went to London as an apprentice to his father, who had again taken to shoemaking. His apprenticeship

---

[1] *Memoirs*, vol. i., p. 50. [2] *Ibid.*, vol. i., p. 140.

was not successful, because "his time was idled away in reading," and at "spouting clubs." At the age of twenty, with no prospects whatever, he married very happily. Holcroft's domestic life seems always to have been ideal. After trying several occupations he was on the point of enlisting for the wars in despair, when a friend persuaded him to join a company of strolling actors. This was in the year 1770. Holcroft remained on the stage for many years thereafter, acting chiefly comedy parts, with moderate success. He began to eke out his uncertain income with hack writing, as his family responsibilities increased. Ultimately he withdrew from the stage, and began to earn his living entirely by his pen, writing novels and plays, and translating from the French and German.

Meanwhile his passion for reading continued unabated. Hazlitt's account of his literary tastes is interesting. Here, as in everything else, Holcroft was untainted by Sentimentalism.

Pope always held the highest place in his esteem after Milton, Shakespeare, and Dryden. He used often, in particular to repeat the character of Atticus, which he considered as the finest piece of satire in the language. Moral description, good sense, keen observation, and strong passion, are the qualities which he seems chiefly to have sought in poetry. He had therefore little relish even for the best of our descriptive poets, and often spoke with indifference approaching to contempt of Thomson, Akenside, and others.[1]

[1] *Memoirs*, vol. i., p. 253.

In 1789 Holcroft suffered the greatest grief of his life, the suicide of his only son, to whom he was devotedly attached. Hazlitt says:

The shock Mr. Holcroft received was almost mortal. For three days he could not see his own family, and nothing but the love he bore that family could possibly have prevented him from sinking under his affliction. He seldom went out of his house for a whole year afterwards, and the impression was never completely effaced from his mind.[1]

Possibly the best-known incident in Holcroft's life was his trial for treason, in 1794. The exact nature of his political opinions we shall consider in connection with the novels. For the present it is sufficient to say, that Holcroft was too earnest and independent a thinker to have remained entirely orthodox in his convictions. In the literary circles of London he came in contact with all the newer currents of thought. He became a member of the Society for Constitutional information, and frequently attended their meetings; but not altogether approving of their proceedings, he took little part in the debates. The views expressed in his published works differ somewhat from those held by the majority of the members; in any case, they form rather a system of social ethics than a political manifesto. But when the tide of popular feeling turned against France and the Government became alarmed for

[1] *Memoirs*, vol. ii., p. 102.

its own safety, there was no limit to the spirit of persecution.[1]

The Constitutional Society had no idea that their obscure, semi-metaphysical discussions could possibly attract official attention. But rumours began to be afloat that the Government intended to take action against them. Holcroft was utterly amazed. "Surely," he said, "there have been practises of which I am totally ignorant, or men are running mad."[2] And after the lapse of a century, we cannot but feel that his latter supposition was entirely correct. Official insanity reached its crisis when a warrant was issued naming twelve members of the society[3] on the absurd charge of High Treason. A rumour of this warrant got abroad, was contradicted, began again, and was again contradicted. Holcroft, who was on the point of leaving town, changed his plans at the first report and remained in London, lest he might seem to avoid inquiry. He wrote to his daughter with characteristic firmness:

The charge is so false and absurd it has not once made my heart beat. For my own part, I feel no enmity against those who endeavour thus to injure me; being persuaded that in this, as in all other instances, it is the guilt of ignorance. They think they are doing

[1] We have already quoted (in Chapter I.) Hazlitt's vivid account of this reign of unreason.
[2] *Memoirs*, vol. ii., p. 153.
[3] Holcroft, Horne Tooke, and Thomas Hardy were the best known of these.

their duty: I will continue to do mine, to the very utmost of my power; and on that will cheerfully rest my safety.[1]

Without waiting for an arrest, Holcroft surrendered himself to the Lord Chief Justice, demanding to know the charge against him; a display of dignity and fortitude which considerably embarrassed the authorities, and exposed him to the sneers of the venial press. The paragraph in the *St. James Chronicle* was typical:

Mr. Holcroft, the playwright and performer, pretty well known for the democratical sentiments which he has industriously scattered through the lighter works of literature, such as plays, novels, songs, etc., surrendered himself on Tuesday at Clerkwell Sessions House, requesting to know if he was the person against whom the Grand Jury had found a bill for High Treason. . . . We do not understand that he is in any imminent danger, and suppose from his behaviour he has the idea of obtaining the reputation of a martyr to liberty at an easy rate.

On which Hazlitt comments sarcastically:

What a pleasant kind of government that must be, which is so fond of playing at this mock tragedy of indictments for High Treason, that the danger arising from their prosecution is made a subject of jest and buffoonery even by their own creatures.[2]

[1] *Memoirs*, vol. ii., p. 157.   [2] *Ibid.*, vol. ii., pp. 174, 175.

The story of the trials is too well known to need repetition. After the acquittal of Thomas Hardy and Horne Tooke, the rest were dismissed without trial; which Holcroft regarded as a grave injustice, since, having been publicly accused, he wished to be publicly heard in his own defence. But after examining the report of the evidence against him, one does not wonder that the Government was not anxious to expose its own imbecility by a public trial. Here is a sample of the evidence on which he was indicted:

Mr. Holcroft talked a great deal about Peace, of his being against any violent or coercive means, that were usually resorted to against our fellow creatures; urged the more powerful operation of Philosophy and Reason, to convince man of his errors; that he would disarm his greatest enemy by those means, and oppose his fury.—Spoke also about Truth being powerful; and gave advice to the above effect to the delegates present who all seemed to agree, as no person opposed his arguments. This conversation lasted better than an hour, and we departed.[1] [The witness adds:] Mr. Holcroft was a sort of natural Quaker; but did not believe in the secret impulses of the Spirit, like the Quakers.[1]

Holcroft published the testimony and his defence immediately upon his acquittal. But if he made the Government ridiculous, the Government was amply avenged. Hereafter he was branded

[1] *Memoirs*, vol. ii., pp. 186, 187.

everywhere as an "acquitted felon." He was an object of suspicion to the authorities at home and abroad, so that passports were actually refused him, on the charge of being a spy. Most serious of all to a professional dramatist, the whole force of popular prejudices was turned against his plays; so that finally he was forced to publish under a friend's name in order to gain a hearing. For years he was forced to live abroad because of the general feeling against him in England. It was only at the close of his life that he returned to his own country, where he died, in 1809, surrounded by his children and the friends of his younger days.

It is pleasant to know of such a life. In all the years of struggle against poverty, ill health, and misfortune one finds no records that one would like to forget. When critics declare that his "Frank Henley" and "Hugh Trevor" represent an impossible nobility of character, we hesitate, remembering the stainless gentleman who drew them. All the responsibility of a numerous family with the added care of his aged parents, never forced him to the mean and petty expediencies so common among the literary men who were his friends. Coleridge and Godwin thought the world owed them a living; and they were not backward in asking for it. Holcroft's only remedies for the ills of poverty were self-denial and hard work. He never begged or borrowed. Looking at the long list of his writings, one is amazed at the industry of the man. Malice and persecution brought from him a dignified protest, but no aftermath of complaining. As he formulated his political idealism before the flood-tide of Revolutionary popularity, so he held it unchanged through the long years of the Reaction. When Wordsworth, Coleridge, Southey, and even Blake had recanted, Godwin and Paine had fallen silent, and all the world seemed to have forgotten its vision of Democracy, Thomas Holcroft kept the faith, true knight without fear and without reproach. In his diary for 1798 there is a record of a friend who asked him "whether the universal defection had not made him turn aristocrat?"

I answered [writes Holcroft], that I supposed my principles to be founded in truth, that is, in experience and fact: that I continued to believe in the perfectibility of man, which the blunders and passions of ignorance might apparently delay, but could not prevent; and that the only change of opinion I had undergone was, that political revolutions are not so well calculated to better man's condition as during a certain period I with almost all thinking men in Europe had been led to suppose.[1]

Holcroft was the author of four novels. Two of these, the first and the last, we may pass over lightly. The other two[2] contain the full expression of Holcroft's Revolutionism.

[1] *Memoirs*, vol. iii., p. 65.
[2] *I. e.*, *Anna St. Ives* and *Hugh Trevor*, which we shall consider in their proper chronological order.

Alwyn, or The Gentleman Comedian (1780) was received with only moderate success, and distinctly unfavourable reviews. The plot as a whole is of little interest to us.[1] The political theories are the same as in the later novels, only not so completely worked out. The characters are worth comment, however. Holcroft himself appears as the friend of the hero, under the name of Hilkirk, a young man who betakes himself to the stage on being discharged from his position as a clerk "for his frequenting spouting clubs and billiard rooms": a portrait without vanity, certainly. The other interesting character is Handford, a sentimental gentleman whose ruling passion is the prevention of cruelty to animals. He establishes a humane asylum for cats, and finds himself frightfully imposed on. He says in despair:

I believe all the cats in Christendom are assembled in Oxfordshire. The village where I live has become a constant fair. A fellow has set up the Sign of the Three Blind Kittens, and has the impudence to tell the neighbours that if my whims and my money only hold out for one twelve-month, he will not care a fig for the king.[2]

This not unkindly satire, Hazlitt conjectures, was directed by the author against his friend Ritson's

[1] This novel is summarized by Hazlitt, *Memoirs*, vol. ii., pp. 2 to 13.
[2] *Ibid.*, vol. ii., p. 10.

arguments "on the inhumanity of eating animal food."

Holcroft's second novel, *Anna St. Ives* (1792), is the story of two young persons who do some quixotic things and say a great many foolish ones, bringing down upon themselves a great deal of well-deserved ridicule. But somehow they keep their idealism while they learn wisdom, and in the end win the respect of their keenest opponent.

The action centres in three figures; Anna St. Ives, the daughter of a baronet, a thoughtful girl with a capacity for fine enthusiasms; Coke Clifton, whom her family intend her to marry; and Frank Henley, the son of her father's overseer. As this is a novel in letter form, there are several minor characters with whom they correspond, but the action is simple and there is no sub-plot.

Frank Henley is a young man with a vigorous intellect and a habit of thinking for himself. He has reached certain conclusions as to the relative values in life, with the result that he takes for the vital principle to which all his thought and action is referred, not self-interest, but service. Just what there was in this to bring down such a storm of protest from Holcroft's opponents one is at a loss to discover. It is a point of view about life which found expression many centuries earlier, on a much higher authority than that of Thomas Holcroft. But from the tone of contemporary criticism one would supose that in Frank Henley the author was promulgating a highly original and dangerous doctrine, instead of merely illustrating the practice of a principle that was safely embalmed in the creeds of the orthodox.

Frank Henley's father, a shrewd business man, represents what was apparently the more usual point of view. Frank says of him: "He despises my sense of philanthropy, honour, and that severe probity to which no laws extend. He spurns at the possibility of preferring the good of society to the good of self."[1]

To this basic ideal of a life consecrated to the service of society Henley adds certain conclusions which he has reached as to the way of greatest usefulness. He writes to a friend, with wistful whimsicality:

I half suspect, indeed, that the world is not quite what it ought to be. [Then, more seriously], In order to perform my duty in the world, I ought to understand its manners, its inhabitants, and principally its laws, with the effects which the different legislation of different countries has produced. I believe this to be the most useful kind of knowledge.[2]

Ignorance and prejudice are at the bottom of all the ills of the world, he believes. "How inconstant are the demands and complaints of ignorance! It wishes to tyrannize, yet complains against

[1] *Anna St. Ives*, vol. i., p. 27.
[2] *Ibid.*, vol. i., p. 185. Holcroft had, of course, no conception of social evolution, and the historical method as we understand it. But to break with the past was no part of his intention.

tyranny. . . . There is no tyranny but that of prejudice."[1] Therefore his strongest efforts must always be directed towards the spread of education, and of right ways of thinking. But he recognizes that forms of government have much to do with the progress and happiness of nations. He concludes:

Among the many who have a vague kind of suspicion that things might be better are mingled a few who seem desirous that they should remain as they are. These are the rich; who having plundered the defenseless, say to the hungry who have no food, "Labour for me, and I will return you the tenth of your gain. Shed your blood in my behalf, and while you are young and robust I will allow you just so much as will keep life and soul together. When you are old, and worn out, you may rob, hang, rot, or starve,"—yet let us not complain. Men begin to reason and think aloud; and these things cannot always endure. Let men look around and deny if they can that the present wretched system of each providing for himself instead of the whole for the whole, does not inspire suspicion, fear, and hatred. Well, well!—another century, and then

Henley loves Anna St. Ives, and feels that they two might find the perfect friendship; as Holcroft says finely, "the friendship of marriage. Surely if

[1] *Anna St. Ives*, vol. ii., p. 46.
[2] *Ibid.*, vol. iv., p. 42. Holcroft's having fixed upon *our*-century as the date for the millennium seems like one of life's little ironies.

marriage be not friendship according to the best and highest sense in which that word is used, marriage cannot but be something faulty and vicious."[1] Anna is aware of his love; but she hesitates, because her world would not consider him her equal. Her reasoning here is worth noting as an illustration of Holcroft's attitude on questions of propriety and expediency. He has an excellent sense of proportion; he gives these things their full value, although he declines to make them the centre of his ethical code. Anna reflects:

My family and the world are prejudiced and unjust. I know it. But where is the remedy? Can we work miracles? Will the prejudices vanish at our bidding? . . . Though I earnestly desire to reform, I almost as earnestly wish not unnecessarily to offend the prejudices of mankind. . . . No arguments, I believe, can show me that I have a right to sport with the feelings of my father and friends, even when those feelings are founded in prejudice.[2]

At this juncture Coke Clifton makes his appearance. He is a young man of the world, clever, fascinating, keen of intellect, and with a strong aversion to all forms of cant. He falls in love with Anna's beauty and genuine goodness, but he has no patience with her solemn priggishness. Henley he finds quite intolerable. The letters in which Clifton describes these two young dreamers are brilliant bits of satire. We who criticize

[1] *Anna St. Ives*, vol. i., p. 107.   [2] *Ibid.*, vol. ii., p. 156.

Holcroft's heroes for their tendency to preach need not plume ourselves upon any special discernment; Holcroft was perfectly capable of criticizing himself with greater discernment than his opponents have ever shown. Godwin, having neither imagination nor a sense of humour, caricatures his own theories unconsciously. Holcroft had both, and some knowledge of the world to boot. His faith in the ultimate triumph of social idealism was so deep and serene that he could afford to laugh at the well-meaning tiresomeness of himself and his fellow idealists. Here is a sample of Clifton's account of Frank Henley:

I cannot deny that the pedagogue sometimes surprises me with the novelty of his opinions; but they are extravagant.—The rude pot-companion loquacity of the fellow is highly offensive. He is one of your levellers. Marry! His superior! Who is he? On what proud eminence can he be found? On some Welsh mountain, or the peak of Teneriffe? Certainly not in any of the nether regions. Dispute his prerogative who dare! He derives from Adam; what time the world was hail fellow well met! The savage, the wild man of the woods is his true liberty boy; and the ourang-outang his first cousin. A lord is a merry andrew, a duke a jack-pudding, and a king a tomfool: his name is Man!

Then, as to property, 'tis a tragic farce; 'tis his sovereign pleasure to eat nectarines, grow them who will. Another Alexander he; the world is all his own! Aye, and he will govern it as he best knows how.

He will legislate, dictate, dogmatize, for who so infallible?

As for arguments, it is but ask, and have: a peck at a bidding, and a good double handful over. I own I thought I knew something; but no, I must to my horn-book. Then for a simile, it is a sacrilege; and must be kicked out of the high court of logic! Sarcasm too is an ignoramus, and cannot solve a problem with a pert puppy who can only flash and bounce. The heavy walls of wisdom are not to be battered down with such pop-guns and pellets. He will waste you wind enough to set up twenty millers, in proving an apple is not an egg shell; and that homo is greek for a goose. Duns Scotus was a schoolboy to him.[1]

Suspecting Anna's partiality for Henley, Clifton takes occasion to quarrel with him, challenges him to a duel, and when Henley refuses, calls him a coward and strikes him. Henley answers quietly: "No man can be degraded by another. It must be his own act."[2] Soon after, Henley vindicates his courage by saving Clifton's life at the risk of his own.

Fortified by the knowledge of former conquests, Clifton thinks he need only ask and Anna will be his. To his utter surprise, she answers serenely that he must wait for her decision until they are better acquainted. Clifton, falling into the usual rant on such occasions, offers to "do and dare anything for her sake." This brings a spirited reply:

[1] *Anna St. Ives*, vol. i., p. 116 f.   [2] *Ibid.* vol. iii., p. 42.

Dare you receive a blow, or suffer yourself falsely to be called liar or coward, without seeking revenge, or what honour calls satisfaction? Dare you think the servant that cleans your shoes is your equal, unless not so wise and good a man, and your superior, if wiser or better? Dare you suppose mind has no sex, and that woman is not by nature the inferior of man? Dare you make it the business of your whole life to overturn these prejudices, and to promote among mankind the spirit of universal benevolence which shall render them all equals, all brothers? [Seeing his amazement she adds somewhat sadly], Your opinions and principles are those which the world most highly approves and applauds; mine are what it daily calls impracticable and absurd.[1]

This is perhaps the strangest love scene in all eighteenth century fiction. But there is stranger yet to follow. Appreciating Clifton's real powers of intellect, Anna decides that she will marry him, if by so doing she can influence him to a truer way of thinking. Whereupon she goes to Henley, admits she loves him, then tells him the whole situation, asking him to put aside his own love for her and help her win his rival to the truth they serve! Henley, after a struggle with his own disappointment, promises to help her; telling her, however, that he thinks her sacrifice a useless and mistaken one.

Henley and Anna do their best to win Clifton by argument. He, naturally enough, does not

[1] *Anna St. Ives*, vol. iii., p. 156 f.

enjoy this perpetual sermonizing, and soon becomes disgusted with the idea of marrying Anna. But he determines to be revenged upon her for his humiliation. For purposes of his own, he feigns conversion, and proceeds to carry their argument further than they intend. He thinks:

> She starts at no proposition, however extravagant, if it do but appear to result from any one of her favourite systems, of which she has a good round number. Is it not possible to prove marriage a mere prejudice?—All individual property is evil—marriage makes woman individual property—therefore marriage is evil—Could there be better logic?[1]

Intending to persuade Anna that it is her duty to "be a heroine and defy present necessity," Clifton entraps her with this argument. He puzzles, but cannot convince her. As she writes afterward, she "knew there was an answer, a just and irrefragable one, though she could not immediately find it." Hearing of this brilliant piece of wisdom on Clifton's part, Henley supplies the answer of common sense, dismissing the whole matter as simple absurdity.[2]

Baffled in this, Clifton resorts to force. He has Anna kidnapped and concealed in a country house of his from which Henley rescues her. Clifton is dangerously wounded, and is almost

[1] *Anna St. Ives*, vol. v., p. 20 f. William Godwin takes up this very argument in all seriousness, two years later.

[2] Thereby proving his penetration superior to that of William Godwin, who did not know a *reductio ad absurdum* when he saw it.

insane with remorse for the crimes he has attempted. Anna and Frank visit him, assuring him, not of their forgiveness, but that they have nothing to forgive.

Of what have you been guilty? Why, of ignorance, mistakes of the understanding, false views which you wanted knowledge enough, truth enough to correct. "Exemplary punishment is necessary"—so they say—But no,—'tis exemplary reformation.[1]

Anna and Henley are married, of course. The book ends, not with a sudden conversion of Clifton to the principles of altruism—Holcroft is far too wise for that—but with his acknowledgment of an unwilling respect for these two extraordinary young philosophers. He adds, however, with a touch of his old spirit:

These wise people should leave us fools to wrangle, be wretched, and cut each others throats as we list, without intermeddling; 'tis dangerous. But Truth is a zealot; Wisdom will be crying in the streets; and Folly meeting her seldom fails to deal her a blow.

Hazlitt's criticism of this novel is worth noting:

Of the difficulty of exhibiting the passions under the control of virtue, religion, or any other abstract principle, let those judge who have studied the romances of Richardson.[2] To have made Clarissa a natural character with all her studied attention to

[1] *Anna St. Ives*, vol. vii., p. 250. [2] *Ibid.* vol. vii., p. 120.

prudence, propriety, etc., is the greatest proof of his genius. Yet even she is not free from affectation. In Sir Charles Grandison, he has completely failed.[1]

This is a comparison which we cannot altogether admit. Anna's social idealism is heaven-high above the prudence of Clarissa as a controlling virtue. Moreover, Anna and Frank are much less enhaloed by the author than their prototypes in Richardson. One feels that this is the criticism of the age of Reaction, which worshipped prudence and propriety, but was inclined to think that after all there was something rather commendable in having perfectly undisciplined emotions.[2]

Holcroft's next novel, *Hugh Trevor*, is much less open to the charge of exhibiting virtuous abstractions.[3] In fact, Hazlitt's criticism here is just the reverse. He has to defend Holcroft from the charge of too great realism and satire.

As a political work [he says] it may be considered as a sequel to *Anna St. Ives;* for as that is intended to develop certain general principles by exhibiting imaginary characters, so the latter has a tendency to enforce the same conclusions by depicting the vices

[1] Hazlitt carries this comparison a step further; Clifton and Lovelace are the same being, and are often placed in situations so similar that the resemblance must strike the most cursory reader. *Memoirs of Holcroft*, vol. ii., p. 107.
[2] An age, for instance, that was shocked by the opinions of Shelley, while it revelled in the heroes of Byron.
[3] Published 1794 to 1797.

and distresses which are generated by the existing institutions of society.[1]

The hero is not introduced to us here with principles already formed. We are allowed to watch an ambitious, hot-headed youth, with more aspirations than judgment, while he learns prudence through weary years of disillusionment. But this novel is in no sense a recantation. The social idealism that remains to Hugh Trevor in the end is the same as that of Frank Henley.

Hugh Trevor's childhood is drawn from Holcroft's own.[2] But Trevor is adopted by his wealthy grandfather and sent to Oxford. He takes the university life with exaggerated seriousness; finally falls under the influence of Methodism; is seen at a meeting of that sect by the university authorities, and rusticated for a year in consequence. The account of Methodism as Holcroft saw it is worth quoting.

The want of zeal in prayer and every part of religious duty, the tedious and dull sermons heard in the churches, and what Methodists call preaching themselves and not their Saviour, were the frequent topics of our animadversion.

This was a doctrine most aptly calculated to inflame an imagination like mine, which was ardent and enthusiastic. Besides, it relieved me from a multitude

[1] *Memoirs of Holcroft*, vol. ii., p. 134.
[2] Perhaps there is more of autobiography in this novel than these early incidents. Hugh Trevor's life is not Holcroft's, but the progress of his mental development seems not dissimilar.

of labours. For as I proceeded, Thomas Aquinas and his subtilizing competitors were thrown by in contempt. I had learned divinity by inspiration, and soon believed myself fit for a reformer. The philosopher Aristotle with his dialects and sophisms was exchanged for the philosopher Saint Paul, from whom I learned that he who had saving faith had everything, and he who wanted it was naked of all excellence as a new born babe. To these mysteries which all the initiated allow are suddenly unfolded, descending like lightning by inspiration of the Spirit and illuminating the darkened soul, to these mysteries no man was ever a more combustible kind of convert than myself. I beamed with gospel light. It shone through me. I was the beacon of this latter age; a comet sent to warn the world. I mean, I was all this in my own imagination, which swelled and mounted to the very acme of fanaticism.

But although Trevor refused to recant under pressure, he admits afterwards:

My dereliction of intellect was of short duration, my attachment to Methodism daily declining and at last changing into something like aversion and horror.[1]

During his year of rustication, Trevor goes to London as secretary to the Earl of Idford, a young lord of the minority party, who says he is "a friend to the philosophy of the times, and would have every man measured by the standard of individual merit."

[1] *Hugh Trevor*, vol. i., p. 154.

These liberal sentiments [says Holcroft] were delivered on the first visit he received from the leader of the minority.[1] Anger, self-interest and the desire of revenge had induced him to adopt the same political principles; anger, self-interest, and the desire of revenge had induced him to endeavour after the same elevation of mind. Esop is dead, but his frog and his ox are still to be found.[2]

Holcroft was perfectly aware of the motives affecting many of the followers of the new philosophy. He would have been the first to admit that Lucas's satire was not without foundation in fact.[3] The Earl of Idford and Lord Marauder are close akin.

Trevor also gets an introduction to a bishop, and in a furious fit of orthodoxy, writes a "Defence of the Thirty Nine Articles." The bishop invites him to a dinner (of which Holcroft gives a highly satirical account),[4] and proposes to print this polemic under his own name. Trevor replies by denouncing the amazed bishop, and rushes away, shocked at the discovery that all Churchmen are not worthy of reverence.[5]

[1] Probably Fox.   [2] *Hugh Trevor.*
[3] *Cf.* discussion of *The Infernal Quixote*, in Chapter V. of this thesis.
[4] Holcroft often satirizes the intemperance of his time in the matter of eating and drinking. Simple to the point of austerity in his own tastes, he had a fastidious disgust for all forms of self-indulgence.
[5] As we have quoted Holcroft's account of Methodism, we may also examine his views on orthodoxy, in the person of the

Trevor has written in the Earl's name a series of political letters, opposing the ministry. At about this time the Earl comes to terms with the ministry, deserts the minority party, and wishes Trevor to change the tone of his letters accordingly. Trevor replies indignantly that "when he wrote against the minister it was not against the man," and that he "cannot hold the pen of prostitution." So end all his prospects, and his faith that churchmen and statesmen are *ex officio* superior to common mortals.

There is something so winning in the very blunders of this hot-headed young idealist that one is willing to excuse his melodramatic rant on the ground of his extreme youth. But Holcroft does not spare him. He comments:

And yet, when the Earl had asked me to write letters that were supposed by the public the production of his own pen, I had then no such qualms of conscience. When deceit was not to favour but to counteract my plans, its odious immorality rushed upon me.[1]

bishop. "He was so sternly orthodox as to hold the slightest deviation from Church authority in abhorrence. What he meant by Church authority, or what any rational man can mean, it might be difficult to define; except that Church authority and orthodox opinions are, with each individual, those precise points which that individual makes part of his creed. But as, unfortunately for Church authority, no two individuals ever had or ever can have the same creed, Church authority is like a body in motion. No man can tell where it rests." (*Hugh Trevor*, vol. i., p. 285.)

[1] *Hugh Trevor*, vol. ii., p. 24.

There is in London an old schoolmate of Trevor's named Turl, who was expelled from the University for heresy, and is earning a contented livelihood as an engraver. Trevor rushes to him in an agony of rage and disillusionment, and tells him his plans for exposing Bishop and Earl in a scathing pamphlet. Turl calmly replies, Trevor was a fool to expect a lord to be more honourable or a bishop more righteous than other men. As for exposing them he adds, even if it could be done successfully:

"You will be to blame—you may be better employed."
"What! than in exposing vice?"
"The employment is petty; and what is worse, it is inefficient. Such attacks are apt to deprave both the assailant and the assailed. They begin in anger, continue in falsehood, and end in fury. I repeat, you may be better employed, Mr. Trevor."[1]

Trevor returns to Oxford, but the Earl of Idford manages to have him expelled without a degree. He learns that the bishop has actually published the polemic as his own, without the writer's consent. Trevor alienates the sympathy he might have had in the University at large by his violent and incoherent attack on both Bishop and Earl.

Almost penniless, Trevor returns to London and devotes himself to writing a pamphlet denouncing

[1] *Hugh Trevor*, vol. ii., p. 65.

Earl, Bishop, and University. Turl again tells him he is in the wrong; that his troubles are more than half due to his own ungoverned temper; and finally that it is absurd to blame the whole structure of society because his own individual happiness and ambition have been thwarted.

There are, indeed, wrongs and injustices in the world which men must not pass by in silence. Speak, but speak to the world at large, not to insignificant individuals: Speak in the tone of a benevolent and disinterested heart, not of an inflamed and revengeful imagination. Otherwise you endanger yourself and injure society.[1]

Another friend of Trevor's, Wilmot, after wretched years of hack writing at starvation pay[2] attempts suicide. Turl rescues him from the river, and tries to bring him to a truer sense of the value of life. This passage is so characteristic of Holcroft's philosophy that it is worth quoting entire:

You demand that I should communicate to you a desire of life. Can you have a perception of the essential duties you are fitted to perform, and dare you think of dying?
You have been brooding over your own wrongs, which your distorted fancy has painted as perhaps the most insufferable in the whole circle of existence!

[1] *Hugh Trevor*, vol. ii., p. 172.
[2] Holcroft describes this very vividly. He knew it from experience!

How can you be so blind? Look at the mass of evil by which you are surrounded! What is its origin? Ignorance. Ignorance is the source of all evil; and there is one species of ignorance to which you and men like you have been egregiously subject; ignorance of the true mode of exercising your rare faculties; ignorance of their unbounded power of enjoyment.

You have been persuaded that this power was destroyed by the ridiculous distinction of rich and poor. Oh mad mad world! Monstrous absurdity! Incomprehensible blindness! Look at the rich! In what are they happy? In what do they excel the poor? Not in their greater store of wealth; which is but a source of vice, disease and death; but in a little superiority of knowledge, a trifling advance towards truth. How may this advantage be made general? Not by the indulgence of the desires you have fostered but by retrenching those false wants that you panted to gratify; and thus giving leisure to the poor, or rather, to all mankind, to make the acquirement of knowledge the grand business of life.

Holcroft is quite aware of his opponents' answer to such an ideal, and supplies it: "The self-denial you require is not in the nature of man." To which Turl gives his answer: "The nature of man is senseless jargon. Man is that which he is made by the occurrences to which he is subjected."[1]

Trevor becomes acquainted with an eccentric philanthropist, Mr. Evelyn, who, struck by a certain honesty of intention under all Trevor's

[1] *Hugh Trevor*, vol. ii., 280 f.

mistakes, offers to help him to enter some profession where he can be of real service to society. The passage in which Mr. Evelyn explains his views of the times is more than any other passage, perhaps, an answer to the charge that Holcroft countenanced the violent factions of his time.

It is the moral system of the time [he says], that wants reforming. This cannot be suddenly produced, nor by the effort of any individual; but it may be progressive, and every individual may contribute: though some more powerfully than others. The rich, in proportion as they shall understand their power and their duties, may become peculiarly instrumental; for poverty, by being subjected to continual labour, is necessarily ignorant; and it is well known how dangerous it is for ignorance to turn reformer.

Let the rich therefore awake. They are not, as they have long been taught to suppose themselves, placed beyond the censure of the multitude. It is found that the multitude can think, and have discovered that the use that the wealthy often make of what they call their own is unjust, tyrannous, and destructive. The spirit of inquiry is abroad.—But when they expect to promote peace and order by irritating each other against this or that class of men, however mistaken those men may be, and by disseminating a mutual spirit of acrimony between themselves and their opponents, they act like madmen; and if they do not grow calm, forgiving, and kind, the increasing fury of the mad many will overtake them.[1]

[1] *Hugh Trevor*, vol. iv., p. 93 f.

Holcroft knew, as few literary men did, what forces were stirring below the surface of the social order. He calls upon the so-called upper classes to set their own house in order, lest a worse thing befall them. His faith in the saving power of social idealism was not in spite of his knowledge of the world, but because of it.

Hugh Trevor, having reluctantly consented to accept financial aid from Mr. Evelyn for a time, the question of a profession for him is discussed. The law is decided upon, as giving rare opportunities for serving society by uprightness. Trevor accordingly goes to London to read law. Gradually he becomes convinced that, however noble and necessary law may be in theory, in practice it is a mass of chicanery. Very regretfully he tells Mr. Evelyn that for him the way of service does not lie in the practice of law.

Mr. Evelyn has a relative, Sir Barnard, who has the disposal of two seats in Parliament. One of these he occupies himself, and the other he gives to some young man who will vote as he does, *i. e.*, in opposition to the ministry. Trevor is, of course, of the minority party from conviction; so he accepts Sir Barnard's offer of a seat and is duly elected. During the pre-election canvassing he finds himself forced into many practices of which he cannot approve. There are no money bribes; but he is expected to make valuable presents to the voters. He develops a considerable gift of oratory, however, and Sir Barnard is delighted with him.

In London, the young M.P. attends a banquet where he meets his old enemies, the Earl of Idford and the Bishop. Idford is worn with dissipation, and the Bishop is aged by his life of self-indulgence and petty intrigues for power. As Trevor looks at them all traces of his old hatred vanish and give place to a deep sadness that these men should have so missed the durable satisfactions in life.

Trevor's career in Parliament comes to an abrupt end. Sir Barnard had opposed the ministry only from pique at being refused a baronetcy. This being granted him he suddenly changes sides, and on Trevor's indignant refusal to follow him, a violent quarrel ensues. Unfortunately, Trevor's patron, Mr. Evelyn, is dead; Sir Barnard has inherited his estate. Trevor had insisted on giving a note for all the money he received. This note comes into the hands of Sir Barnard, who uses it to have Trevor imprisoned for debt. Trevor might plead exemption from arrest, as an M.P., but he feels bound in honour to resign as soon as he can no longer vote as Sir Barnard wishes.

Trevor accepts imprisonment quietly. But help comes from unexpected quarters. A man who has cheated him out of a large sum of money, compelled to an unwilling respect for his principles, makes restitution. Soon after, a legacy makes Trevor comparatively wealthy, and he marries Olivia, one of the most charming of Revolutionary heroines, whose lifelong love for him has woven a thread of romance through this somewhat overserious novel.

By way of criticism we can perhaps do no better than to give Holcroft's own comment on a French review of the book.[1]

Read a criticism in *La Décade Philosophique* on a French translation of *Hugh Trevor*, containing great praise and some pointed blame. The chief articles of the latter are,—that the plan proposed is incomplete, (true), that some of the conversations are too long (true), that my satire on professions is unfounded (false), that I have not put my morality sufficiently into action (false again, the law part excepted), that probability is not quite enough regarded (perhaps not), and that, to make Trevor so suddenly a wealthy man is entirely in the novel style (true; blamable). The following are the concluding remarks: "Malgré ces défauts qu'on peut reprocher, comme nous l'avons vu, à beaucoup de romans, celui-ci mérite assurément d'être distingué par la justesse des observations, la vérité des tableaux et des caractères, le naturel du dialogue, la peinture exacte des mœurs et des ridicules. En un mot, c'est l'ouvrage d'un homme de talent, d'un observateur habile et exercice, d'un ami des mœurs et de la vertu; disons encore d'un écrivain patriote, hardi défenseur des droits sacrés du peuple, et de telles productions sont toujours faites pour être bien accueillies."

Holcroft had to go outside of his own country for a just estimate of his work. The praise of

[1] *Memoirs*, vol. iii., pp. 134 f.

this French critic is well deserved. We are concerned here with novels as an expression of ideas rather than from the standpoint of literary excellence; but it may not be amiss to observe that of all the novels here considered those of Holcroft are the only ones whose obscurity is in any way to be regretted.

For the last of his novels, *The Memoirs of Brian Perdue* (1805), Holcroft has chosen the favourite theme of humanitarian radicals: the evils of the English penal system. In this he shows himself truly a representative Revolutionist, for no other form of social injustice so appealed to imaginations quickened by the new ideas. From *Caleb Williams* to *The Prisoner of Chillon* there was a continuous stream of literature inspired by the wrongs of the criminal and the convict. It might almost be said that the injustice and cruelty of social punishment is a corollary of the Virtuous Outlaw, dear to Sentimentalists. We shall encounter both themes frequently in the fiction under discussion.

Holcroft's novel directed against frequent and indiscriminate capital punishment shows his characteristic moderation. The subject is one on which he as an "acquitted felon" was peculiarly entitled to a hearing. The true source of *Brian Perdue* is not the Sentimentalists' Virtuous Outlaw, but Holcroft's own experience when he was on trial for his life eleven years before.

The purpose and method in *Brian Perdue* are best stated in the author's own words:

Whenever I have undertaken to write a novel I have proposed to myself a specific moral purpose. This purpose,—in the present work [is], to induce all humane and thinking men, such as legislators ought to be and often are, to consider the general and adventitious value of human life, and the moral tendency of penal laws.

To exemplify this doctrine it was necessary that the hero of the fable should offend those laws, that his life should be in jeopardy, and that he should possess not only a strong leaven of virtue, but high powers of mind, such as to induce the heart to shrink at the recollection that such a man might have been legally put to death.[1]

There is little in the development of this theme that merits especial attention. There are significant attacks upon the ruthless and unscrupulous methods of the rising capitalist class; there are some characteristic pleas for tolerance, for forbearance in dealing with those whose opinions seem to us mistaken; for the rest, Holcroft reverts in style to his eighteenth-century models. He digresses in passages of Addisonian reflection, interlarded sometimes with Sterne-like whimsicalities. Now and again he indulges in conscious neo-classical "beauties," or attempts somewhat laboured satire after the manner of Pope.

The reason is not far to seek. Holcroft is writing as an old man, with a meditative detachment impossible in the stirring days that inspired

[1] Holcroft, *Brian Perdue*, Preface, p. i.

his earlier novels. Freed from youthful urgency in defence of a losing cause, he becomes more of a conscious artist in his attitude. Unfortunately for *Brian Perdue*, it is not Holcroft's mannered and mediocre artistry that appeals to us now, but the sincere and gentle personality of the author himself.

We have called Holcroft a representative Revolutionist. But it will be observed how seldom in his works we find specific mention of the Revolutionary philosophies. Once, in *Anna St. Ives*, the hero is seen reading the *Nouvelle Héloïse;* he half apologizes for it, adding, "I think I know what were the author's mistakes."[1] Again, we have Holcroft's own comment on *Political Justice*, that: "The book was written with good intentions, but to be sure nothing could be so foolish."[2] These are the only direct evidences we have of his Revolutionary reading.

This does not mean of course, that Holcroft was not influenced by the new philosophies. His intimate association with the Revolutionists in London literary circles and his connection with the Society for Constitutional Information would insure his being acquainted with all the radical ideas afloat, at second hand, if not from his own reading.

What it may indicate is, that Holcroft's social idealism was less associated in his mind with

[1] *Anna St. Ives*, vol. iv., p. 154.
[2] Paul, *William Godwin*, vol. i., p. 116.

metaphysical conceptions of Reason and Justice or with the political crisis in a neighbouring country than with his intimate knowledge of the social conditions in his own. For Holcroft knew the life of his time at first hand, whatever may have been the case with its philosophies. The profession of actor-dramatist has shown itself a good school of observation since the days of the Mermaid Tavern. And probably no other writer among the Revolutionists knew from personal experience so many layers of society; from the life of a stable boy to the choicest literary circles of London, with a trial for High Treason thrown in!

Holcroft's Revolutionism, then, may be taken as representative, not alone of a small group of closet-philosophers, but of the more vitalizing currents of social idealism which had their source in the social unrests of the time.

CHAPTER III

REVOLUTIONARY PHILOSOPHERS

SECTION I: WILLIAM GODWIN

AMONG our philosophical novelists the second in order of time (and, to my mind, also in order of importance), is William Godwin. As we have already observed, there has been a decided tendency, especially among critics somewhat hostile to political idealism, to regard him as the central figure of the entire movement; an interpretation which greatly simplifies the task of dismissing the Revolutionists as a group of amiable fanatics. If, therefore, the present discussion seem to minimize his originality and underestimate his influence, there will be found no lack of commentators who do him justice.

William Godwin[1] was the son of a dissenting minister, of Cambridgeshire. The account Godwin gives of his father is, as Paul says, "amusing and characteristic."[2] "Aiming at the most scrupulous fairness he succeeds only in giving a very distinct impression that he had but little love for

[1] William Godwin, born 1756, died 1836.
[2] Paul, *William Godwin*, vol. i., p. 7.

his father and no very high opinion of his mental powers."[1] Godwin's early reading consisted principally of books of sermons, the *Pilgrim's Progress*, and the *Pious Deaths of many Godly Children*. In this "hotbed of forced piety" he grew up a precocious, self-conscious child, whose most characteristic features were, as he says himself, "religion and the love of distinction."[2]

Godwin's schooling was regular, and the instruction probably somewhat above the average; but not of a sort to counteract his unwholesome childhood. His principal teacher, by whom he was greatly influenced, was, as he tells us, "a disciple of the supra-Calvinistic opinions of Robert Sandeman."[3] In consequence, we hear later of the boy Godwin being rejected from Homerton Academy on the suspicion of Sandemanian heresy. In 1773 he entered Hoxton College. We have his own account of his interests during the five years he spent there:

During my academical life, and from this time forward, I was indefatigable in my search after truth. I read all the authors of greatest repute for and against the Trinity, original sin, and the most disputed doctrines; but I was not yet of an understanding sufficiently ripe for impartial discussion, and all my inquiries

[1] Paul adds a significant passage from Godwin's account of his mother: "After her husband's death her character became considerably changed; she surrendered herself to the visionary hopes and tormenting fears of the methodistical sect."

[2] Paul, *Godwin*, vol. i., p. 9.   [3] *Ibid.*, vol. i., p. 13.

terminated in Calvinism. I was famous in our college for calm and impassionate discussion. For one whole summer I rose at five and went to bed at midnight, that I might have sufficient time for theology and metaphysics. I formed during this period from reading on all sides a creed upon materialism and immaterialism, liberty and necessity, in which no subsequent improvement of my understanding has been able to produce any variation.[1]

Soon after this began Godwin's friendship with Joseph Fawcett, another young dissenting minister, "one of whose favourite topics was a declamation against the domestic affections, a principle which admirably coincided with the dogmas of Jonathan Edwards, whose works I had read a short time before."[2] It will be remembered that Godwin ranks Joseph Fawcett first among the four oral instructors to whom he acknowledges particular indebtedness; the others being Holcroft, George Dyson, and Samuel Taylor Coleridge.

After a few not altogether successful years as a dissenting minister and tutor, Godwin went to London and became a political writer for the liberal side, contributing regularly to the official organs of Fox and Sheridan. Of the progress of his opinions during these years he has, as usual, left us a careful record. He was always deeply interested in the processes of his own mind.

[1] Paul, *Godwin*, vol. i., p. 15.   [2] *Ibid.* vol. i., p. 17.

In 1782 I believed in the doctrine of Calvin—The *Système de la Nature*, read about the beginning of that year, changed my opinions and made me a Deist. I afterwards veered to Socinianism, in which I was confirmed by Priestley's *Institutes*, in the beginning of 1783. I remember having entertained doubts in 1785, when I corresponded with Priestley. But I was not a complete unbeliever until 1787.[1]

Godwin's life thenceforward was that of the typical London literary man of the period. He attended the Constitutional and Revolutionary societies, was intimate with Holcroft, Coleridge, and Lamb, and acquainted with the rest of the Revolutionary circle. There is hardly a name of literary, philosophical, or theatrical interest that does not appear in his diary.

The publication of *Political Justice* (1793) raised Godwin at once to a position of recognized eminence among the radical thinkers of the time. We shall see (in the next chapter) that the literary opponents of Revolutionism seized upon *Political Justice* as embodying the very essence of the radical heresies, the accepted creed of democratic opinion. But it will be observed that practical statesmen saw more danger in Paine's popular discussions, and Holcroft's gentle appeals to an awakening

[1] Paul, *Godwin*, vol. i., p. 26. "Unbeliever" is not to be taken in an extreme sense here. Godwin later states that he "finds the idea of God so easy, obvious, and irresistible as instantly to convert mystery into reason and contradictions into certainty." As a systematic metaphysician, Godwin never could tolerate any loose ends in his universe.

social sense, than in all the metaphysical subtleties of Godwin. It was not pure chance that Holcroft was brought to trial while Godwin escaped arrest.[1] As a matter of fact, it is a mistake to suppose that *Political Justice* was at any time accepted by the Revolutionists themselves as the true and orthodox presentation of their philosophy. Ample proof of this is afforded by the opinions Godwin quotes in his journal (for March 23, 1793):

Dr. Priestley says my book contains a vast extent of ability—Monarchy and Aristocracy, to be sure, were never so painted before—he admits all my principles, but cannot follow them into all my conclusions—Horne Tooke tells me my book is a bad book, and will do a great deal of harm—Holcroft had previously informed me, that he said the book was written with good intentions, but to be sure nothing could be so foolish.[2]

The latter part of Godwin's life need not detain us. In 1797 he married Mary Wollstonecraft.[3] Within the year she died, leaving two children under his care. By this time Godwin's views on the political injustice of marriage were completely

---

[1] Paul, *Godwin*, vol. i., p. 80. *Political Justice* escaped prosecution because of the expensive form in which it was published. Pitt is said to have observed, when the question was debated in the Privy Council, that "a three guinea book could never do much harm among those who had not three shillings to spare." The wily Pitt was perfectly aware of the distinction between the philosophy of the study and the propaganda of social unrest.

[2] Paul, *Godwin*, vol. i., p. 116.

[3] *Cf.* Chapter VII., Section 2, of this book.

forgotten; he seems to have proposed to half the literary women of his acquaintance before he was finally married by a scheming widow with two children of her own. A son, William Godwin, junior, was soon added to his responsibilities. From this time on, the diary and letters form an ungracious record of financial and domestic difficulties, shabby expediencies, querulous complaints, squabbles with his friends, fading ideals, and increasing literary obscurity. Not Godwin but the young Shelley was to be the Light-bearer of political idealism during the dreary decades of the Reaction.

Such, so far as it need concern us, was the life of William Godwin. A greater contrast to that of his friend Holcroft could hardly be imagined. All his occupations, as student, preacher, tutor, tended to restrict his experience of life and foster his natural tendency to introspection. Surrounded from childhood by an atmosphere of somewhat fussy piety, schooled in metaphysical and theological hairsplitting, there is small wonder that such natural common sense and judgment as he may have had were reduced to a minimum. The traits which he recognized in himself as a child—"religion and a desire for distinction,"—remained the dominant characteristics of the man. His "religion" (by which he probably meant his theological bent; his writings show little trace of any genuine religious sense), appears in the metaphysics of *Political Justice*. The "desire for distinction"—true mark of the egoist—became an introspective self-consciousness that intensified his extreme individualistic philosophy. It is this latter quality that appears most strongly in his novels.

The novels of William Godwin which we shall consider are six in number.[1] The first in time, in merit, and in importance is *Caleb Williams*. This was published in the year following *Political Justice*, when the author, as he himself tells us, was still fully in the spirit of that work. The preface announces it as a novel with a purpose:

It was proposed in the invention of the following work, to comprehend, as far as the progressive nature of a single story would allow, a general review of the modes of domestic and unrecorded despotism by which man becomes the destroyer of man. If the author shall have taught a valuable lesson, without subtracting from the interest and passion by which a performance of this sort ought to be characterized, he will have reason to congratulate himself on the vehicle he has chosen.[2]

[1] *Caleb Williams, or Things as They Are* (1794); *St. Leon* (1799); *Fleetwood, or The New Man of Feeling* (1805); *Mandeville* (1817); *Cloudesley* (1830); and *Deloraine* (1833). Godwin was also the author of a few earlier romances, but they were little known even in his own time. Paul, his biographer, dismisses them with a word, and Meyer omits them altogether from the very comprehensive bibliography appended to his thesis. The plots of two of them are outlined in Fargeau's *Revue des Romans*, vol. i., pp. 284, 285. But they have little significance for our discussion.

[2] *Caleb Williams* (Frederick Warne ed., not dated), p. 1.

The first line strikes a keynote: "My life has for several years been a theatre of calamity. I have been a mark for . . . etc." Before we leave Godwin's novels we shall be very familiar with that mode of introduction. This particular Jeremiad might serve to begin any one of the others equally well. Caleb Williams is of humble birth (a rather unusual circumstance, for our republican friend Godwin likes to write chiefly about people of wealth and title), and has a Rousseauistic education, "free from the usual sources of depravity." He becomes secretary to a Mr. Falkland. Here ensues a characteristic description of a recluse. Williams's curiosity being aroused concerning his employer, a friend obliges him with a hundred pages or so of information. Falkland was, it seems, a young man of great talents and liberal culture (no "child of nature" when we come to the real hero, observe). He outshines a boorish neighbour, Tyrrel, thereby arousing in him implacable hatred. Falkland is warned against Tyrrel by a dying friend, Clare, supposedly a portrait of Godwin's friend Fawcett, but he is unable to avoid continual entanglements with him, culminating in a public insult. Almost immediately afterwards Tyrrel is assassinated. Two of his tenants are accused and hanged. Falkland is completely cleared but lives a recluse ever after, nursing his wounded honour. Here ends Collins's account. Caleb Williams promptly suspects that Falkland's trouble is a guilty conscience. His amateur detective activities culminate when Falkland catches him trying to investigate a mysterious chest. What the chest contained the author takes no trouble to explain, although it seemed important enough to Mr. Colman to furnish the title to the play he based on this story.[1] Like the writers of Gothic romance, Godwin seems to think it enough to concoct a riddle; he owes no answer to his readers. But at all events, Falkland suddenly changes his policy, confesses to Williams, and warns him of the consequences of his curiosity. Falkland's master passion is a desire for the world's approbation. He will go to any lengths to preserve his good name, and he proposes to keep Williams in his power henceforth. After a time, Williams grows nervous and tries to quit Falkland's service. Then we come to the point of the story. Williams discovers that the laws are completely at the service of the powerful, and that the very machinery of justice can be wrested to Falkland's purposes. Falkland accuses him of theft. Williams's protestations of innocence are worthless against a man of Falkland's position. He is imprisoned pending trial.

This gives Godwin an opportunity for describing the English penal system, and he makes the most of it. Here, to my mind, is one of the rare instances in which Godwin's eloquence rings true.

[1] George Colman the Younger, *The Iron Chest*, cf. Chapter IX., Section 2, of this book.

Usually, as we shall see hereafter, he is interested in emotion for its own sake. He taxes himself to invent situations that may give occasion for it. Consequently his elaborate tirades seem to us utterly insincere and wearisome. Here he is talking of actual conditions. He writes as a humane and intelligent observer. And here, without apparent effort, he attains to real power. The philosopher and the novelist are forgotten for the time; the man Godwin writes simply and understandingly of the lives of men in prison. He shows us the squalid room, the "prison dirt that speaks sadness to the heart," the prisoners, innocent and guilty, condemned and untried, herded together, the young prisoners learning their trade from old offenders, the noisy appearance of mirth with ever-present fear beneath, the horror of the slow, monotonous days in lonely cells, and the bitterness that enters into the soul of a man and makes him indeed an enemy of the society that has so fearfully wronged him. Behind the clear and forceful words the moral earnestness of the writer shows plainly. The facts he writes of, of which he has not told the half, have been improved since his day. But when he speaks out against the system he carries us with him not by force of logic but by the great spirit of humanitarianism which belongs to all times.

"Thank God," exclaims the Englishman, "we have no Bastile! Thank God, with us no man can be punished without a crime!" Unthinking wretch! Is that a country of liberty, where thousands languish in dungeons and fetters? Go, go, ignorant fool! and visit the scenes of our prisons! witness their unwholesomeness, their filth, the tyranny of their governors, the misery of their inmates! After that, show me the man shameless enough to triumph, and say, England has no Bastile! . . . I have felt the iron of slavery grating upon my soul. I looked round upon my walls and forward upon the premature death I had too much reason to expect; and I said, "This is society. This is the object, the distribution of justice, which is the end of human reason. For this sages have toiled, and midnight oil has been wasted. This!"[1]

Williams escapes from prison, and after various adventures in eluding a relentless pursuit, falls in with a band of thieves led by a philosophic and loquacious person named Raymond. The philanthropic brigand, a familiar figure in literature ever since the days of Robin Hood, was an especial favourite with the Romanticists. It is worth remarking that Schiller's *Die Räuber* had been translated into English in 1792, just two years before the publication of *Caleb Williams*. It may also be remembered that notes for a treatment of Eugene Aram in that character were found among Godwin's papers.[2] Raymond protects Williams, recognizing in him a victim of tyranny. But Godwin's treatment of the brigand is only half sympathetic. He had no notion of

[1] *Caleb Williams*, p. 80.   [2] Paul, *Godwin*, vol. ii., p. 305.

changing society by isolated individual rebellions, and he believes in an appeal to reason rather than violence.

In one of the brigands Williams makes an enemy who adds an element of personal animosity to the powers of the law in tracking him down. After a prolonged chase, Williams suddenly turns the tables. He boldly accuses Falkland of murder, and they are brought face to face before a court.· There the unexpected happens. Williams's purpose fails on seeing how broken Falkland is, and he declares himself a miserable wretch. Whereupon Falkland confesses his crime, clears Williams, and dismisses him, not to live happily ever after, but to be a prey to remorse.

Such is the story of Caleb Williams, and such, too, is the measure of Godwin as a novelist. He never equalled his first attempt. Most of his later novels are here in germ; situations, ideas, and characters repeat themselves again and again. He searches laboriously for original plots and explains conscientiously in his prefaces. For his was not a facile vein.

Caleb Williams had an immediate success, arousing a storm of conflicting criticism. It was recognized as one of the significant novels of the time. It appeared almost immediately in French and German translations. But there were some dissenting voices. Godwin's friend James Marshall declares "the incidents ill chosen, the characters unnatural, distorted, everything on stilts, the whole uninteresting."[1] Mrs. Inchbald, another intimate friend, herself a novelist, finds it sublimely horrible, captivatingly frightful."[2] Hazlitt (*On English Novelists*) is more discriminating.

There is little knowledge of the world [he says], little variety, neither an eye for the picturesque nor a talent for the humorous in *Caleb Williams;* but you cannot doubt for a moment of the originality of the work and the force of the conception. The impression made upon the reader is the exact measure of the author's genius.[3]

Later commentators are apt to be still more cautious. De Quincey, reviewing Gilfillan's panegyrics on the book, says: "Other men of talent have raised *Caleb Williams* to a station among the first rank of novels, while others, amongst whom I am compelled to class myself, see in it no merit of any kind."[4]

Finally, Sir Leslie Stephen voices the criticism of our own time:

Caleb Williams can still be read without the pressure of a sense of duty. It has lived—tho' in comparative obscurity—for over a century—and must have had some of the seeds of life. Mysterious crimes are always

---

[1] Paul, *Godwin*, vol. ii., p. 90.   [2] *Ibid.*, vol. i., p. 139.
[3] Hazlitt, *Collected Works* (1902), vol. viii., p. 130.
[4] De Quincey, *Biographical Essays* (Fireside ed.), vol. vi., p. 339.

interesting. But given the situation, and shutting our eyes to impossibilities Godwin shows the kind of power manifested by *Political Justice*.[1]

Pressure of public interest aroused by *Caleb Williams*, to some extent forced Godwin to continue his career as a novelist. There is a certain note of hesitancy in the preface to *St. Leon*, however, that suggests that he dimly felt his own limitations.

I was solicited to try my hand again in a work of fiction. I hesitated long. I despaired of finding a topic again so rich of interest and passion. At length, after having passed some years in diffidence and irresolution, I ventured on the task. It struck me that if I could "mix human feelings and passions with incredible situations," I might thus attain a sort of novelty that would conciliate the patience, at least, of some of the severest judges.[2]

The "incredible situation" he has hit upon is nothing less than the possession of the Philosopher's Stone and the Elixir of Life. It is only fair to observe, however, that the subject was in Godwin's time neither so remote from public interest nor so hackneyed as it would be to-day. In the second half of the eighteenth century the "Brotherhood of the Rosy Cross" had been revived, and professed to have the Stone and Elixir in its possession. The exploits of Count Cagliostro who gave himself out as their agent were common talk

[1] Leslie Stephen, *Studies of a Biographer*, vol. iii., p. 121.
[2] *St. Leon*, vol. i., p. 2.

within the memory of Godwin. Further, Godwin was the first of his contemporaries to treat the subject, which had enough life in it to furnish material later for Shelley's *St. Irvine* and Bulwer's *Zanoni, Strange Story,* and a host of others.

Godwin's treatment is, briefly, as follows: Count St. Leon is a youth of great promise. He conducts himself with gallantry in battle, takes a picturesque part at the Field of Cloth of Gold, and proves himself, in short, quite the proper hero for a novel. After a brief whirl of dissipation—also quite the proper thing for a hero—he reforms and marries Marguerite de Damville, supposedly intended for a portrait of Mary Wollstonecraft. Really she is somewhat more lifelike than most of the "exemplary females" who serve as the pegs upon which Godwin hangs his love scenes. The ensuing period of domestic bliss is broken up when St. Leon goes to Paris to put his son in a school—(shades of Émile! what heresy! Could he not afford a tutor?)—and incidentally loses all his fortune at cards. Marguerite arrives at the critical moment to wind up her husband's affairs for him while he indulges in a fit of insanity. The couple moralize exhaustively on the compensations of poverty (Godwin had tried it too often himself to have any delusions as to its advantages), and betake themselves to Switzerland, beloved of Romanticists for its scenery and of Republicans for its government. Here they settle down quite resignedly until their property is destroyed by a storm. Thereupon they are forcibly driven away by the inhabitants. Just why is not clear; but mark the tyranny of even a republican government. They find another home where they enjoy seven years of domestic happiness. Godwin really does these little Swiss Family Robinson scenes very well. His own happy married life had awakened his latent domesticity. He was genuinely fond of children; no man who was not could have written the preface to *Baldwin's Fables*.

To this model family comes a mysterious stranger who imparts to St. Leon the secret of eternal youth and unlimited wealth. He insists that St. Leon must not reveal the process even to his wife. St. Leon perceives that this will mean the end of mutual confidence. Again, the reason is not clear; but the circumstance furnishes opportunity for extended introspective moralizing.

Calamity after calamity follows, because St. Leon seems utterly unable to find a plausible excuse for having money. One becomes exasperated at his inability to construct a good lie. His son leaves him, his wife dies of grief, he is pursued from place to place by the fury of mobs. Finally he settles his daughters on his old estate and starts out alone, a Byronic hero without the fascination of Byron.

He falls into the hands of the Inquisition, escapes, rejuvenates himself, and sets methodically about his favourite project of benefiting mankind.

He decides to finance a famine-stricken Hungarian province. Here follow some very sound economic reflections on gold actual *versus* wealth; did ever alchemist invoke such laws before! It really begins to look as though St. Leon were going to do something interesting at last. But like all Godwin's heroes he is obsessed by the need of a confidential friend. The man he hits upon, Bethlem Gabor, is one whose wrongs have made him an enemy of mankind. Gabor finds St. Leon rather tiresomely priggish (we cannot blame him) and imprisons him. After another long interlude of moralizing St. Leon is freed by his son. This son he really does manage to benefit by giving a dowry to his sweetheart, Pandora, another "beauteous female." Here the book ends; for no particular reason. But we are too much relieved to care for that.

This novel also was a success, although not so decidedly as the first. Godwin's friend Holcroft writes to him:

> You have repeated to me times innumerable the necessity of keeping characters in action and never suffering them to sermonize, yet of this fault *St. Leon* is particularly found guilty by all whom I have heard speak of the work . . . yet men must have arrived at an uncommon degree of wisdom when *St. Leon* shall be no longer read.[1]

I think we are inclined to agree with the first part of Holcroft's criticism at least, although modesty

[1] Paul, *Godwin*, vol. ii., p. 25.

may forbid us to claim for our own age "an uncommon degree of wisdom." For certainly *St. Leon* is no longer read. Hazlitt writes: "*St. Leon* is not equal in plot and groundwork to *Caleb Williams*, tho perhaps superior to it in execution."[1] It "ventures into the preternatural world, and comes nearer the world of common sense." Later, Shelley, on Godwin's saying that writing another novel would kill him, replied in a burst of enthusiasm: "What matter, if we have another *St. Leon!*"[2] But Sir Leslie Stephen calls it "a semi-historical novel, with all manner of improbable adventures and coincidences, which yet contrives to miss the moral."[3] And we are rather inclined to let it go at that.

In *Fleetwood* Godwin tries yet a third type of interest. He says in his preface:

Caleb Williams was a story of very surprising and uncommon events, but which were supposed to be entirely within the laws and established course of nature as she operates in the planet we inhabit. The story of *St. Leon* is in the miraculous class, and its design to "mix human feelings and passions with incredible situations"[4] and thus render them incredible and interesting. The following story consists of such adventures as for the most part have occurred to at least half of the Englishmen now existing who are of the same rank of life as my hero.

[1] Hazlitt, *Collected Works* (1902), vol. viii., p. 131.
[2] Hazlitt, *The English Novel*.
[3] Leslie Stephen, *Studies of a Biographer*, vol. iii., p. 151.
[4] *Fleetwood*, vol. i., p. v.

Fleetwood is educated among the wild scenery of Wales in a manner that Wordsworth would quite approve. He goes to Oxford a perfect young Rousseauist, naturally benevolent and good, and full of "sensibility." He gets some of the bloom knocked off his benevolence in the student life there. His education finished, he goes to Paris for the usual period of dissipation, like St. Leon. Then he looks up an old friend of his father's, M. Ruffigny,—in Switzerland, of course. This M. Ruffigny turns out to be a Republican of the old school, living in a cottage, all virtue and simplicity. He had known Rousseau personally— the only direct mention of him in these novels. This sage gives Fleetwood news of the death of his father. Grief restores him to his original sensibility. M. Ruffigny tells his own story, perhaps as human and enjoyable a bit of narrative as Godwin ever wrote. He was left an orphan in the care of the traditional wicked uncle, who appropriates his property and puts the child into the silk mills in Brussels. The description of the silk mills is to my mind one of the few really fine passages in these novels. Here again, as in the prison passage in *Caleb Williams* Godwin is really interested in a situation for its own sake, not as an excuse for an emotion; he is looking out, not in. Godwin was a man who really loved children, in spite of his dry philosophy. At the very time he was writing this, there were children growing up about him—his own little Mary

Wollstonecraft, and the stepchildren of his adoption. He writes of the children in the mills with a high sincerity and perfect naturalness, for once, too much in earnest to sentimentalize.

Several of the children appeared to me, judging from their size, to be under four years of age. I never saw such children. . . . Some were not tall enough with their little arms to reach the swift; these had stools which they carried in their hands, and mounted when occasion offered. They were all sallow; their muscles flaccid, and their form emaciated.

· · · · · · ·

The child from the moment of his birth is an experimental philosopher: and it is equally necessary for the development of his frame that his thoughts and his body should be free from fetters. But then he cannot earn twelve sous a week. These children were uncouth and ill-grown in every limb, and were stiff and decrepit in their carriage, so as to seem like old men. At four years of age they could earn salt to their bread; but at forty, if it were possible that they should live so long, they could not earn bread to their salt.

· · · · · · ·

But be it so! I know that the earth is the great Bridewell of the universe, where spirits descended from heaven are committed to drudgery and hard labour. Yet I should be glad that our children, up to a certain age were exempt; sufficient is the hardship and subjection of their whole future life; methinks, even Egyptian taskmasters would consent that they should grow up in peace until they had acquired the strength necessary for substantial service.[1]

More than a hundred years have passed since Godwin wrote that passage. Much that seemed to his contemporaries worthy of admiration serve only to amuse or bore us now. But this is modern. To our shame be it said, it might be incorporated as it stands in the next report of the National Committee on Child Labour.

From this mill the child Ruffigny makes his escape, and wanders to Versailles in search of the king—a pathetic little figure that Dickens would have loved. He finds that the king is not as he had fancied, the father of his people. But he attracts the notice of Ambrose Fleetwood, grandfather of our hero, who takes him to England and brings him up as the companion and equal of his own son. Ruffigny makes a fortune, saves his foster-brother from bankruptcy, and retires to his native country to live, as we found him, "a Republican of the old model."

At the news of his father's death, Fleetwood shows his "sensibility," like the typical hero of the period, by an utter absence of restraint and a long tirade against the heartless stoicism of any self-control. Ruffigny accompanies his *protégé* on his return to England, but, finding him again drifting into dissipation, leaves him. This effectively sobers Fleetwood. He retires to Wales and

[1] *Fleetwood*, vol. i., pp. 164–68.

"the pleasures of memory and imagination." But he is lonely: he desires a friend after the Romantic pattern. For, like most egoists, Godwin's heroes bore themselves fearfully when left alone. He goes to London and mingles with literary men. At the age of forty, he meets a delightful family named MacNeil, and falls in love with the youngest daughter, Mary. The others go on a voyage and are lost at sea. Fleetwood marries Mary, whose attractions are enhanced by her grief and "sensibility." He resolves to devote himself to consoling her. But he finds it hard to adjust his old-bachelor ways to even a well-loved young wife. (Query: is this autobiography?) He invites two young kinsmen to visit him. One, Kenrick, is virtuous and lovable; the other, Gifford, is a perfectly conventional stage villain after the model of Iago. The obvious misunderstanding ensues. Gifford contrives to make Fleetwood jealous. He banishes his wife, disinherits his child, and starts divorce proceedings. Mary protests her innocence and vows she will never see Fleetwood again. But matters are cleared up. She forgives him in spite of her vow, he is properly remorseful, "and they all lived happily ever after."

Not a very powerful novel, certainly. Godwin never had the gift of writing of the real doings of real people so as to make them live and hold our interest. Nevertheless, to my mind this is one of the pleasantest of his novels. There is less straining after effect, and there are some really likable people in it; Ruffigny, for instance, and the girl-wife Mary.

In the preface to his next novel, *Mandeville* (1817), Godwin gives as his sources Joanna Baillie's *De Montfort* and *Wieland* by C. B. Brown of Pennsylvania.[1] There is a historical background of the time of Cromwell, but it is handled rather perfunctorily. The story begins with a massacre in Ireland in which Mandeville's parents are killed when he is a child of three. He is saved by his nurse and brought up in the desolate seacoast manor of a misanthropic invalid uncle. Mandeville's tutor is a bigoted Presbyterian clergyman who trains him in the fear of the Lord and implacable hatred of the Catholic Church. Godwin writes of the horrors of theology from experience. The dark childhood of the little Mandeville, "who never was a boy," is drawn with a masterly stroke. Godwin is a thorough believer in environment as an influence in the formation of character. He misses no detail contributing to the gloomy consistency at which he aims. This novel is really a study in abnormal psychology.

The Reverend Hilkiah's nagging severity crushes the natural self-confidence of his pupil, producing in its place a rankling self-conscious pride. The one bright spot in Mandeville's life is a visit from his sister who is growing up in a happier environment. After a time young Man-

[1] Preface to *Mandeville*, p. ix; *De Montfort*, pub. 1798.

deville is sent to school. Here the results of his abnormal childhood and unfortunate disposition appear. His egoism is intense. Behind a morose and repellent manner festers a morbid self-consciousness. He is obsessed with a desire for admiration. A schoolmate, Clifford, wins easily the popularity Mandeville longs for, and he hates him with a jealous intensity. He sees the unreasonableness of this with painful clearness; but his hatred becomes a mania. Accidents increase it. Mandeville is falsely accused of having an anti-royalist book in his possession. Clifford presides at his trial. Later, at the university Mandeville is promised a secretaryship to a royalist leader only to find that the place had previously been assigned to Clifford.

Mandeville retires from the Cause. To his diseased imagination it seems that he is permanently disgraced. A fit of madness ensues. He is nursed to health by his sister who tries to reconcile him to Clifford. Clifford does all in his power to humble himself and appease Mandeville. But circumstances continually throw them together and Mandeville cannot endure seeing the admiration his rival wins. It soon appears that Clifford is betrothed to Mandeville's sister. The rest of the book is a melancholy record of mania. The climax is reached when with the acuteness of a deranged mind Mandeville discovers that his own bride is related to Clifford. His violent reproaches cause her death; he goes in search of

Clifford and finds him at her grave. They fight, and both are killed.

So ends a sombre, powerful, tedious novel. The character of Mandeville is developed with painfully minute consistency. But we feel that the author has no right to trouble us with the psychology of such a person on any terms. The method is introspection carried beyond the verge of sanity. It needs the light touch of a Meredith to anatomize an egoist; even then it is not a pleasant picture.

Strange to say, this novel found a warm admirer in no less a person than Shelley. He writes:

> It is of that irresistible and overwhelming kind that the mind in its influence is like a cloud borne by an impetuous wind. In style and strength of expression *Mandeville* is wonderfully great, and the energy and sweetness of its sentiments can scarcely be equalled.[1]

Though Godwin's last two novels are passed over by most commentators as mere pot-boilers, I must confess that I see in them no falling off. But as the others have been discussed in considerable detail, perhaps these two may be somewhat more briefly treated.

The preface to *Cloudsley* gives a rather fanciful statement of its origin:

> When I wrote *Caleb Williams* I considered it as in some measure a paraphrase on the story of Bluebeard

[1] Leslie Stephen, *Studies of a Biographer*, vol. iii., pp. 138-39.

by Charles Perrault. The present publication may in the same sense be denominated a paraphrase on the old ballad of the Children in the Wood.[1]

At first sight it suggests rather a paraphrase on the Arabian Nights' Entertainment, or on a Chinese "nest of boxes"; a story within a story within a story, and all in the first person until one forgets which "I" is supposed to be speaking.

Briefly, the plot is as follows: Meadows, son of poor parents, becomes a sailor, is abandoned in Russia, incurs the enmity of the powers there by falling in love in the wrong place, is banished, and comes home looking for employment. Lord Richard Danvers engages his services for a dangerous mission, with the following confession: Richard was a younger son; his elder brother was killed in a duel, leaving his wife in Richard's care. She dies at the birth of her son. Richard appropriates the estate, giving the child, Julian, to an accomplice named Cloudsley to be brought up in obscurity. Richard marries and has four children. But the children die one after another of a mysterious curse. Richard is troubled by his guilty conscience. Meanwhile Cloudsley has taken Julian to Italy and brought him up as his own son. But Cloudsley too is troubled with remorse. He goes to England to remonstrate with Richard. Julian in his father's absence quite innocently falls in with a company of ban-

[1] *Cloudsley*, vol. i., p. iv.

ditti. (Once more our old friend the philosophic brigand appears.) These accidentally kill Cloudsley on his return.

The mission Lord Danvers assigns to Meadows is to go in search of Julian and bring him to England to restore him to his estate. Meadows arrives in Italy just in time to save Julian from being executed with the brigands and brings him back in triumph. Lord Danvers abdicates in his favour. Meadows is retained as confidential adviser.

The last of Godwin's novels, *Deloraine* is allied in its general scheme to the first. It is the story of a murder and a long and fantastic flight from the law. Deloraine is a brilliant young nobleman. After some years of ideal married life his wife dies and his only daughter, Catherine, goes to live with friends on the continent. Deloraine falls in love a second time, with a young woman—I beg her pardon, a "female of exquisite sensibility" —who has been crossed in love. Her accepted lover William was lost at sea. Deloraine falls in love with her melancholy, and she marries him to please her parents. He becomes very unhappy because his wife does not return his love.

William, the lost lover, was not dead after all. He appears most inopportunely in search of Margaret. Finding them together, Deloraine in a fit of insane jealousy shoots William. Margaret dies of shock (or more properly, of the author's desire to get her out of the story), and Deloraine accompanied by his devoted daughter begins a long flight from justice. Here too the arm of the law is reinforced by personal vindictiveness. A friend of William's dedicates himself to avenging the murder. The chase leads them all over Europe, into an abandoned castle on the Rhine in true Gothic romance style, ending only when Deloraine in despair returns to England to give himself up. This Catherine prevents by going to their pursuer and appealing to his reason and magnanimity. This device is as successful as it was in *Caleb Williams*. Deloraine is permitted to retire with his daughter to live in contented obscurity.

Whatever was the secret of the success of these novels whose road to oblivion was beset by so many contradictory estimates, it certainly was not Godwin's ability to tell a story. His plots are poorly constructed and worse managed. Godwin is in his literary ideas a Sentimentalist; he is interested in feeling for its own sake. He seems laboriously to invent a situation merely as a peg on which to hang an emotional paroxysm. We are perfectly ready to be interested in a novel of psychology rather than of incident, if the author chooses; but even on those terms we feel that the motivation is inadequate, the emotion insincere, and the psychology unsound. Godwin's style, however, we can praise with a clear conscience. It is clear, direct, easy to read; simple, yet with a sustained dignity of manner; the style of a logician rather than of an artist.

In recalling these six novels, one is struck by a certain similarity of impression. The theme, in spite of Godwin's conscious efforts not to repeat himself, does not vary greatly. It has been defined by some of his commentators as "Man, the enemy of man," or, "The Victim of Society." I prefer to call it "The Sentimental Individualist," or, "The Egoist." The type-hero is usually a man of considerable talents, all the advantages of birth and breeding, and a disposition of Rousseauistic benevolence. Like all egoists, he is totally dependent on the approbation of his world. This takes two forms; a craving for general admiration, and the need of a very exclusive and exacting type of friendship. This latter he speaks of always from the standpoint of the one receiving, not of the one giving. Usually he passes through a period of ideal married life. *Caleb Williams* is the exception, of course, being written under the influence of the ideas in *Political Justice*. But the next novel is frankly a recantation of Godwin's earlier attitude towards domestic life. Before *St. Leon* was written, he had married Mary Wollstonecraft and learned a great many things. Godwin's characters are all more or less lay figures, with the possible exception of the type-hero; but women compare very favourably with the men in point of reality. They are all tiresomely good and monotonously beautiful, but occasionally they show considerable force of character. St. Leon's Marguerite and Deloraine's Catherine, for instance, take charge of very trying situations and manage their respective husband and father quite efficiently. Godwin always succeeds better in treating domestic affection than in passionate love episodes. Some of his pictures of married friendship are rather fine. Surely when Dickens and Scott make most of their heroines prigs, we may pardon Godwin.

The type-hero puts an end to his own possibility of happiness by some crime or act of folly, concerning which he moralizes morbidly, but into which he is forced, apparently by his own nature when circumstances present the occasion.[1] The remainder of his life is involved in the consequences, external and internal. The nature of this dominant characteristic and the resultant act varies. It is Falkland's obsession of "honour" and his murder of Tyrrel; Williams's curiosity and his prying into the chest; St. Leon's desire for wealth and his acceptance of the stone and elixir; Fleetwood's desire to monopolize the entire attention of his young wife and his yielding to jealousy; Mandeville's craving for admiration and his hatred of Clifford; Richard's wish to be Lord Danvers, and his wrong to his brother's child; Deloraine's longing for Margaret's love, and his shooting of William.

In all these cases, be it observed, the type-hero is not the victim of society primarily, but of his own character. Godwin's view of society

[1] Godwin is a necessarian, with a Calvinist training.

enters into his novels (excepting of course the first), only incidentally. Even in *Caleb Williams* we should hardly recognize social theory as the main purpose if it were not for the preface and the sub-title. But we catch occasional glimpses of the author of *Political Justice*. The point oftenest emphasized is the fallacy of regarding our judicial system as impartial or just to the individual. We have already considered the treatment of this subject in *Caleb Williams;* the same ideas are glanced at in all the others.

Economic theories are discussed specifically in one place only: St. Leon's attempt at improving the condition in Hungary by using his gold as a lever to start the production of real wealth. But the Swiss Ruffigny exemplifies in his conduct Godwin's theory of justice in the matter of property rights. In *Political Justice* Godwin declares that the individual's rights over property are of three sorts: (1) each man has a right to the means of subsistence, and to that portion of the general goods which will yield its maximum of pleasure by being appropriated to his use; (2) he has a right of stewardship over that property which he produces; (3) his ownership of property such as lands, and capital in general is recognized for the present, because any system is preferable to the chaos that would ensue if every man appropriated what he thought he had a right to. Ruffigny, it will be remembered, makes a fortune by his own ability and industry, and proposes to retire on a reasonable income regarding himself as merely a steward of the rest to be used for others. But he is satisfied to make over his surplus to a single individual, his friend, instead, in order that that friend may continue in the position of a capitalist to which he is accustomed.

A further point upon which numerous passages may be found in the novels of Godwin is education. Here more than ever one catches echoes of a greater individualist, Rousseau. The child is to be interested, drawn out; on no account is his spontaneity to be repressed. But Godwin had been a fairly successful tutor and had also brought up children of his own, which Rousseau never did; so there are hints of discipline here and there which would have shocked the author of *Émile*.

But it is in his general attitude toward culture that we find the greatest divergence between Godwin and the pure Rousseauists. Godwin does not regard civilization as the sole source of corruption; he cherishes no delusion of the noble savage in an ideal state of nature. Perhaps his early Calvinism had eaten into his soul too deeply. At all events, he is out of harmony with the school of inspired ignorance, as the following passage shows; Marguerite tells St. Leon she is reconciled to poverty:

But she could never bring herself to believe that ignorance was a benefit. She wished her children to attain intellectual refinements, possess fully the attributes of a rational nature, and be as far removed as possible from the attributes of stocks and stones, by accumulating a magazine of thoughts and a rich and cultivated sensibility.[1]

So far, our treatment of Godwin as a novelist seems to have been devoted entirely to the ungracious task of pointing out his failings. But if it is true, as Hazlitt says, that: "The impression made upon the readers is the exact measure of the author's genius," then we must allow these novels some tinge of greatness. They have undoubtedly in parts a sombre power. They produce in the reader a sense of oppressive, morose intensity; a force of individualism verging toward that evil borderland of reason whereon mania casts its first faint shadow of unwholesomeness. The very dullness of the minute introspective analyses adds to the effect. For there is no depth of soul-weariness like a Cosmos filled with Ego.

It will doubtless be objected that this very unsympathetic treatment of William Godwin's personality leaves unexplained the strong influence which he undoubtedly exerted over some of the finest minds of his time. By no means. William Godwin was a powerful reasoner, with a gift for clear and forcible argument. Certain revolutionary principles he found ready to his hand in the works of earlier French and English

[1] *St. Leon*, vol. i., p. 180.

philosophers. To these he added certain ideas gathered from theologians like Jonathan Edwards, and carried the resultant theories to their extreme conclusions with a grim, irresistible logic. His only original contribution to Revolutionism was an unconscious *reductio ad absurdum.* Nevertheless, *Political Justice* is an eminently reasonable book; much more reasonable than life ever is. Moreover, it is written in a style that carries conviction. It is only when one deserts the methods of logic for those of common sense that its absurdity appears.

This very forcible work might, however, have remained unknown outside the circle of logic-chopping metaphysicians but for one important fact. It came at a time when the age was ready for it. It was, as we have seen, one of a large group of books expressing similar philosophies, all of which found their audience awaiting them. Of this group *Political Justice* was the most extreme, though not the most representative. Hence its pre-eminence.

Political Justice stands alone among William Godwin's works; a book dominated by rather than dominating the spirit of the time. It is safe to say he could not have written it in any other year. During the period of the Reaction he employed himself in writing novels which are, as we have seen, the creatures of literary sentimentalism, touched only with an afterglow of Revolutionary ideals.

SECTION 2: THE YOUNG SHELLEY

One does not usually think of Shelley as a novelist. In fact one is apt not to think of him as anything but a poet. That is indeed all-inclusive if one's conception of poetry is high enough. Too often however poet and thinker are used as separate terms, with an implication that to the poet's imaginative and emotional appeal a sound intellectual basis is unessential. From criticism of this type no poet, perhaps, has suffered more than Shelley. In his own time his poetry was condemned because of the underlying doctrine, but at least it was taken seriously. Now criticism has gone to the other extreme. The poetry is accepted, the doctrine patronized or apologized for. We are all so obsessed with Matthew Arnold's fine phrase for Shelley—"Beautiful and ineffectual angel, beating in the void with his luminous wings—in vain"—that we quite forget to listen fairly to what Shelley may have to say for himself. Perhaps, then, by way of restoring the balance, it may not be amiss to turn for a little from Shelley the poet to that younger and almost unknown Shelley before the publication of *Alastor*,[1] whose work consisted chiefly of radical pamphlets and prose romances.

[1] *Alastor*, 1816. Shelley's first poetical work with the exception of the lost juvenilia and *Queen Mab*, which he afterwards wished to repudiate. The poet Shelley belongs to a period rather later than the one under discussion. But Shelley the novelist and pamphleteer was still living under the shadow of the Revolution.

Only two of the novels of Shelley were completed: *Zastrozzi* (1810) and *St. Irvyne* (1811). These are of interest chiefly as they may serve to mark the progress of the poet's mind. They are extraordinary only as the work of a schoolboy of eighteen. We may perhaps pause for a moment to summarize them.

The action in *Zastrozzi* centres in three persons: Verezzi, a young nobleman; Matilda, a lady who is infatuated with him and to whom he is indifferent; and Zastrozzi, a mysterious stranger who pursues Verezzi with relentless hatred. Zastrozzi aids Matilda to win Verezzi's love by a deception, using her as the (unconscious) means of reducing him to despair and suicide. Zastrozzi is seized by the Inquisition and accepts torture with calm defiance, saying that his life was dedicated to the task of avenging on Verezzi a wrong done to his mother.[1]

St. Irvyne, or the Rosicrucian has two plots, very superficially connected. 1. A young lady is captured by bandits. One of them, Wolfstein, kills the captain and rescues her. They escape by the aid of a mysterious stranger, Ginotti, who thereafter possesses a powerful influence over Wolfstein. It appears that Ginotti possesses the gift of eternal

---

[1] Dr. Hancock (*French Revolution and the English Poets*, p. 52) says: "Zastrozzi is his (Shelley's) ideal of a virtuous man." This is hardly a fair interpretation. Zastrozzi is merely the conventional villain of the time. He is described as: "A soul deadened by crime" (*Zastrozzi*, p. 73), which was hardly Shelley's ideal of virtue.

life and can only end his wretched existence by inducing another to accept it. He imparts the secret to Wolfstein, but Wolfstein refuses to complete the transaction by "denying his Creator." Thereupon fiends kill Wolfstein and carry Ginotti living to eternal torment. 2. The other plot is merely the story of a girl who has fallen under the fascination of one Nempere, who, it is explained at the end, was Ginotti under another name.

Shelley says of these novels in a letter to Godwin in 1812[1]:

I was haunted with a passion for the wildest and most extravagant romances. . . . From a reader, I became a writer of romances; before the age of seventeen I had published two, *St. Irvyne* and *Zastrozzi*, each of which, though quite uncharacteristic of me as I now am yet serves to mark the state of my mind at the period of their composition.

Describing the change effected in him by the reading of *Political Justice*, he adds:

I was no longer the votary of romance: till then I had existed in an ideal world—now I found that in this universe of ours was enough to excite the interest of the heart, enough to employ the discussion of reason. . . . You will perceive that *Zastrozzi* and *St. Irvyne* were written prior to my acquaintance with your writings. I had indeed read *St. Leon* before I wrote *St. Irvyne*, but the reasonings had then made little impression.

[1] Dowden, *Life of Shelley*, vol. i., pp. 220–25.

From this it is clear that we need look for no conscious social theorizing in these early romances. Both have heroes of a type very common in the age immediately following the Revolution; the mysterious defiant outcast from society. This is the type of titanism which later became somewhat identified in England with the poetry of Byron. Its source, however, is to be found among the German Romanticists. Shelley's treatment of Zastrozzi and Ginotti is in no way characteristic. At most, they merely indicate the appeal of this type to a young individualist in a state of schoolboy revolt against authority.

In this connection a suggestion in Buxton Forman's preface[1] becomes significant. On the ground of certain references in letters and certain internal evidence of phraseology, he believes that these are not original compositions, but adaptations and translations from the German.

There is mention of several other novels which were planned and even begun, at about this time. Among them was "a fragment of wild romance about a witch," begun in conjunction with Medwin about the beginning of 1809 and "a novel which was to be the deathblow to intolerance, projected at the end of 1810."[2]

But the only fragment of unfinished novel which remains to us is *The Assassins*, written in Switzerland in 1814.

[1] *Works of Shelley*, Forman ed., vol. v., pp. xii f.
[2] *Ibid.*, p. xxvii.

The Assassins are described as an ancient tribe of Christians driven into exile at the fall of Jerusalem. They take refuge in the beautiful valley of Bethzatanai, where they live for generations in the loving communism of the Golden Age. Gradually their religious beliefs are modified, "corresponding with the exalted condition of their being." They "esteem understanding to be the paramount rule of conduct."[1] Shelley comments on the extent to which the sincere directness of such a people would be at variance with the time-serving policies of civilized society. "No Assassin would submissively temporize with vice and in cold charity become a pandar to falsehood and desolation."[2]

Albedir, a member of this gentle tribe, wandering in the forest finds a man impaled among the branches of a cedar, and watched by a serpent and a vulture. He overhears a part of a titanic soliloquy:

The great tyrant is baffled even in success! Joy! Joy! to his tortured foe! Triumph to the worm whom he tramples under his feet! . . . Thousands tremble before thy throne who at my voice shall dare to pluck the golden crown from thine unholy head![3]

The Stranger calls to Albedir in a voice "as the voice of a beloved friend." "In the name of God,

[1] *Works of Shelley*, vol. vi., p. 229. [2] *Ibid.*, p. 232.
[3] *Ibid.*, p. 235

approach. He that suffered me to fall watches thee;—the gentle and merciful spirits of sweet human love delight not in agony and horror."[1] Albedir bears the stranger to his home and cares for him tenderly. The fragment ends with a picture of the two children of Albedir playing by the lake with a tame serpent. "The girl sang to it and it leaped into her bosom and she crossed her fair hands over it as if to cherish it there."[2]

In this fragment there are foreshadowings of Prometheus and of Cythna. Forman says of it:

Intellectual brilliancy, earnestness, great ease in the use of rhetoric, and an egregious practical energy are already among the qualities to be credited to Shelley. But in the *Assassins* there is a touch of a new quality,—trace of an infinite yearning over the miseries of suffering humanity, the divine tenderness which is eventually and forever the distinguishing characteristic of Shelley. . . . In every composition dating after the middle of the year 1814 a new tone prevails.[3]

These novels may be considered as marking the beginnings and the end of Shelley's early prose period. *Zastrozzi* is the work of a precocious boy, disliking restraint, whose imagination has been captured by a certain type of titanism in the romantic literature of the time. With *St. Irvyne* the influence of Godwin through *St. Leon*, if not

[1] *Works of Shelley*, vol. vi., p. 235.   [2] *Ibid.*, p. 242.
[3] *Ibid.*, vol. v., preface, p. xxii.

through *Political Justice*, has begun. In *The Assassins*, Shelley 'sRevolutionary political theory is already passing over into a social idealism whose imaginative and emotional intensity forces poetic expression.

The most significant part of Shelley's early work however is not the romances but the political pamphlets. These give explicitly and in its true proportions the political belief underlying the later poetry.

In the light of these prose tracts it becomes apparent that Shelley's political writings fall into three distinct groups, only one of which is adequately represented in the poems. 1. In the first group are those writings which form a serious and coherent expression of Shelley's theory of the nature and function of government. 2. In addition to these there are a number of articles and pamphlets directed against some specific abuse or in favour of specific reforms. 3. The third class, consisting chiefly of poems, we may call the expression of Shelley's social religion. Shelley believed devoutly in the ultimate perfectibility of humanity through the principle of universal love, and looked forward to a time when mankind fulfilling its highest possibilities might live without restraint. But be it observed, perfect liberty was to be the result of moral and spiritual perfection, not perfection the result of immediate liberty.[1]

[1] This gives the doctrine of Godwin a somewhat different emphasis. The nature of Shelley's indebtedness to Godwin, Rous-

In considering any social or political doctrine of Shelley's it should be made quite clear in which of these classes it belongs. Shelley is not inconsistent. But if his recommendations as to the most effective method of dealing with the specific abuses in his own time are to be confused with his statements of underlying governmental principles, or if his impassioned yearning for the kingdom of heaven on earth is to be perverted into propaganda for immediate political anarchy, obviously it will make a considerable difference in our estimate of the soundness of his judgment.

In this connection it may be well to recall the character of Shelley given by his friend Jefferson Hogg (who despised poetry) and endorsed by another intimate friend, Trelawney, as "the only written likeness he ever knew of him." Hogg says:

It was his rare talents as a scholar that drew me to him. The greatest men are those who compose our laws, and judges to minister them, and if Shelley had put all his mind into the study of law, instead of writing nonsensical rhapsodies, he would have been a great benefactor to the world, for he had the most acute intellect of any man I ever knew.[1]

With this estimate by way of counterbalancing ancient prejudice against poets in practical affairs

seau, Holbach, Helvetius, and the Encyclopaedists is treated in some detail by Dr. Hancock in his *French Revolution and the English Poets*, chap. v. For this reason all question of sources is omitted from the present discussion.

[1] Trelawney, *Records*, preface, p. x.

we may consider briefly the three divisions of Shelley's political theory. Perhaps it may be well to select one document to represent each class and let Shelley speak for himself as far as possible.

The fullest expression of Shelley's principles of government is to be found in the *Declaration of Rights*, a broadside printed in Ireland in 1812.[1] Much of this wise and liberal manifesto seems commonplace now. But many of its passages are strikingly modern in their application. One might undertake to find parallels for all of them in the leading sociological publications of the past decade.

We may quote the most characteristic sections:

1

Government has no rights. It is a delegation from several individuals for the purpose of securing their own. It is therefore just only so far as it exists by their consent, useful only so far as it operates to their well being.

7.

The rights of man in the present state of society can only be secured by some degree of coercion to be

[1] "In an article in the *Fortnightly Review* for January, 1871, Mr. Rossetti points out the resemblance between this declaration and two such documents of the French Revolution, the one adopted by the Constituent Assembly in August, 1789, and the other proposed in April, 1793, by Robespierre." *Works of Shelley*, vol. v., p. 392.

exercised on their violator. The sufferer has a right that the degree of coercion employed be as slight as possible.

9.

No man has a right to disturb the public peace by personally resisting the execution of a law however bad.

17.

No man has a right to do an evil thing that good may come.

18.

Expediency is inadmissible in morals. Politics are only sound when conducted on principles of morality. They are in fact the morals of nations.

19.

Man has no right to kill his brother. It is no excuse that he does so in uniform.

20.

No man has a right to monopolize more than he can enjoy.

29.

Every man has a right to a certain degree of leisure and liberty, because it is his duty to attain a certain degree of knowledge. He may before he ought.[1]

These are the main points insisted upon in the *Declaration of Rights*. Twelve of the thirty-one sections are devoted to the right of perfect freedom of belief and discussion.

[1] *Works of Shelley*, vol. v., pp. 393-98.

In the same classification may be included the fragments *On A System of Government by Juries* and *On Reforms*, together with numerous passages in works belonging primarily to the other groups.

Of the second group, Shelley's propaganda for specific reforms in his own time, the two *Marlow Pamphlets* may be taken as representative.[1] The first of these is *A Proposal for Putting Reform to a Vote Throughout the Kingdom*. The closing paragraph may be quoted as a fair sample of Shelley's practical wisdom:

> With respect to Universal Suffrage, I confess I consider its adoption, in the present unprepared state of knowledge and feeling, a measure fraught with peril. ... The consequences of the immediate extension of the franchise to every male adult would be to place power in the hands of men who have been rendered brutal and torpid and ferocious by ages of slavery. ... Mr. Paine's arguments are unanswerable; a pure republic may be shown by influences the most obvious and irresistible to be that system of social order the fittest to produce the happiness and promote the genuine eminence of man. Yet, nothing can less consist with reason or afford smaller hopes of any beneficial issue, than the plan which would abolish the regal and aristocratic branches of our constitution before the public mind, through many gradations of improvement, shall have arrived at the maturity which can disregard these symbols of its childhood.

[1] Published in 1817, under the signature "The Hermit of Marlow."

The second of these pamphlets, *An Address to the People on the Death of the Princess Charlotte*, is a noble example of almost lyric eloquence in dealing with questions of the hour. Shelley merges the lament for the death of a beloved princess in the deeper and more solemn lament for the death of three ignorant workmen executed on a trumped-up charge of conspiracy through the machinations of government spies:

Mourn then people of England. Clothe yourselves in solemn black. Let the bells be tolled. Think of mortality and change. Shroud yourselves in solitude and in the gloom of sacred sorrow. Spare no symbol of universal grief. Weep—mourn—lament. A beautiful princess is dead,—she who should have been the queen of her beloved nation and whose posterity should have ruled it forever. *Liberty* is dead. Slave! I charge thee disturb not the depth and solemnity of our grief by any meaner sorrow. . . . Let us follow the corpse of British Liberty slowly and reverentially to its tomb; and if some glorious phantom should appear and make its throne of broken swords and sceptres and royal crowns trampled in the dust, let us say that the Spirit of Liberty has arisen from its grave and left all that was gross and mortal there, and kneel down and worship it as our queen.[1]

In this group of occasional propaganda belong *An Address to the Irish People* (1812), *Proposals for an Association* (1812), and *A Letter to Lord Ellenborough Occasioned by the Sentence which he*

[1] *Works of Shelley*, vol. vi., p. 113.

Passed on Mr. D. I. Eaton as Publisher of the Third Part of Paine's "Age of Reason" (1812).

The final phase of Shelley's Revolutionism, his social faith, finds its complete expression only in the poems. Shelley was perfectly aware that the choice of prose or verse as a medium is not a matter of the writer's caprice but is inherent in the nature of the idea. He abhorred didactic poetry.[1] It is the soul of his Revolutionism that is to be found in his poems. On our own heads be it if we forget to look for the body of his practical teachings where it may be found, in his prose works.

Chronology assumes here a certain relevancy. If we take the period of the Revolution (including the opposition to it in England) as it is frequently taken, to extend from the summoning of the States General to the Battle of Waterloo, it may be said that during this period Shelley belongs among the Revolutionary prose writers. When the last sparks of radicalism had been so completely crushed by the Holy Alliance that even Conservatism lost its defensive vigour, Shelley's Revolutionism, instead of fading to a mood of half-sceptical revolt like that of Byron, reaches the tragic intensity of faith in the social ideal that gives to *Prometheus Unbound* its unearthly beauty.

The poetry of Shelley does not properly fall within the limits of our discussion, either in point

---

[1] *Cf.* Shelley's preface to *Prometheus Unbound*.

of time or of form.[1] We may say in closing that Shelley the poet lived in an age of conservatism but he was not of it. His poetry is the fine flower of the age of Revolution. His own time felt this and repudiated him. He himself was conscious of it, and has left a perfect analysis of his own relation to the age in the lines from *Adonais:*

> Midst others of less note came one frail form,
>   A phantom among men; companionless
> As the last cloud of an expiring storm
> Whose thunder is its knell.[2]

[1] Revolution in the poetry of Shelley has, moreover, been fully treated by Dr. Hancock. A list of the poems which contain Revolutionary doctrines is added to the bibliography of this chapter.
[2] *Adonais*, verse xxxi.

CHAPTER IV

SOME OPPONENTS OF THE REVOLUTIONARY PHILOSOPHERS

HOLCROFT, Godwin, and Shelley; these three are the true and orthodox exponents of the Revolutionary doctrines. Of all the phases of that complex philosophy, nothing essential remains entirely unrepresented in their writings. In succeeding chapters[1] we shall see what variations the main tenets received at the hands of novelists who did not accept them in their entirety. These, however, add little that is original. They are like ripples spreading in circles that grow ever broader and less distinct, until one is finally puzzled to trace their relation to the central force that troubled the surface of the age.

Before we pass on to these secondary radicalisms, there remain a number of novels which deal with the original philosophies directly but from an opposite point of view. These add very considerably to our understanding of the period. Unfriendly criticism is often not the least acute. The absurdities of the Revolutionary philosophies

[1] Especially in Chapters V. and VI.

were numerous; he who runs may read them. But besides satirizing the obvious fallacies of their opponents, some of these novels offer, as we shall see, valuable analyses of the systems which they are attacking. They also give explicit lists of the authors identified with the Revolution, and throw some light on the extent to which their doctrines had spread in the nation at large. Finally, and not least important, they indicate the extent to which the age was aware of the economic basis of its own unrests. Veiled under a zeal for law, order, monarchy, religion, or what not, one catches ever and anon strange echoes of the primitive, snarling hatred, born of fear, with which the Classes who Have regard all that threatens to arouse that sleeping beast, the Masses who Have Not. Political and religous bigotry are but feeble motives compared with the bitter unreason awakened by any discussion in which Property is involved.

Two of these anti-Revolutionary novels are of sufficient interest to warrant a somewhat detailed discussion. These will be treated first at some length before passing on to the less important novels of the same group.

The Vagabond, or, Whatever is Just is Equal, but Equality not always Just[1] was, as the preface announces:

written with a desire of placing in a practical light some of the prominent absurdities of the many self-

[1] By George Walker, published in 1799.

important reformers of mankind who, having heated their political imaginations, sit down to write political romances,—and turn loose their disciples upon the world to root up and overthrow everything that has received the sanction of ages. On this subject it is impossible to exaggerate, so inimical are the doctrines of Godwin, Hume, Rousseau, etc., to all civilized society. Can we wonder at the vices and crimes of a neighboring people? Or can we wonder that the generality of shallow-thinking men embrace and support them with ardour?[1]

This was apparently a "best seller" in its time. In the preface to the third edition the author comments upon the fact that, in spite of his refusal to print a cheap edition like *The Rights of Man*, two editions have been sold within six months. "It gives me considerable hopes that the destructive torpor of the rich is evaporating, and that they have begun to take an active interest in the present crisis."[2] Evidently the worthy Walker perceived quite clearly the economic nature of "the present crisis," and to whose interest it was to avoid changes.

In the first chapter the philosophic Dr. Alogos, while walking near his estate reflecting upon the unreasonableness of private property, is attacked by a youth who eloquently defends his right to take whatever he needs. The good Doctor, perceiving that he has met with a kindred spirit, takes the youth home with him, and listens

[1] *The Vagabond*, vol. i., p. xix.   *Ibid.*, p. xxii.

to his story. Fenton (the youth's name) had, it appears, a natural desire for learning. He "did not then know that profound ignorance is the real and only state in which man can enjoy felicity." At the university he had a tutor, Stupeo by name, who instructed him in modern philosophy as represented by Tom Paine, Godwin, Hume, Voltaire, and Rousseau. He learned, among other things, that: "To doubt is the first step to be a great philosopher. . . . Those who believe anything certainly are fools. (Hume, *On Human Nature*, vol. i., p. 168.)"[1] Also, that as he had never consented to the government under which he lived, to him it was an absolute despotism. He objected at first that the government could not possibly consult every individual as he came of age, but was soon convinced that: "Surely Voltaire, Rousseau, and Tom Paine knew what was for the best."[2] He "deserted Aristotle, Grotius, Puffendorf, and even Locke, and ceased to study Latin and Greek."[3] He adds:

My imagination was warmed by the glorious and brilliant spectacle of superstition tumbling down and crushing tyranny in its ruins. . . . The time shall come when knowledge is disseminated in all ranks, when the plowman shall sit on his plow reading the rights of man. Then aristocracy and property shall tumble together.[4]

[1] *Vagabond*, vol. i., p. 16–21.
[2] *Ibid.*, p. 25.
[3] *Ibid.*, p. 30.
[4] *Ibid.*, pp. 45–47.

He was expelled from college, to the great grief of his affectionate father, who said: "Stupeo could never sophisticate the common sense dictates of a mind willing to do right."[1] A fire broke out near his home; he kept the firemen away from the ladders while he meditated which of the inmates was best worth saving, according to the teachings of Godwin. Attacked by his indignant neighbours, his answer was to doubt whether there ever was any fire at all, according to the method of Hume.

Fenton then left his home and became a vagabond, consoling himself with the thought: "Were I fit to live in society, I should be no real philosopher." In his wanderings, he came upon a gathering in a barn where a political ranter was lecturing on the rights of man and the evils of the time. (A note declares this address to be quoted from a real political lecturer.) He winds up with a denunciation of government spies. The crowd applauds vigorously, and departs with a firm conviction that: "England be gone to the dogs as we heard Citizen Ego say, and it will never be as it ought to be until we have another Alderman Cromwell, and no tithes."[2] Afterwards Fenton heard "Citizen Ego" planning to forge letters from imaginary corresponding clubs in other cities. The author adds a note denouncing all political clubs.

Fenton harangued against the luxury and ex-

[1] *Vagabond*, vol. i., p. 64.   [2] *Ibid.*, p. 84.

travagance of the rich, and was answered by a noble lord (the author's mouthpiece), in the following manner:

Luxury fosters arts and sciences, and employs the mechanic, the shop-keeper, the merchant. Without luxury, none of these could meet employ. . . . In the present condition of society, it is in the power of every man possessing real abilities to rise to a station equal to those abilities; and therefore we reverence the exteriors of wealth, tacitly bestowing it upon all possessors.[1]

Next, Fenton fell in with a "No Popery" mob, which forced him into a boxing contest. To the account of this the author adds a note:

See the elegant reasons for boxing, in *Anna St. Ives* and *Hugh Trevor*, two novels which the democratic Reviews hold up as examples of virtue and morality. 'Tis true, if blasphemy be virtue and morality, these offspring of the new school have ample claim.[2]

Finding that the "No Popery" mob was being roused by the new philosophers, Fenton joined in it. There he encountered his old friend Stupeo, who urged him on to the destruction of property. "As long as one single cartload of property remains in any country, there can be no true equality."[3]

---

[1] *Vagabond*, vol. i., p. 114. The unconscious irony of all this must have appealed very forcibly to thinkers of the type of Holcroft and Mary Wollstonecraft.
[2] *Ibid.*, p. 129.   [3] *Ibid.*, p. 144.

Fenton next associated himself with a woman who harangues him on the rights of women. He says of her: "She reasoned little, but adopted one principle and rejected another by a sort of tact." A note points out that this is quoted from Godwin's *Life of Mary Wollstonecraft*, and adds: "Those who reason much will readily believe this."[1] Fenton's Mary soon left him, however.

On one occasion, while inciting a mob of farmers to protest against the enclosure of public lands, he was arrested. The magistrate at his trial repeats the argument of the noble lord, with additions:

What can be more easy than to lead people to desire to live without labour, to plunder the rich, and to live without regard to those laws which were made purposely to restrain their passions? . . . The accumulation of individual property is the natural and certain consequence of society. The rich, by their luxuries, give employment to the poor. The rich would do much better without the poor than the poor without them. . . . In fact it is the middle class of people who bear the great burden of the state. The poor were exactly the same a hundred years ago, and will be always the same under any form of government. Moreover, no Englishman can die of absolute want if he will appeal to the charitable institutions.[2]

To which astonishing piece of complacent economic nonsense Fenton replies, that, "There is no

[1] *Vagabond*, vol. i., p. 181.   [2] *Ibid.*, p. 213.

wealth but the labour of man." But the people have been convinced by the magistrate, and eagerly consent to have their public lands fenced in.[1]

Soon after this, Fenton turned highwayman, since robbery is "merely asserting the Rights of Man by force," and so met Dr. Alogos.

Dr. Alogos and Fenton determine to enlighten their community. They establish a Temple of Reason in a barn, where they read moral lectures with such effectiveness that the curate soon finds himself obliged to sue for his tithes and the neighbouring public houses each have a Revolutionary Club where the labourers meet and drink, until: "They now clearly perceived that the times were the worst that ever old England had witnessed; for they every day found themselves less able to maintain their families."[2]

Dr. Alogos has a very sensible niece who is much opposed to the new philosophies, and especially to Mary Wollstonecraft's doctrines. Her argument is, that women cannot be equal to men in anything because their lives must be confined exclusively to the bearing and rearing of children, "a humbling difference." It will be observed that it was left for the opponents of the new femin-

[1] Fenton was not so altogether in the wrong here as the author would have us believe. Gibbins says, in his *Industrial History of England* (p. 199): "The enclosure of the common fields was effected at a great loss to the smaller tenant, and when his common of pasture was enclosed as well, he was greatly injured, while the agricultural labourer was permanently disabled."

[2] *Vagabond*, vol. ii., p. 19.

ism to discover anything "humbling" in this. Mary Wollstonecraft herself would have considered potential motherhood a strange proof of inferiority.

Dr. Alogos, Fenton, and Stupeo resolve to emigrate to America in search of a virtuous and primitive society. They meet a storm at sea, and terror convinces Dr. Alogos that: "There is more in religion and in commonplace maxims of good and evil than the great Stupeo would allow."[1]

They find Philadelphia very uncomfortable. "Property is much regarded, and the maxim is 'work or starve.' There is political equality here, but not equality of property."[2] They immediately set out for the wilds of Kentucky. There they have some experience of real savages. Stupeo is killed. The Doctor declares: "Rousseau was a fool. I begin to think the savage state of nature was not conducted on philosophical principles." To this the author adds a note:

> It is the practice of the new school to extoll everything savage. Why is this but to loosen men from the bonds of society, and sap the foundations of governments? . . . The emancipation of the negroes, and the inhumanity of Christians is an excellent stalking-horse for those who pretend to finer feelings than the rest of mankind.[3]

Fenton and Dr. Alogos finally discover a fantastic land of philosophers, conducted on the

[1] *Vagabond*, vol. ii., p. 105. [2] *Ibid.*, p. 132.
[3] *Ibid.*, pp. 158–73.

principles of *Political Justice;* and a most wretched community it is. Lack of incentive has checked the development of talents; no one will work; and no one will study. All property in common has resulted in no property at all. To this account there is a note appended:

I know that many of the new school will say that I misrepresent the meaning of equality; that they do not mean equality of property, but equality of *rights*. The truth is, they mean both, though the fairest pretence is held out.[1]

In this community, Alogos and Fenton see men starving while they are trying to decide by pure reason where the daily half-hour of work, which according to Godwin is all they need do, can best be applied for the general good. Thieves and criminals destroy everything; for there is no "politically just" mode of punishment. The women are forced to share in the roughest work, until they petition for a return to the "ancient slavery." Poverty, hunger, and disease are rapidly destroying the entire population.

This [says the author], is a philosophic republic. The ancient republics were fighting republics; the Americans and Hollanders are trading republics. But men seem neither better satisfied, nor better governed, nor better fed in any of them; nor in fact do they enjoy so many benefits as in a limited monarchy.[1]

[1] *Vagabond*, vol. ii., p. 209.

Fenton and Dr. Alogos, quite convinced of their folly, return to warn England of the dangers of the principles which they formerly advocated.

The Infernal Quixote: A Tale of the Day has for its motto: "Better to reign in Hell than serve in Heaven."[1] Walker at least did Godwin and his followers the honour of believing them sincerely mad; Lucas will not allow them even the merit of self-deception. He considers them demagogues one and all, willing to overturn society if thereby they may come into power.[2]

There is a Miltonic prologue[3]; an address of Satan to the peers of hell.

The reign of Antichrist is begun, thanks to the daring, restless sons of France inspired by me and mine! Yet there is still a spot resists my utmost efforts,—too well ye know the place. In vain that Imp Voltaire and yonder miserable group—on earth, conceited prating, proud philosophers—gifted with all our learning, tried; in vain Robespierre. . . . Our Hell-born virtues nor art nor force can graft upon their tree of civil and religious liberty.

[1] By Charles Lucas, A.M. London, 1801.

[2] While we are on this question of disinterestedness, we might observe Lucas's own disgustingly fulsome dedication to royalty. Is it possible that our worthy Master of Arts was judging other men by himself?

[3] Milton was having an especial vogue when this was written. *Cf.* the following passage from the *Memoirs of an Old Wig:* "It was much the rage, not only to write the life of Milton, but to hunt out busts, paintings, prints, nay, to trace him through all his different places of residence."

But there remains one scheme untried; of which this novel is an account, as foretold by Satan.[1]

Lord Marauder and Wilson Wilson, the son of a virtuous farmer, are born on the same day (for purposes of antithesis). Marauder is from his youth devoted to evil.

> He seemed to have imbibed an inveterate dislike to religion [but on the other hand, although], he was not ignorant of the wonderful arguments of William Godwin, and though, if it suited his purpose, he would make use of the conceit and folly of another, he had too much sense to be led by them himself.[2]

Marauder corrupts Emily, the girl Wilson loves, by keeping her supplied with all the new books. "Among the first of these was Mary Wollstonecraft's *Rights of Women*.[3] To this he adds Voltaire's *Tales*, and Diderot's novels. He reads to her extracts from "that first of writers, that most rational, philosophic, learned, modest, and ingenious of all human naturals, William Godwin; taken from his scientific work, *The History of the Intrigues of his Own Wife*."[4] Emily is induced to elope with Marauder to London, where her education in vice is completed by the noble *émigrés* with whom Marauder associates. She becomes an adept in the Voltairean philosophy, with a

---

[1] *Infernal Quixote*, vol. i., p. 4.   [2] *Ibid.*, p. 152.
[3] *Ibid.*, p. 153.
[4] *Ibid.*, p. 170. *Memoirs of the Author of a Vindication of the Rights of Women*, of course.

charming marchioness to explain it to her. The author comments on the fact that:

> The *ci-devant* nobility were perfectly acquainted with the works of Spinoza, Hobbes, Shaftesbury, Hume, Voltaire, Diderot, D'Alembert, and the whole gang of modern sceptics in the English, French, and German languages, and . . . frequently dispute with great civility on the use of titles. From the conversation of many of them a stranger would suppose that they were of the democratic party. Many of the first abilities actually joined the popular cause; for . . . the present infamous factions (in France) must not be confused with the first noble emancipators of their country.[1]

The duke, whose heir Marauder believed himself to be, dies, a long-lost son appears, and Marauder finds his hopes of rank and title vanished. His aristocratic ambitions thwarted, he changes sides immediately, resolving to make the hell of democracy his heaven. In this he is compared to Cromwell, "except that Cromwell's enthusiasm rather got the better of his hypocrisy," while Marauder's only principle is, that "all principle is folly."[2] He becomes a leader in all seditious and treasonable plots, finally joins in the Irish uprisings, and is there defeated and killed by Wilson.

[1] *Infernal Quixote*, vol. i., pp. 125–37. The last sentence is significant as an indication that English observers were fully aware of the fundamental change in the nature of the Revolution, the passing from bourgeoise to proletarian control.
[2] *Ibid.*, p. 295.

Such is the main plan of the novel. All this is of interest, aside from the author's main thesis (the ambitious motives of the Revolutionary leaders), for the lists of Revolutionary writers it gives, and for the light it throws on the attitude of the French *ci-devant* nobility. There are also various passages satirizing the mummeries of "Those Secret Societies, who by some general name and open profession of constitutional purpose conceal their attempt to overthrow Church and State."[1]

But there are certain other digressions which are of more interest to us than all the rest of the novel. Lucas was evidently of a keenly analytical turn of mind; not content with merely disliking all the newer tendencies of his time, he seeks to discover the common basis of his dislikes. In so doing he gives us a very illuminating discussion of the underlying affinities between the apparently opposite principles of Sentimentalism and Pure Reason.

The question is one which suggests itself inevitably. Sentimentalism (which we have defined as an interest in feeling for its own sake, tending to make feeling the test of opinion), and the Pure Reason philosophies, with their negation of feeling, would seem to be opposite poles of thought. Yet there are certain curious parallelisms. It is at about the same time (the close of the seventeenth century), that both Sentimentalism and

[1] *Infernal Quixote*, vol. ii., p. 212.

Scepticism begin to make their influence felt in English literature. Furthermore, it is in the writers directly influencing the Revolutionists that both come to their fullest expression. Hume, the complete Sceptic, and Rousseau, the complete Sentimentalist, were born within a couple of years of each other.[1] We have already commented on the fact that Godwin, apostle of Pure Reason in his theory, is a thorough Sentimentalist in his literary practice. Certain books like the *Social Contract* are puzzling to classify.

There is another puzzling element in the thought of the eighteenth century. The growth of Methodism and similar forms of dissent, whose followers were grouped under the general heading of religious enthusiasts, were seriously threatening the dry bones of Establishment. And, again a coincidence in dates: the first Methodist preaching place was opened in Bristol in 1739, the year of the publication of Hume's first work, *A Treatise on Human Nature*.

We must not be misled by an instinctive desire for synthesis; yet it is difficult to believe that these curious interactions and chronological parallelisms are altogether without significance. Hence their discussion and analysis by a contemporary critic is of especial interest.

[1] Hume, b. 1711; Rousseau, b. 1712. These coincidences in dates are, of course, noted merely to illustrate the fact that Sentimentalism, Scepticism, and Methodism were exactly contemporary.

Infidelity and enthusiasm, Lucas admits, are opposite extremes; but they often reach the same conclusions. Godwin, he points out, began as a dissenting preacher, and there are many similarities between his doctrines and those of Methodism.

The author of the *Spiritual Quixote*, speaking of religious enthusiasm ere the irreligious was yet matured, said "Enthusiasm is deaf to all the calls of nature," etc. Did not the wretches in France boast the murder of fathers, brothers, and sons? Does not Godwin renounce those ties?[1]

In further illustration of this similarity Lucas gives a mock sermon, based he declares on one he has actually heard, which with a few changes in names is adapted either to a democratic ranter or to a Methodist preacher. He defies the reader to tell which was the original form.

Faith, Grace, Hope, and Charity make it the one; Liberty, Equality, and Justice make it the other. Call Saints Democrats; Sinners, Aristocrats; for Satan, read Tyrants; and for more sacred names, take Nature, and so forth.

Oration

{Satan and his imps of darkness / Tyrants and their ministers of tyranny} are on the watch, my {beloved Brethren / fellow Citizens} to fasten you in the eternal chains of {Hell / Slavery} Be therefore ever vigilant.

---
[1] *Infernal Quixote*, vol. ii., p. 176.

Put on the { Gospel Armor } and defy the powers of
         { Liberty Cap   }
Evil
Tyranny.   etc., etc., *ad libitum*.[1]

Lucas then passes on to a classification of the new philosophies of infidelity and enthusiasm, which he groups under the comprehensive heading of "Diabolism." This he defines as, "A species of wisdom which man discovers by the aid of his own individual powers, corporal and mental, without owning the aid of any superior being, directly or indirectly."[2]

Diabolism he divides into nine sects, as follows:

Stoics.
Epicureans.   } of ancient origin, but modernized.
Peripatetics.
Virtuosos.

Illuminati.
Libertinians.
Naturals.   } Moderns.[3]
Reasoners.
Nothingers.

The first three "ancients" he dismisses as being sufficiently well understood, and proceeds to define the others, with satirical comment. The "Virtuosos" are the lovers of Wonder; their

[1] *Infernal Quixote*, vol. ii., p. 177–78.
[2] *Ibid.*, p. 222.
[3] *Ibid.*, p. 225.

delight is to rake in the past for things forgotten, which they hail as novelties.[1] "Libertinians," as might be supposed, are the political theorists, anarchistic or republican, who are insane on the subject of liberty. "Illuminati" include not merely the society of that name, but all religious sects which claim an especial enlightenment, including Quakers and Methodists.[2]

The "Naturals" are the philosophers of the Return to Nature, and the worshippers of "natural" feeling.[3] This sect, Lucas thinks, are more sincere and less dangerous (because more obviously mad) than the others. "Like the Quakers, they are more admired by the rest than imitated."[4] He adds, the name "Natural" is rendered especially appropriate by the bedlam appearance presented by the followers of this sect in their "Return to Nature" costumes.

Lucas comments on the strange alliance between

[1] *Cf.* frequent definitions of Romanticism as "The Rennaissance of Wonder" and as "A Return to the Middle Ages."

[2] Society of the Illuminati; "Founded in 1776, by Adam Weishaupt with the ostensible object of perfecting human nature, of binding in one brotherhood men of all countries, ranks and religions, and of surrounding the persons of princes with trustworthy advisers. The mysteries related to religion, which was transformed into naturalism and free thought, and to politics, which inclined to socialism and republicanism." (Article on Illuminati, in the *American Encyclopædia*.) *Cf.* also my note on St. Simon, in Chapter VI.

[3] *Infernal Quixote*, vol. ii., p. 263.

[4] *I. e.*, Sentimentalists, and Rousseauists of the Thomas Day type.

the "Naturals" and the "Reasoners" (*i. e.*, the Sentimentalists and Sceptics) of his time. "The Reasoners deceive the Naturals by making them think the Reasoners' whims and fancies are the genuine offspring of nature."[1] Like the Naturals, the Reasoners exalt an ideal primitive man; especially when attacking religion. "The most common method of the Reasoner is to write a dialogue on the subject between himself and the savage. He, very kindly, for Christianity; the savage for himself. Oh, how the savage cuts him up!"[2]

Hume is a perfect specimen of the Reasoner. "Rousseau is so strange a compound between a Natural and a Reasoner (which rarely happens) that his brethren never knew what to make of him."[3]

Most detestable of all Diabolists are the Nothingers. These are the people whose pride it is to have no principles whatever; who are swayed entirely by self-interest. In this group Lucas classified Godwin. "Every Jacobin is of this sect, and they generally also embrace most of the others, except the Naturals, and that they endeavour to make 'Le Souverain Peuple.' "[4]

Having demonstrated the real unity in Diabolism, however various its forms, Lucas proceeds to indicate his own philosophy. He favours a definite and centralized authority in matters of

[1] *Infernal Quixote*, vol. ii., p. 263. [2] *Ibid.*, vol. ii., p. 279.
[3] *Ibid.*, vol. ii., p. 283. [4] *Ibid.*, vol. ii., p. 291.

government and of belief; Constitutional Monarchy and the Established Church.

Establishment [he says], is a requisite form of religious worship. What in the abstract cannot be defended may in the whole be of the highest benefit.[1] In Church, in State, I fear schisms and oppositions as the harbingers of confusion, and from them I dread the introduction of every species of evil.[2]

In all matters of belief, he recognizes the principle of authority.

If everyone were free to make the articles of his own faith, little would remain of the original institutions of Christ. . . . The majority of the world are composed of the ignorant, the designing, the indolent, and the open reprobate;—how dark and gloomy is the prospect of the human mind left to itself! It is absolutely necessary that our minds as well as persons should have some law.[3]

Such is Lucas's analysis of the thought of his time. On the one side authority, tradition, a fixed standard, in belief as in conduct. On the other side, individualism, revolt, disorganization. The Sentimentalist and Pure Reason philosophies

[1] But Lucas is not quite so sound a Pragmatist as one might infer from his method of defending Establishment. He defines Christianity as "That purity of principle which will not, by any mental persuasion, commit that which is wrong, even if it is to produce the greatest benefit." *Infernal Quixote*, vol. iii., p. 68.
[2] *Ibid.*, vol. ii., pp. 183–86.
[3] *Ibid.*, vol. ii., p. 295.

in all their forms have this in common: they are a revolt from the principle of authority. Their ethical systems are formed by each man for himself, subject to no discipline by recognized superiors. Having cast aside the principle of authority, one group is guided by pure feeling, the other by pure reason; but that is merely a subdivision of the main classification on the basis of their common revolt.

A number of other novels written in opposition to the Revolutionary philosophies may be mentioned, but none of them merit any detailed consideration. They are merely significant of the prevalence of the opinions which they represent.[1]

It will be remembered that Lucas classified the Methodists among the Sentimentalists, as having revolted from the principle of authority in favour of purely subjective standards. This classification is curiously corroborated by an earlier novel, *The Fair Methodist, or, Such Things Are* (anon., 1794). This is announced as "a serious novel, founded on truth." A passage in the dedication (to Sir Rowland Hill) is worth quoting:

---

[1] *Edmund Oliver*, by Charles Lloyd (the friend of Charles Lamb, to whom the book is dedicated), should be mentioned here. Dowden says of it: "The reproduction in fiction of some of S. T. Coleridge's early adventures has given the book an interest which its literary merits fail to justify. The heroine, Lady Gertrude Sinclair, is a disciple of *Political Justice*" (*English Literature and the French Revolution*, p. 89).

And the English Novel 155

The word Gospel in divinity, like Liberty in politics, is intoxicating in its sound to those who know little of its genuine signification. . . . That ignorance is the mother of devotion is manifested in the very temper of methodistical enthusiasm, which denies human learning as useless and gives a preference to the Spirit as alone sufficient.[1]

The novel itself deals with a young woman who behaves very treacherously to all her friends, and then becomes a Methodist and assumes airs of great sanctity. There are numerous passages directed against all forms of belief in which faith and an emotional experience are considered as an equivalent for works. The author is not opposed to all the newer tendencies, however. He speaks with great respect of Hume and Priestley.

Before we leave the subject of Methodism, there is an interesting passage in *The Memoirs of an Old Wig* (Richard Fenton, 1815), indicating that the charge of Sentimentalism was a common one. The Old Wig says of one of its owners: "His religion was made up of Rousseau and H——h M——e [Hannah More?], the worst sort of Methodism, that is, Methodism with a disproportionate mixture of the philosophy of feeling."

There are several novels written at about this time in rather truculent defence of orthodoxy. Among the best of these is *Memoirs of a Female*

---

[1] *The Fair Methodist*, p. ii.

Philosopher, by a Modern Male Philosopher (anon., 1818). This is an imitation of Hume's *Dialog of Four Philosophers*. It is in the form of an argument between four ladies representing the Stoic, Epicurean, Platonist, and Christian philosophies. The Christian has the best of it, of course. The semblance of narrative form is kept by having each of the ladies tell the story of her life by way of illustration.

A similar novel of argument is *Edward and Sophia* anon. (188–,), in which a deist is reconciled to the Established Church.

In *Walter Kennedy, an American Tale* (1805), John Davis gives some realistic pictures of Indian life in opposition to the belief in a Rousseauistic state of nature and the noble savage.

Two novels with prefaces bewailing the use of fiction to corrupt the age with Revolutionary doctrines, but confining themselves to commonplace morality, are *Cypher, or The World as it Goes* (anon., 1791), and *Romulus: A Tale of Ancient Times*, an adaptation from the German, by Rev. P. Mill (not dated).

The Last Man, or, Omegarus and Syderia: A Romance of Futurity contains certain passages on the Revolutionary philosophies as they are supposed to be regarded by a remote posterity. "Experience is the only reason of man. Maxims more pernicious than the plague were supposed beneficent by ages which deemed themselves enlightened. The evils which these maxims create cannot be described."[1] The only other points worth noting in this novel of prophecy are the forecasts of the development of machinery, and the art of flying, and a Malthusian terror of over-population.[2]

I'll Consider of It (anon., 1812), a novel written in obvious imitation of Sterne, has for its unifying principle the exaltation of aristocratic birth, and the evils of *mésalliances*. A typical speech of the hero is: "Such are the maxims of those who are fond of innovations, that 'virtue alone is true nobility,' and all such commonplace ideas. I am for different orders and degrees of men."[3]

Turning from the noisy warfare over ideas, religious and political, to the underlying realities of the economic conflict, we come upon one novel at least that merits attention. *The Magic of Wealth, an Antibank Novel*[4] is a protest, from the standpoint of the landed classes against the growing supremacy of capital. It may serve to indicate the extent to which the age was aware of the real nature of the changes taking place.

There are three principle figures in the novel: Oldways, Flimflam the banker, and Lyttleton, the mysterious stranger. Mr. Oldways is an Old

[1] *The Last Man*, anon., 1806.
[2] This particular bogy continued to cast a dark shadow over the future for sociologists as late, certainly, as Tennyson's second *Locksley Hall*. In the twentieth century we seem to prefer the race suicide bogy.
[3] *I'll Consider of It*, vol. ii., p. 179.
[4] By E. T. Sun, author of *A Winter in London*, etc., 1815.

Whig, of the school of Burke, who has "the sincerest admiration of the principles of the British Constitution as recognized at the era of the Revolution," and points triumphantly to "the mortifying lesson to the bigoted worshippers of any human theory or system afforded by the horrors of the French Revolution."[1] Oldways was

born and bred the true old English gentleman; he possessed no part of the trafficking spirit of the times. It never occurred to him that the revenues of his estates were to be considered only so much capital. . . . He never contemplated the necessity of engaging in such projects, to save himself from being overwhelmed by the effects of that power, which paper circulation imparted to every dealer in every article of general consumption.[2]

Oldways finds, however, that as the cost of living rises his expenses are enormously increased through no fault of his own. Also, his tenantry are becoming steadily poorer and less able to pay even his moderate rents. He refuses to follow the general practice of raising rents. He likewise refuses to speculate. Consequently, he is fairly driven out of the country, "until principles of sound policy shall induce the government to adopt such reforms as shall restore to its natural and wholesome influence among the other orders of

[1] *Magic of Wealth*, vol. i., p. 174.
[2] *Ibid.*, vol. i., p. 179.

the state, the ranks of *independent country gentlemen.*"[1]

Oldways's estate, his influence, and his seat in Parliament fall into the hands of the upstart banker Flimflam.

Dangerous crisis when a skilful manoeuvrer by speculative art can wrest from the descendants of the ancient nobility the means of supporting with necessary dignity that rank and influence in the state which the wisdom and experience of their ancestors considered and confirmed as a most salutary balance between the monarch's power and the people's will.[2]

The *deus ex machina* who interferes at this crisis to save the nation from the consequences of wild speculation and a loss of the balance of power is the mysterious stranger, Lyttleton.[3] He has gained possession of the hidden treasure of the Jesuits. Returning after years of absence, he reflects: "With wealth that gives me over millions of my fellow creatures the powers of the genii of romance I am here in England where poverty and wealth are terms almost synonymous with vice and virtue."[4] He decides that the best way in which he can serve mankind is to "apply the magic

[1] *Magic of Wealth*, vol. ii., p. 134.
[2] *Ibid.*, vol. ii., p. 124.
[3] Of course he turns out to be Oldways's long-lost nephew. In novels of this period one may always rest assured that any person not otherwise accounted for will turn out to be someone's long-lost something-or-other, before the end of the book.
[4] *Ibid.*, vol. i., p. 27.

of real wealth in order to counteract the evils which have originated from the tricks and delusions of selfish impostors." He straightens out the banking system and the currency, assists Oldways and his friends, and exposes Flimflam. The novel ends with a moral:

Happy will it be for Old England, for the British Empire, for the civilized world, when the manoeuvres of such mischievous speculators as Flimflam shall no longer be successful; and when the character and conduct of such men as Mr. Oldways shall be rightly understood, duly honored, and generally imitated.[1]

[1] *Magic of Wealth*, vol. ii., p. 240.

CHAPTER V

REVOLUTIONISTS AND RADICALS OF VARIOUS DEGREES

SECTION I: THE NOVELS OF ROBERT BAGE

IN considering the novels of Godwin we observed a certain divergence between the personalities shown in his life, in his novels, and in his philosophical writings. In the case of Robert Bage, the man, the literary artist, and the thinker are so identified that it is hard to separate them even for convenience in discussion. His six novels are the spontaneous expression of the observations and ideas collected in a long and useful life. One no more wishes to consider them apart from the biography of the author than one would read *The Old Benchers of the Inner Temple* without wishing first to make the personal acquaintance of Elia.

Fortunately there are few among our little group of novelists whom we may know more intimately than Bage. The accounts of his friends Godwin and Hutton, letters, and the memoir which Miss Hutton supplied for Scott's preface to his edition of Bage's novels help us to give form to the personality that so pervades his work.[1] Robert

[1] Paul, *William Godwin*, vol. i., p. 263.

Bage himself comes clearly before us,—a successful manufacturer and the son of a manufacturer, belonging with Shakespeare and Chaucer in that honourable minority of imaginative writers who have had the practical qualities necessary to make their way in the world of business. After a good common school education, where he early distinguished himself by his proficiency in Latin, he entered his father's paper-mills. When he had gained the necessary experience, he set up for himself as a paper manufacturer at Elford. He married early and very happily. His efficient management left him time for wide reading and study; at the age of fifty-three, as he told Godwin, the failure of a business venture "filled him with melancholy thoughts, and to dissipate them he formed the idea of a novel which he endeavoured to fill with gay and cheerful ideas. At first he had no idea of publishing what he wrote. He believes he should not have written novels but for the want of books to assist him in any other literary undertaking."[1] The six novels which he published at fairly regular intervals during the next fifteen years were all decidedly and immediately successful.

To this meagre outline of a well-rounded life we may add some sketches of the man as he appeared to those who knew him. In 1797, Godwin, making a pilgrimage to visit the sage, writes of him in a letter to Mary Wollstonecraft:

[1] Paul, *William Godwin*, vol. i., p. 263.

I found him uncommonly cheerful and placid, simple in his manners, and youthful in his carriage. His house at the mill was floored every room below stairs with brick, like that of a common farmer in all respects. . . . He has thought much, and like most of those persons I have met with who have conquered many prejudices and read little metaphysics, is a materialist. His favourite book on this point is the *Système de la Nature*.[1]

A fuller account is given by Miss Hutton, the daughter of Bage's old friend.

In his person, Robert Bage was rather under the middle size, and rather slender, but well proportioned. His complexion was fair and ruddy, his hair light and curling; his countenance intelligent, yet mild and placid. His manners were courteous, and his mind was firm. His integrity, his honour, his devotion to truth, were undeviating and incorruptible: his humanity, benevolence and generosity were not less conspicuous in private life than they were in the principal characters in his works. He supplied persons he never saw with money because he heard they were in want. He kept his servants and his horses to old age, and both men and quadrupeds were attached to him. He behaved to his sons with the unremitting affection of a father; but, as they grew up, he treated them as men and equals, and allowed them that independence of mind and conduct which he claimed for himself. . . . He never had a strong passion for wealth, and he never rose to opulence.[2]

[1] Paul, *William Godwin*, vol. i., p. 262.
[2] *Ballantyne's Novelists Library*, vol. ix., preface, p. xxiv.

The novels of Robert Bage are precisely what we should expect of such a man. His personality pervades them all; kindly, humorous, even whimsical; keenly observant of life, and genuinely enjoying his fellow-men. He belongs rather to the tradition of Goldsmith than with the Gothic Romancers. There is enough plot to keep the action in his novels from stagnating, but little more. The author is principally interested in the personalities his imagination has created. It speaks volumes for his ability that neither the meagreness of plot nor the frank didacticism are at any time felt as a defect. The form chosen (four out of the six novels are series of letters), is admirably adapted to the genial and sympathetic characterization in which Bage excells. It is not a crowded canvas that he presents us; rather, a group of a dozen or so pleasant people, with a background of events and a few unsympathetic types lightly sketched in. We look over their shoulders at the clever letters they write about each other. We are interested in the various strands of their lives, and not less interested in their shrewd observations on the world of contemporary thought. The zest with which the author created these people is contagious.

The general framework of the plots of each novel may be given in a few words. *Mount Henneth* (published 1781), derives its title from an old castle in Wales bought by a wealthy and intelligent merchant who proposes to retire there with his daughter and such congenial people as he can gather about him. After two volumes of accidents and incidents in which they become acquainted, the book closes with a quadruple wedding, and some twelve or thirteen people settle at Mount Henneth in a sort of pre-Coleridgean Pantisocracy, where the gentlemen work for a short time each day, and in the afternoon join their wives in studies and amusement. Bage is so fond of these multiple weddings, that often, as the last chapter of a novel approaches, the reader feels with Touchstone that: "There is, sure, another flood towards, and these couples are coming to the ark!"

Barham Downs (1784), is a similar earthly paradise, only with a more prominent villain, who complicates matters by carrying off one of the heroines to force her into a *mariage de convenance*. All the main strands of plot in this novel find their counterpart somewhere in the first. Most of them are the usual stock in trade of the novelists of Bage's time.

James Wallace[1] (1788) has a somewhat more unified plot, centring in an individual rather than a place. The hero, setting out to make his own way in the world, fails as a lawyer on account of his over generous and trusting disposition. After sundry adventures he becomes the servant of a

---

[1] *The Fair Syrian* (1787), is the next in chronological order. But as all efforts to secure a copy of this novel have hitherto been unsuccessful, it must be omitted from our discussion for the present.

young lady of rare charm and intelligence. Finding that he loves her, and that her kindness to him is causing gossip, he leaves her. After various wanderings, he turns out to be the long-lost nephew of a certain Irish gentleman who has befriended him, wins great honour in a sea fight, and returns to marry his Judith. This happy love story is interwoven with a sad one. A boy and girl attachment between a certain young gentleman and the daughter of his tutor is broken off by his being sent abroad to travel. He returns no longer capable of finding happiness in right living, and his attempt at kidnapping his former sweetheart being foiled by the intervention of James Wallace, the young man goes back to Paris and a life of dissipation. Several very interesting personalities appear in the course of the book—Judith's benevolent, gruff old uncle; a sea captain, his friend; and Paracelsus Holman, an apothecary of great scientific attainments, a rare mixture of kindliness and shrewd good sense.

The last two of Bage's novels were written during the Revolution in France, at a time when the reaction against liberal ideas had already begun in England. As the titles indicate, these two novels are more distinctly and consciously doctrinary than the earlier ones. Yet so skilful a literary workman is Bage, and so genuine and vigorous his creative ability, that instead of degenerating into mere arguments these show a steady gain in literary merit. Miss Hutton comments with some surprise on the fact that "of six different works comprising a period of fifteen years, the last is unquestionably the best."

Man As He Is (1792) is frankly announced by its preface as a novel with a purpose. In plot and treatment it is the simplest of the six. Bage has deserted the letter form with its opportunities for detailed characterization and its many threads of interest, in favour of direct narrative. A fashionable youth of good average character falls in love with a young woman of rare intellect and refinement. She refuses to receive his addresses until he can win her respect. He goes to France and there falls into the usual dissipations, all of which report brings to the knowledge of his lady-love. After several futile attempts at reform, he returns to England and actually falls ill from despair of ever winning her. Naturally (in a novel), the lady forgives him, waives her impossible demands, marries him, and he reforms, more or less. There is a good deal of social satire in the book, and many long discussions of contemporary ideas and events. Two of the minor characters are worthy of note: Mr. Lindsay, a man of high principles and culture whom the hero rescues from a debtors' prison and chooses for his tutor; and Miss Carlil, a spirited young Quakeress who accompanies the heroine.

The last of Bage's novels was published in 1796, a black year for English sympathizers with the French Revolution. France had disappointed political idealists, and the reaction in England against their principles was at its height. The note of wistfulness in Bage's novel of the ideal man, *Hermsprong, Or Man As He Is Not*, accords well with the time. The sharp conflicts of ideas arising from the political crisis have at last crystallized Bage's very liberal sentiments into a genuine radicalism. The book not only shows abundant evidences of the influence of the most extreme political thinkers of his time, but contains numerous direct references to such writers as Rousseau, Thomas Paine, and Mary Wollstonecraft. Here gentle satire of social follies and shams takes on a note of bitterness, and there are passages of vigorous denunciation directed against specific evils in the body politic. Here only in the six novels does the plot itself seem chosen primarily as a vehicle for the expression of the author's politico-philosophical doctrines.

Hermsprong, the protagonist of Bage's social philosophy, is a mysterious young man who has passed the first twenty years of his life among the American Indians. After some four years of travel through Europe, chiefly on foot, and a brief residence in France, he arrives somewhat abruptly upon the scene of the story, just in time to rescue the heroine from a runaway horse. When his independence of manner incurs the enmity of her father, Lord Grondale, a wealthy and dissipated old nobleman, our stage setting is complete. The rest of the novel consists principally of Hermsprong's comments upon the evils of the time in politics and manners, his conflicts with prejudiced persons, and his philanthropic activities. In the end, of course, he turns out to be the missing heir of Lord Grondale's estate, and marries his daughter. So much for the plot. Our interest here is with the character of Hermsprong, admittedly the exponent of Bage's most extreme doctrines.

The conception of introducing a man of unconventional or uncivilized education as a critic of society was no new one in literature. A host of familiar figures occur to one's mind—Crusoe's Friday, The Plain Dealer, the Fool of Quality, Oronooko. Voltaire's *L'ingénu* (1767) offers a parallel so striking that it is difficult to believe Bage was not influenced by this version. Innumerable likenesses in plot and sentiment might be pointed out. With Rousseau's preaching of the virtues of primitive man the satirically naïve comment from the standpoint of a noble savage received a new popularity. Professor Cross writes of this type-figure:

> He was an evolution under the influence of the new philosophy, of Fielding's Mr. Square, who conducted himself according to the "unalterable rule of right and the eternal fitness of things." How far removed the ethics of the revolutionist was from Fielding is seen by their attitude towards essentially the same gentleman. In *Tom Jones* he was a villain; in Bage's *Hermsprong* he was the hero.[1]

[1] Cross, *Development of the English Novel*, p. 92.

Even in treating such a subject as the perfect man in an imperfect state of society, the genial good sense of Bage saves him from the flights of unbridled idealism which were the curse of so many thinkers of his time. Granting the early environment Bage presupposes, Hermsprong is not unplausible. Whenever he tends to become too much the superman, the author provides some other character to voice with sly good humour the criticism of common sense and common kindness. From his savage training Hermsprong has acquired a contempt for weakness. He is fond of long walks, "makes a pipe and ale his luxuries, not habits," and despises self-indulgence in all forms. He is frankly bored by long dinners and the elaborate ceremonies of polite society; by no means an unheard of characteristic in actual life. But Hermsprong does not condemn civilization wholesale in favour of savage life. In real happiness, he thinks, the gain of civilized society is but small. But he would not give up the pleasures of the mind for any of the compensations of primitive life. The political and philosophic views of Hermsprong are much like those expressed in Bage's other novels, except that he is an avowed Republican, as might be expected. Of the French Revolution he says,[1] "it is strange and new as to the causes which animate the French; for as to the means—the destruction of the human species—it has been a favourite mode with power of every denomination ever since

[1] *Man As He Is Not*, vol. i., p. 85.

power was," but he "leaves it to the loyal Englishman to approve by the lump. All the malignant as well as all the better passions are afloat in France; and malignant actions are the consequence. Many of the acts of the Assembly are acts of necessity, and some, no doubt, of folly."[1] America approaches nearer to his ideal state of society: "Yet still at an immense distance from the ultimatum, to attain which manners must change much, and governments more. The first is possible, for manners are addicted to change. The latter is hopeless. Governments do not change, at least for the better."[2] Of England he says sadly: "Your debts and other consequences of having the best possible of all governments impose upon you the necessity of being the first workshop in the world. You labour incessantly for happiness. If you find it, all is well."

Curiously, Hermsprong's manner towards women is one of affected gallantry: he acknowledges that this is an exception to his principle of universal sincerity. But when reluctantly entrapped into a serious discussion of the question, he takes a thoroughly progressive stand for the education and human dignity of women, ending:

Women have minds untrained, which instead of ranging the worlds of metaphysics and logic are confined to these ideas of routs and Ranelaghs. . . . If

[1] *Man As He Is Not*, vol. ii., p. 164.
[2] *Ibid.*, p. 162.

"a firm mind and a firm body" be the best prayer of men to the gods, why not of women? . . . But while they think as much of their charms as you suppose them to do, Mrs. Wollstonecraft must write in vain. . . . Be not angry with me. Be women what they may, I am destined to be their adorer. Be angry with Mrs. Wollstonecraft, who has lately abused the dear sex through two octavo volumes.[1]

In other words, Robert Bage was not very vitally interested in that part of the revolution in thought which pertained to the position of women. It is safe to say that he had done a good deal of thinking about woman. In his earlier novels he theorizes extensively on the attitude of society towards certain phases of the woman question. But in this last novel his interest is centred on other issues. He evades feminism as far as possible or treats the whole matter with a whimsical sentimentality.

After considering Bage's novels separately, it may prove illuminating to summarize those radical principles which seemed to his contemporaries so dangerous. They may be grouped under two general headings: (1) religious and ethical; and (2) political and economic.

[2] (1) Doctrinal disputes seem to Robert Bage

[1] *Man As He Is Not*, vol. ii., pp. 167, 168.
[2] Sir Walter Scott offers a suggestion of considerable importance at this point. "Bage appears, from his peculiar style to have been educated a Quaker, and he always painted the individuals of that primitive sect of Christians in amiable colours,

futile and absurd. His books give abundant testimony to his dislike for all forms of bigotry. He follows the radical opinion of his time in regarding priests and kings as fellow-conspirators to enslave the human mind. References to the ignorance and corruption existing among the clergy of the Established Church are numerous, but not unfair. *Hermsprong* is the only one of his novels in which satire on the clergy seems part of a deliberate purpose, and even here there is a cheerful admission that the type of "Dr. Blick" is by no means universal. Nor is his opposition confined to the abuses of the Established Church: dissenters

---

when they are introduced as personages in his novels. If this was the case, however, he appears to have wandered from their tenets into the wastes of scepticism."

Later authorities (Chalmers's *General Biographical Dictionary*, etc.) state positively that Bage was a member of the Society of Friends. But the accounts of Bage by his contemporaries, Hutton and Godwin, which form the basis of the encyclopaedia articles, say nothing of this. It seems probable that this suggestion of Scott's, which is after all only a suggestion, may have proved misleading. If Bage presents us with some very attractive Quakers it is also true that at times he writes rather scathing criticisms of that sect. The novels themselves can hardly be said, therefore, to offer conclusive evidence on this point. Neither can such characteristics of Bage's as his dislike of war, of duelling, and of extravagances in dress be taken as evidence. There were many opinions which the Revolutionary sympathizers held in common with the Quakers. Mrs. Opie passes quite naturally from Godwin's particular clique into the Society of Friends.

It is interesting to observe that in his *History of Derby* Hutton gives a list of the dissenting denominations represented in the neighbourhood in which Bage lived; and the Society of Friends is not among them.

of all sorts, even Quakers, come in for their share of shrewd criticism. Perhaps the real attitude of Bage in matters of religion is most fully expressed by James Foston, a character whom Bage might well have drawn from the mirror.

The mere ceremonial forms of religion I had learned among you English to think of very little account. The perpetual view of these absurdities engrafted in my mind a strong contempt. Thus I came at length to bound my own religion within the narrow, (though to me comprehensive), bounds of the silent meditation of a contrite heart lifting up its humble aspiration to the Author and Preserver of all being, by what name soever called throughout the universe. All the rest appears to me invention or convention, sometimes useful, sometimes detrimental to mankind. I speak not of moral duties; they are of another class.[1]

But whatever his own belief, the one point which he emphasizes again and again is the necessity of tolerance and courteous open-mindedness in discussing all matters of opinion, religious and political.

Bage is very careful to distinguish between matters of opinion, for which a man is not responsible, and matters of conduct. He is not so clear as to the distinction between feeling and conduct. Occasionally the "bosom heaving with a story of distress" is taken as an incontrovertible proof of moral integrity. But on the whole, in

[1] *Mount Henneth, Ballantyne's Novelists Library*, vol. ix., p. 165.

ethical theory as well as in literary practice, Bage is fairly free of Sentimentalism.

Contrary to Holbach and Helvetius, Bage asserts firmly that: "There do exist motives in human action that cannot be traced to love of self." But the basis of his ethical system is that: "Virtue alone can secure true happiness." Virtue he defines as: "Action directed for the benefit of mankind."[1] The only standards of honour or of courtesy he recognizes are those founded on sincerity, benevolence, and good sense. Hence he consistently opposes duelling, and all the ostentation and formality of the polite society of his time.

In 1824, twenty-three years after the death of the author, Sir Walter Scott included three of Bage's novels in a collection which he was editing.[2] The preface written on this occasion is for our purpose a very significant one. Scott evidently finds himself in the awkward position of enjoying the work of a man whose whole point of view he considers in the highest degree dangerous to society. He is praising under protest; and it speaks well for the critical fairness of the politically conservative Sir Walter that the estimate he gives us of Bage as a man and as a novelist is both just and generous. "But if not vicious himself," says Scott, "Bage's leading principles are such as if acted upon would bring vice into society; such

[1] *Mount Henneth, Ballantyne's Novelists Library*, vol. ix., p. 117.
[2] *Ballantyne's Novelists Library.*

being the case it was the editor's duty to point out the sophistry upon which they were founded."

The charges against Bage are various. He has "wandered into the wastes of scepticism. His religious opinions are those of a sectary who has reasoned himself into an infidel . . . and could be a friend neither to the Church of England nor to the doctrine she teaches." His code of ethics is unsound, based upon "the self-sufficient morality of modern philosophy."[1] Scott had no great opinion of the novel as a vehicle for influencing public thought, or it is questionable whether any amount of literary merit would have induced him to include Bage in his collection.

(2) The extreme nature of the religious and ethical principles we have considered is somewhat less apparent after the lapse of a century. But for the warning preface, we should hardly be in a position to realize how dangerous Robert Bage appeared to his conservative contemporaries. The charge of prejudice which Scott brings against Bage's political point of view must be taken more seriously.

His opinions of state affairs [he shrewdly suggests], were perhaps a little biased by frequent visits of the excisemen who levied taxes on his commodities for the purpose of maintaining a war which he disapproved of. It is most natural that a person who considered tax-gatherers extortioners, and soldiers who were paid by the taxes, as licensed murderers, should conceive the whole existing state of human affairs to

[1] *Ballantyne's Novelists Library*, vol. ix., preface p. xxvi.

be wrong; and if he was conscious of talent and the power of composition, he might at the same time fancy that he was called upon to put it to rights.[1]

This suggestion resolves itself into two separate charges: the first, that Bage conceives the whole existing system to be wrong; secondly, that he bases this opinion upon a wrongness in that portion of the social system that affects him as an individual. If we turn to the novels themselves for evidence, we shall find that while both these statements are to some extent true, neither is true without comment and explanation.

There is a very real distinction, and one which cannot be too constantly borne in mind in our discussion, between the man who denounces the corruptions and abuses into which society has fallen, and the man who believes these abuses to be inherent in the very structure of society, the direct and inevitable result of the existing system. It is the distinction between the Reformer and the Revolutionist. Holcroft, Godwin, and Shelley are Revolutionists by nature, Radicals in the true sense of the word; their axe is laid to the root of society, and no judicious prunings and purifications will satisfy them. Bage, on the contrary, in his first four novels nowhere implies that "the whole existing state of affairs is wrong," and he certainly has no intention of putting it right by propaganda novels.

[1] *Ballantyne's Novelists Library*, vol. ix., preface, p. xxvi.

The following is fairly typical of the nature of his criticisms of society. In *Barham Downs*, Sir Ambrose Archer writes to a friend:

I also, Mr. Councillor Brevity, am a man of importance, a public man sir, of the patriotic gender. I am returned from a meeting called an association, the object of which is to call upon Parliament with a loud voice for the redress of our grievances. And what are your grievances says a well pensioned gentleman, Mr. T'otherside. The Crown hath acquired too much influence in the worst of all possible ways, corruption. That our representatives injure their health—by too long sitting. That as we never saw the least possible benefit from engaging in the American war, we see as little from its continuance. Finally, that the ministers carry their contempt for money (public money, we mean) to an extreme.[1]

Bage considers the Administration corrupt, negligent, and inefficient. He believes that popular elections are reduced to a farce. His final warnings and denunciations, however, are directed not against tyranny and oppression but against the growing extravagance and love of display. The luxury and ostentation of those who have accumulated large fortunes have corrupted all classes of society. He looks back wistfully to the beginning of the century (before the Industrial Revolution), "when nabobs were not."

It is the last two novels, written after the out-

[1] *Ballantyne's Novelists Library*, vol. ix., p. 294.

break of the French Revolution (not included in Scott's collection), which give Scott a certain basis for the first half of his statement. The storm of radical philosophies which accompanied the political phenomena on the continent, and their English interpretations in the works of such men as Godwin and Paine, served to generalize Bage's specific dissatisfactions with the Government. The reaction that came with the outbreak of war in 1793, and the harsh repressive measures adopted toward Revolutionists crystallized his theories into a demand for genuinely radical changes. *Man As He Is* and *Man As He Is Not* are, as we have seen, conscious expressions of a political point of view. Bage at this time endorses the *Rights of Man*, considers the government of the United States on the whole the most perfect in existence, and has good hopes that in the end France will return to liberty and peace. But be it observed that even in the height of his Revolutionary fervour Bage desires no anarchistic Utopia. He merely expresses a growing conviction that the maladjustments of his time lie too deep to be reached by reform. In no single paragraph does he declare it essential that England should become a republic; but that is implied as an alternative to changes in the existing form almost as sweeping.

We may, I think, admit the truth of Scott's second charge, that Bage's political theories are largely the outgrowth of his practical experience, without reflecting at all upon the disinterestedness of our genial paper manufacturer. As a successful business man and a humane and intelligent employer, he was in a position to realize all the maladjustments arising from the Industrial Revolution. Hence there is a definiteness and practicality in his ideals of government that is lacking in the work of professional literary men like Godwin and Holcroft. Moreover, if Bage's opinions were coloured by his life, it is also true that his life conformed to his opinions. It is from the little brick-floored cottage beside his own prosperous factory that he directs his shafts of satire against the money-snobs, great and small.

SECTION 2: NOVELS REPRESENTING MISCELLANEOUS NOVELISTS

In considering the work of those novelists most completely imbued with the Revolutionary philosophies and the novels written in opposition to them, it is apparent that we have by no means covered our field. As in every strongly marked intellectual movement, the opinions of the full adherents of Revolutionism were reflected in varying degrees by a large number of sympathizers. These range from an almost complete acceptance of the doctrines of Paine and Godwin to the merest Whig liberalism, or to a Sentimentalism that vaguely acknowledges a kinship with that of Rousseau.

Robert Bage, the only novelist of this class whose

life and works merit detailed consideration, may be taken as typical. He represents the intelligent and disinterested Radical; unaffected by the absurdities of Pure Reason, yet perceiving a fundamental justice in many of the charges brought against existing conditions. Our discussion of Bage may be supplemented by a brief review of a number of novels illustrating other types of Revolutionary sympathies.

Perhaps the earliest example of tendenz fiction we need examine is a curious old novel entitled *The Man in the Moon: or, Travels Into the Lunar Regions by the Man of the People* (1783, anon.). This is a satire on Charles James Fox, probably by a fellow Whig of a somewhat more conservative temper. Already, it appears, there were foreshadowings of these doctrines which later seemed so dangerous to men of the type of Burke.

The plan of the satire is rather fantastic. The Man of the Moon determines to enlighten and reform C—s F—x, called The Man of the People, a statesman of ability who has been led into demagoguery by his love of power. His education is conducted by a trip to the moon, which a student (the author), is assigned to the duty of reporting. In the moon, Fox meets and converses with great orators and statesmen of the past, and sees the punishments necessary to purify them from the faults of ambition, self-interest, and treachery.

It is significant, however, that throughout the

book there are continual praises of "ancient republican virtues," the "foolish titles which at present prevail in Europe"[1] are denounced, and the forerunners of the Pure Reason philosophers are quoted with approval. Hume is made a sort of tutelary spirit in the moon. "Price, Clarke, Wollaston and others who maintain that moral distinctions are perceived by the active energy of the intellect are right in their speculations."[2] Fox is much impressed by his trip to the moon, and promises "not to have any hand in destroying the constitution of England," or at least that: "It will proceed from a dread of being excluded from office if I shall ever be reduced to so direful a necessity."[3]

In 1789, the date of the actual beginning of the French Revolution, there appeared two novels containing no very startling doctrines but significant of the trend of popular interest. *The Bastile, or The Adventures of Charles Townley* (anon.) is merely a pleasant satire on fashionable France. The author states in the first chapter his nearest approach to a "doctrine":

A vanity of illustrious ancestry is a prevailing and universal passion, though the most cursory observer must perceive that there is much real honour to be met with among men whose arms are not blazoned in the herald's office.[4]

The Amicable Quixote, or, The Enthusiasm of

[1] *The Man in the Moon*, vol. ii., p. 39.   [2] *Ibid.*, vol. i., p. 139.
[3] *Ibid.*, vol. ii., p. 35.   [4] *The Bastile*, vol. i., p. 1.

Friendship (1789, anon.) is a novel of the "ruling passion" variety. Here, too, there is considerable satire directed against pride of birth. The hero wins his lady through serving her in the disguise of a butler.[1] The lady herself is not without interest. She might almost be considered a prototype of "Lady Susan."[2] She had "most noble sentiments and very high ideas of propriety; but this sense of decorum would sometimes evaporate in the vindication of her own liberty."[3] Evidently this type of heroine was not unknown before the *Vindication of the Rights of Women*.

In 1794 appeared an adaptation from the German of Professor Kramer's *Hermon of Unna: A Series of Adventures of the Fifteenth Century*, with a preface pointing out that "the horrors of the Star Chamber, the Inquisition, and the Bastile" are among the "consequences that follow when men yield up their understandings to the dictate of authority. Let us remember this, and congratulate ourselves that we are born in an age of illumination, and at a time when the artifices of superstition and tyranny are fated to vanish before the touch of truth."[4]

The rebellion of the Vendée furnished material for at least one novel, partly historical and partly tendenz in treatment, which has Charlotte Corday

---

[1] *Cf.* Bage's *James Wallace*, pub. the preceding year.
[2] Cf. *Robert and Adela*, discussed in Chapter VII., Sec. 3.
[3] *Amicable Quixote*, vol. i., p. 30.
[4] *Hermon of Unna*, preface, p. i.

for a heroine and Marat for villain.[1] The fictitious part of the story centres in the "Countess de Narbonne," an "Aristocrat" who has been forced by the Commune under Marat to marry a coarse and brutal hanger-on of the Convention. Distrusted alike by her own party and by her husband's Republican associates, the unhappy Countess lives in proud seclusion on her estate in the Vendée. Charlotte Cordet,[2] whose father owns a neighbouring estate, becomes her devoted friend. The Countess gives refuge to a mysterious Princess Victorine, a daughter of Emperor Joseph by a morganatic marriage, whom the Royalists wish to raise to the throne of France. After many vicissitudes the Countess escapes to England, with Victorine and her lover. Marat has persecuted them relentlessly, and finally causes the death of Charlotte's father and lover. The novel closes with his assassination by Charlotte and her execution.

Although the author is evidently more interested in the dramatic than in the philosophical values of the French Revolution, she makes numerous significant comments. Her own attitude towards the Revolution is a Whiggism, conservative when compared with even so mild a radical as Bage, very liberal in contrast to that of the country at large.

---

[1] *Adelaide de Narbonne, with Memoirs of Charlotte de Cordet*, 1800. "By the author of *Henry of Northumberland*" (evidently, a woman; speaks of herself as "she").

[2] This curious spelling of the heroine's name occurs without apparent significance. No effort is made to conceal her identity under a fictitious personality.

The errors committed in its different stages are by no means approved of by me [she writes], but I execrate rather the necessity of the times from which they proceed, than the unfortunate individuals who are forced to have recourse to them.[1]

She quotes Hume with approval; but she nowhere falls into the popular error of dividing her characters into sheep and goats on the basis of their political convictions. Charlotte is described as "a Republican, but a rational one. She wished for reforms in a government which even the most sanguine advocates for monarchy cannot deny wanted them."[2] Her lover, on the other hand, was an aristocrat; "but his principles, like her own, were rational, and of course tended equally to the same end, though the means used for attempting it might vary a little."[3]

Another novel appealing by its title to popular interest in the Revolution is *Arthur Mervin, or, Memoirs of the Year 1793*, by Charles Brockden Brown, 1803. The action takes place chiefly in Philadelphia. The author is obviously somewhat influenced by Godwin; but his interests are humanitarian rather than political.[4]

Less Revolutionary and more distinctively humanitarian in its purpose is *Asmodeus, or, The*

[1] *Adelaide de Narbonne*, vol. i., p. 185.
[2] *Ibid.*, vol. i., p. 31.
[3] *Ibid.*, vol. i., p. 154.
[4] *Cf.* section on Godwin, for connexion between ideas of Revolution and humanitarianism.

Devil in London (1808, anon.). The preface describes this as a novel of anecdote, with machinery borrowed from Le Sage. Few aspects of London life escape the shrewd, satiric comment of Asmodeus, but his severest strictures are directed against the prison system, private mad-houses conducted without supervision, and ostentatious and inefficient charities. Among other subjects discussed are freedom of the press, duelling, fashionable extravagance, the French police, and the evil influences of Methodists, Illuminati, and other types of enthusiast. There is an interesting passage in the discussion of suicide:

Here rest the bones of a woman of uncommon talents and singular opinions. Her writings will be long remembered, although their dangerous tendency will be regretted; for whatever error attached either to her life or opinions was the effect of principle—but of principle founded on the chimeras of a visionary.[1]

Naturally, the anti-slavery movement was one of great significance for both humanitarian and Revolutionary sympathizers. Since the time of Oronooko, the noble-minded negro had been a familiar figure in sentimental fiction. To the Rousseauist he acquired a peculiar interest as exemplifying primitive man in an ideal state of nature. To the Godwinian philosopher, chattel slavery was an especially flagrant violation of

[1] It will be remembered that Mary Wollstonecraft twice attempted suicide.

political justice. To the practical reformer, the slave trade was one of the burning issues of the time. As early as 1780 Burke had prepared a code for the gradual abolition of the slave traffic. In 1788 he "spoke strongly to the effect that the trade was one which ought to be totally abolished, but if this was not now possible it ought to be regulated at once."[1]

In 1792 appeared the best known of the anti-slavery novels, Mackenzie's *Slavery, or, The Times*. The plot is characteristic: Zimza, king of Tonouwah, an eighteenth century Oronooko, sends his son to England to be educated, under the care of his friend Hamilton, with the instruction, "Remind him of his dignity as a man, but let him claim no consequence from his birth."[2] The negro prince, "full of the grandeur of untaught soul," makes the usual naïve comments on civilization, cannot be taught the distinction between courtesy and lies, etc., etc. Meanwhile Zimza is captured and sold as a slave. The prince and Hamilton rescue him, and, after sundry adventures in England and France, they return together to the virtuous (and uncivilized) realm of Tonouwah.

[1] Lecky, *England in the Eighteenth Century*, vol. vi., p. 219. The slave trade was not abolished, however, until 1807. It seems a curious bit of irony that it was the panic created by the French Revolution that delayed this reform. Danton testified that one of the motives of the abolition of slavery in the French colonies was the hope of inciting the negroes in the colonies of England to revolt; hardly a step to conciliate English opponents of emancipation.   [2] *Slavery, or, the Times*, vol. i., p. 4.

Mackenzie's comments on the French Revolution are somewhat adverse; he is a pure Rousseauist, not a Republican. His Frenchmen tell Hamilton: "The liberty we contend for blossoms sweetly in your nation. Had our mode of government been mild as yours, the rights of royalty would have been equally secure."[1] Even an American is made to say: "When I fought in America, it was to protect my property. Even then my heart spoke in favour of monarchy; and though I detest all arbitrary power, I am much against unprincipled liberty."[2]

At about the same time there were published in England adaptations of a somewhat similar novel from the French. At least two versions appeared, under different titles: *Itanoko, or The Noble Minded Negro*, and *The Negro Equalled by Few Europeans*. This is an appeal to the principles of pure reason rather than to Rousseauistic benevolence. The plot is of course a variation of the usual theme: the noble savage kidnapped into slavery.

An indirect method of attacking or defending the institution of monarchy was the publication of semi-fictitious memoirs. In 1794 there appeared an English adaptation of a French work, *Interesting Memoirs of Marie Antoinette, Ci-devant Queen of France*. One would infer from this highly scandalous narrative that her execution was amply justified.

[1] *Slavery*, vol. ii., p. 237. [2] *Ibid.*, vol. ii., p. 215.

Another fictitious memoir, published soon after, presented royalty in a more favourable light. *Henrietta, Princess Royal of England, Daughter of King Charles I.* (1796) professes to be a narrative by the Comtesse de Lafayette (grandmother of the Revolutionary Marquis), which was brought to light by the sacking of the Louvre, and immediately suppressed in France by the Revolutionary government.

The censure of royalty by no means confined itself to that of other nations. In 1812 appeared *The Spirit of the Book, or, Memoirs of Caroline, Princess of Hapsbourg: A Political and Amatory Romance*, by Captain T. Ashe. This makes its appeal rather to a love of scandal than to any political sentiments, and but for occasional spiteful attacks on the morale of courts and kings in general would not call for mention here.[1]

The novels of Thomas Love Peacock have some claim to be included in our discussion. There is scarcely one of them which does not express Revolutionary sentiments. *Maid Marian* (1818) especially contains many passages of political theorizing that might have been written by Shelley or Godwin himself. A detailed consideration of Peacock's novels would, however, add little to our discussion. Peacock's Revolutionism is at best sympathetic and derivative. His intimate association with the Shelley group, together with a

[1] It should perhaps be made clear that the Charlotte of Hapsbourg here mentioned was Princess of Wales.

certain irritable dislike of the established régime in Church and State, gave a Revolutionary bent to his satire. But the vital impetus of Revolutionism had spent itself before it reached Peacock. He is the echo of an echo. In spirit, if not altogether in actual chronology, his novels belong a generation later than the period we are considering.

This part of our discussion might be expanded almost indefinitely. So extensive is the material available and so varied the shades of opinion represented that our selection must necessarily be somewhat arbitrary. Little is to be gained by multiplying illustration. It is already clear that novels dealing with the ideas and tendencies associated with the French Revolution represent almost as many different points of view as there were novelists. We are dealing with very complex reactions to a very complex movement; it is impossible to do more than indicate certain general types of opinion.

CHAPTER VI

SOME TYPICAL LADY NOVELISTS OF THE REVOLUTION

SECTION I: MRS. ELIZABETH INCHBALD

ONE of the literary features of the later eighteenth century in England was the large crop of Lady Novelists. A Lady Novelist, be it observed, is altogether a different thing from a woman who writes novels. The latter may sometimes allow us to forget her sex; the former, never. There is a soft rustle of skirts in every page, from the little bobs and curtsies of her preface to the gentle severity of the sermonette with which she concludes. Her style is redolent of delicate femininity. She is the most charming of Sentimentalists, and withal the most implacable of moralists. Her didacticism lifts hands of demure horror at any suspected laxness of opinion.

She worships the proprieties. Whoso offends against decorum comes straightway to an evil end. Even heroines languishing under a false accusation get small sympathy from the author. They should have been more cautious in avoiding the very appearance of indiscretion. And yet the Lady Novelist has a Christian charity for handsome, rakish heroes if they promise reform in the last chapter.

Her favourite virtues are the domestic ones: filial and parental affection, wifely submission and fidelity, patience, good nature, economy, charity to the poor, devoutness in religious observance. These she thoroughly understands, and never tires of illustrating.

If we must smile over the works of the Lady Novelist, let it be with respect, for these are the virtues of delight without which no fine heroisms can make life tolerable. There was a surprising amount of good sense under her gentility. Her world had no real heights or depths; but at least it was a sane and comfortable one. Moreover, not infrequently her Sentimentalism yields to an exquisite sense of humour, and a rare gift for satirizing the smaller vices and foibles of mankind. All honour to Lady Novelists; for the greatest among them was no less a person than the inimitable Jane.

There was little natural affinity between the Lady Novelists and the Revolution. That movement of revolt was more concerned to demand the rights of women than to exalt the beneficent influence of "the fair sex." But there were some few gentle feminine souls who through their humanitarian sympathies, the influence of Rousseau, or a personal association with the leaders of English Revolutionism, were swept into the heterodox currents of the time.

Among the most prominent of these was the pretty actress and dramatist, Elizabeth Inchbald. Her life was in no way noteworthy. Elizabeth was the youngest daughter of John Simpson, a Suffolk farmer. As a child, her chief characteristics were her beauty and the love of admiration that was always her ruling passion. She seems to have chosen her profession early, and made heroic efforts to overcome the impediment in her speech that threatened to unfit her for it. As a stage-struck little girl of sixteen she began secret negotiations with a local theatrical manager. Apparently he gave her some encouragement, for "Richard Griffiths" appears in her diary in ecstatic childish capitals, with the inscription: "Each dear letter of thy name is harmony." Two years later she ran away to try her fortune in London, where she wandered about for several days before her brother-in-law found her, frightened and penniless, and took her home with him. While visiting her sister she made the acquaintance of a middle-aged actor named Joseph Inchbald, whom she married soon afterwards, apparently in despair of being able to make her way in London alone. Through his assistance she obtained the coveted entrée to the stage. But one fancies she soon perceived the unwisdom of taking a husband when what she really wanted was a chaperon. After seven years of not altogether happy married life and many vicissitudes as an actress, Mrs. Inchbald was left a widow at the age of twenty-six and never ventured into matrimony again. Like Holcroft, she made but an indifferent success on the stage, took to writing plays and novels as a means of increasing her income, and finally gave up acting altogether. By 1783 we find her settled in London, a prominent figure in literary society.

Elizabeth Inchbald had three merits which no one denied: beauty, cleverness, and an unblemished reputation. Of the value of these she was fully conscious. There are rumours of her throwing a kettle of hot water over one not sufficiently respectful admirer, and pulling the hair of another. In telling the story afterwards she concluded: "Oh, if he had wo-wo-worn a wig, I had been ru-ruined!" She received many offers of marriage, but none sufficiently advantageous to tempt her. There was a cool, calculating shrewdness under all her coquetry and caprice.

Perhaps her finest characteristic was her perfect freedom from snobbishness, and her loyalty to the humble ways of her own home. Her style of living was economical in the extreme; she escapes the charge of penuriousness only because of the generous uses she made of her savings. She wore gowns, Mrs. Shelley tells us, "not worth a shilling," and there was one occasion when a carriage bearing a crest waited while she finished scrubbing her attic room, and then drove her to visit her sister who was a barmaid near London. Godwin describes her as "a piquante mixture between a lady and a milkmaid."[1]

The one absorbing passion of Elizabeth Inchbald's life seems to have been her love of admiration; especially masculine admiration, for she was never a woman's woman. She was jealous of rivalry. Once when she found herself beside Mrs. Siddons in the Green Room, "suddenly looking at her magnificent neighbor, she said 'No, I won't s-s-sit by you; you're t-t-too handsome!'"[2] But it was not often that she met with serious rivalry. It was said that: "When Mrs. Inchbald came into a room and sat down in a chair in the middle of it as was her wont, every man gathered around it, and it was vain for any other woman to attempt to gain attention."[3]

The account of Mrs. Inchbald's relations with the other novelists of our group is somewhat amusing. Report said that: "Mrs. Inchbald was in love with Godwin, Godwin with Miss Alderson, Miss Alderson with Holcroft, and Holcroft with Mrs. Inchbald."[4] Reading between the lines, with the aid of the diaries and letters of the parties concerned, one suspects that the truth of the matter was something like this. Both Godwin and Holcroft were Mrs. Inchbald's intimate friends;

---

[1] Paul, *William Godwin*, vol. i., p. 74.
[2] Taylor, *Records of My Life*, vol. i., pp. 347–409.
[3] Paul, *William Godwin*, vol. i., p. 74.
[4] Brightwell, *Memorials of Amelia Opie*, p. 60.

there is ample indication that, at one time, had she chosen to marry an impecunious literary man, she might have had either of them. But when Amelia Alderson came to London, in 1794, she made quite an impression on these too-susceptible disciples of pure reason. Elizabeth Inchbald was not the woman to give up an admirer willingly. She resorted to crude, tale-bearing methods, which aroused Amelia's resentment and inspired her with a natural and laudable feminine desire to spoil Elizabeth's monopoly.[1] Fortified with this noble motive and a becoming new bonnet[2] Amelia Alderson entered the lists against the veteran coquette, with such success that before she left London, Holcroft had been refused outright and the austere Godwin was cherishing her discarded slipper as a tender relic.[3]

Before we leave this digression into the gossip of a century ago, there is a more serious charge of jealousy that must be brought against Elizabeth Inchbald. It is said that she wept at the news of Godwin's marriage. Whatever her real feelings were, she, bohemian of bohemians, suddenly developing scruples for the proprieties, took oc-

[1] She writes: "Mrs. I. appears to me jealous of G.'s attention to me, so she makes him believe I prefer H. to him. . . . Is not this very womanish?" Brightwell, *Memorials of Amelia Opie*, p. 60.

[2] Mrs. Brightwell describes the bonnet, in her *Memorials*. It was light blue, with blue plumes.

[3] Thackerary, *Book of Sibyls*, pp. 161 f.: "Will you give me nothing to keep for your sake?" says Godwin, parting from Amelia, "not even your slipper?"

casion to insult Mary Wollstonecraft publicly, and injure her by private report.

One source of Mrs. Inchbald's Revolutionism is obvious: the influence of her friendship with Godwin and Holcroft. There is another, not quite so obvious. We have noted the curious affinity between Revolutionism and the various dissenting bodies. Mrs. Inchbald was a devout Roman Catholic. At first glance it seems rather contradictory that the creed which adheres most rigidly to the principle of authority should have tended to produce a sympathy with the political doctrines of revolt. But Catholics and dissenters suffered alike under legal discrimination. Fellowship in oppression produces strange alliances.[1]

Whatever the source, Mrs. Inchbald's Revolutionism was of the mildest. One of her plays, *Every One Has His Fault* (1793), was absurdly accused of having a seditious tendency, by a periodical called *The True Briton*.[2] On the other hand, in 1792, another play of hers, *The Massacre*, dealing severely with the atrocities of the Terror, was seriously objected to by Holcroft and Godwin. It was written without any doctrinary intention, however, for Mrs. Inchbald writes to Godwin: "It was your

[1] Lest this seem a fanciful connexion, we may quote a passage from Elwood's *Memoirs of Literary Ladies* (vol. i., p. 20): "Belonging as she did to the Roman Catholic community—Mrs. I. necessarily advocated liberal opinions."

[2] Tobler, *Elizabeth Inchbald*, p. 39. The humanitarian tendencies of her other plays we will discuss in Chapter IX., Section 2, of this thesis.

hinting to me that it might do harm which gave me the first idea that it might do good by preventing future massacres."[1]

There is a record of a *Satire on the Times* (now lost), of which she writes:

> I said to myself, how pleased Mr. Godwin will be at my making the King so avaricious, and—how pleased the King will be at my making him so good at the conclusion. He will . . . generously pardon me all that I have said about equality in the book, merely for giving him a good character.[2]

Mrs. Inchbald was the author of two novels, both of which are generally credited with Revolutionary tendencies. The first, *A Simple Story*, was begun in 1777, but was not published until 1791. This is really two novels thrown together. In the first part, Miss Milner, an orphan, is left as a ward to a young priest named Dorriforth. The frivolous, pleasure-loving girl leads her guardian an anxious life of it, and ends by secretly falling in love with him. Dorriforth unexpectedly falls heir to an earldom. The Pope dispenses him from his vows in order to keep the succession in a Catholic family. He marries Miss Milner. An interval of seventeen years elapses before the second part of the novel begins. Meanwhile, Miss Milner has

---

[1] Paul, *William Godwin*, vol. i., p. 74. The publisher liked the subject no better than Godwin did, and the play was suppressed, though printed, before publication.

[2] *Ibid.*, vol. i., p. 141.

proved unfaithful to her husband, and he has cast her off, together with his infant daughter. On the death of her mother the Earl consents to let Lady Matilda live in a secluded part of his castle, but only on condition that he is never to see her. The Earl's nephew, Rushbrook, whom he has made his heir in Matilda's place, falls in love with her. Of course the novel ends with a reconciliation and a wedding. The moral is, "the pernicious effects of an improper education, in the destiny which attended the unthinking Miss Milner. On the opposite side, what may be hoped from that school of prudence through adversity, in which Matilda was bred."[1] On the ground of this moral, of which we hear nothing until the last page, *A Simple Story* has been commonly classified among the tendenz novels written to illustrate the educational theories of Rousseau. As there is absolutely no emphasis on education anywhere else in the novel, it seems more probable that the moral was merely tacked on in an attempt to give unity to what is obviously two separate stories.

A more genuine interest lies in the fact that Miss Milner is supposed to represent the author herself, and Dorriforth, John Kemble (the actor), who left a Catholic seminary to go on the stage, and for whom Mrs. Inchbald is credited with a decided partiality.

The second of Mrs. Inchbald's novels, *Nature and Art* (1796), shows more clearly defined Re-

[1] *A Simple Story*, p. 372.

volutionary doctrines. The story is built on the favourite device of two brothers with contrasting dispositions. Henry, the younger, helps William to an education and a start in the Church. As William obtains ecclesiastical preferment and makes a wealthy marriage, he neglects his humbler brother, who is only a fiddler by profession. Henry goes to Africa, taking with him an infant son. After several years of Robinson Crusoe adventures among more or less noble savages, he sends young Henry, then a boy of twelve, to England to be under his uncle's care. William also has a son of about the same age. Here begins the contrast between the fashionable and the Rousseauistic education. Young William has been trained, parrot-like, by tutors who have never taught him to think. Young Henry, on the contrary, sees the world through unsophisticated eyes and formulates his own opinions.

> He would call compliments, lies—reserve he would call pride—stateliness, affectation—and for the words war and battle, he constantly substituted the word massacre.[1]

He cannot seem to grasp the conception that the poor are born to serve the rich. Nor can he perceive how really comfortable the poor would be but for their laziness and thriftlessness. A lord speaks of his charitable gifts:

[1] *Nature and Art*, p. 412.

"How benevolent!" exclaimed the Dean.
"How prudent!" exclaimed Henry.
"What do you mean by prudent?" asked Lord Bendham.
"Why, then my Lord," answered Henry, "I thought it was prudent in you to give a little, lest the poor, driven to despair, should take all."[1]

The two boys grow to manhood. Both fall in love with village girls. William deserts his sweetheart, Agnes, whom he never intended to marry. She attempts to kill her child. Henry saves it, and gives it to his fiancée Rebecca to care for. Agnes is driven out of the village by the rigid virtue of the lady of the manor. She wanders to London, and there, unable to find employment, drifts from bad to worse. William meanwhile has become a successful lawyer, and finally risen to the bench. Agnes is brought before him for trial on a charge of counterfeiting. He does not recognize her.

But when William placed the fatal velvet on his head and rose to pronounce her sentence, she started with a kind of convulsive motion, retreated a step or two back, and lifting up her hands, with a scream, exclaimed—

"Oh, not from YOU!"

Serene and dignified as if no such exclamation had been uttered, William delivered the fatal speech, ending with "Dead, dead, dead."

She fainted as he closed the period, and was carried

[1] *Nature and Art*, p. 433.

back to prison in a swoon; while he adjourned court to go to dinner.[1]

Agnes leaves a letter which makes William's subsequent life a prey to remorse. Henry, less successful but more happy, rescues his father from Africa, marries his faithful Rebecca, and settles down as a contented farmer.

Professor Cross classes this novel with *Caleb Williams* as "the best examples of the distinctively 'victim-of-society' story."[2] The presence of other characteristic features of Revolutionary fiction is obvious. Young Henry is the unsophisticated critic of civilization of the type of Hermsprong.[3] The satire on lawyers and clergy recalls *Hugh Trevor*. The efforts of Agnes to find employment resemble those of Jemima, in *Maria or the Wrongs of Women*.[4]

On the whole, however, we must conclude that Mrs. Inchbald is a Revolutionist only in her humanitarian sympathies and her dislike of certain specific oppressions and intolerances. She has more in common with Robert Bage than with men of the type of Godwin and Holcroft who are Revolutionists from theory and conviction as well as from sympathy.

[1] *Nature and Art*, p. 527. Mrs. Inchbald's sense of the dramatic value of this situation has recently been justified by the success of a play built on the same idea. (*Madam X*.)

[2] Cross, *The English Novel*, p. 91.

[3] *Cf.* note on *Hermsprong*, in Chapter VI., Section 1, of this thesis.

[4] *Cf.* Chapter VIII., Section 2, of this discussion.

SECTION 2: MRS. AMELIA ALDERSON OPIE

Perhaps the pleasantest of our Lady Novelists, in personality and in literary style, is Mrs. Opie (1769–1853). Throughout her long life she was always in sympathy with the progressive movements of the time. The most interesting people of two generations figure in the pages of her biography.

Amelia Alderson was the only child of a Norwich physician, a Unitarian, of radical political principles. Her parents were deeply interested in various humanitarian movements. It is to these early influences that Mrs. Opie ascribed her lifelong zeal for the cause of negro emancipation.

In 1794 she went to London for a visit, and there became acquainted with all the literary Radicals of the Joseph Johnson circle. It was on this visit that she aroused the jealousy of Mrs. Inchbald by her flirtations with the Pure Reason philosophers, of which the letters of the two ladies have left us an amusing account. Miss Alderson attended the trials for High Treason of Hardy, Tooke, and Holcroft. She wrote home indignant accounts of ministerial oppression: "What a pass are things come to when even dissenters lick the hand that oppressed them! Hang these politics! How they haunt me! Would it not be better, think you, to hang the framers of them?"[1] Later, she writes to a friend:

---

[1] Brightwell, *Amelia Opie*, vol. i., p. 47.

I had reason to believe that if the "felons" about to be tried were not "acquitted felons" certain friends of mine would have emigrated to America, and my beloved father would have been induced to accompany them.[1]

On a second visit to London, Miss Alderson met the portrait painter John Opie, to whom she was married in 1798.

In 1805 she visited France, where she went with Ann Plumptre to visit Helen Maria Williams.[2] She also met Fox and Kosciuszko, the Polish patriot, and saw Buonaparte, then First Consul. In 1807 the death of Mr. Opie ended her entirely happy married life, and the young widow returned to her father's home in Norwich. The rest of her life was uneventful. She made the acquaintance of Wordsworth, Southey, Sidney Smith, Sir Walter Scott, Mme. de Staël, and Mme. de Genlis, all of whom thought well of her literary work. But her closest friends were the Gurneys, especially Elizabeth Gurney Fry, Howard's successor in prison reform. It was undoubtedly through the influence of Elizabeth Fry that Mrs. Opie was led in 1825 to become a member of the Society of Friends.

We may say a word here on the subject of Mrs. Opie's previous sectarian affiliations. In 1814 she left the Unitarians with whom her earliest connex-

---

[1] Brightwell, *Amelia Opie*, vol. i., pp. 48 f.
[2] Two literary ladies of well-known Revolutionary sentiments. For Ann Plumptre, *cf.* following Section.

ions had naturally been formed. Her biographer says:

> Many of her relations on her mother's side had been united for generations past to the Wesleyan Methodists, which consideration naturally disposed her to a union with that sect of worshippers.[1]

Her final decision in favour of the Society of Friends was a very natural one for a Revolutionist. Since the time of William Penn that sect had been noted for their sympathy with the most liberal political opinions. It will be remembered that Algernon Sydney helped draft the constitution of Pennsylvania. Many of the finest doctrines of the Revolutionists were identical with those of the Friends. Bage has been generally credited with being a member of that Society, and Holcroft was referred to as "a sort of natural Quaker."[2]

Mrs. Opie must have made a somewhat amusing Friend, one fancies. The fondness for pretty clothes that was one of her most endearingly human characteristics was not laid aside when she put on the "plain" dress. She wore the gown of grey, but it was of pale grey satin, with a modish little train, and we hear of "the crisp fichu crossed over the breast, which set off to advantage the charming little plump figure with its rounded

---

[1] Brightwell, *Amelia Opie*, p. 193.
[2] *Cf.* Chapter II., Chapter IV., and Chapter V., Section 1, note p. 172, for previous discussion of Friends in this thesis.

lines."[1] Her calling cards bore her name "Amelia Opie," in the "plain" style, scrupulously without prefix: but there was an embossed wreath of pink roses about the name! But if the vanities did rather cling to her after she had renounced the world, there was one sacrifice which she made in all seriousness. She gave up writing fiction, and even recalled a novel which was in the hands of her publisher, at no small loss and inconvenience to herself. A book of anecdotes, under the title *Illustrations of Lying*, was her nearest approach to fiction after she joined the Friends.

In 1830 Mrs. Opie revisited Paris. She records her emotion in seeing again the scene of her youthful enthusiasms in some verses, very popular in her own time, beginning: "At sight of thee, O Tricolor, I seem to see youth's hour return." She met Lafayette, whom she calls, "The hero of my childhood, the idol of my youth!"[2]

One incident of this visit to Paris is worth recording. Mrs. Opie writes to a friend:

The Paris intellectual world runs mad just now after a new sect, (a new religion they call it), the Saint Simoniennes: the founder is a St. Simon, of the Duc de St. Simon's family. His disciples preach up equality of property. The thing is, I suspect, more political than anything else in its object; but on a first day there is a religious preaching, and the room overflows; so it does on a week day evening when there are only

[1] Thackeray, *Book of Sibyls*, p. 189.
[2] Brightwell, *Amelia Opie*, p. 234.

lectures. . . . I have vainly tried to read their book of doctrine. I could not get on with it. But as they agree with the Friends in two points, I am sometimes tempted to go one evening. *Nous verrons.*[1]

This comment of one of the last survivors of the older group of Revolutionists is not without a certain interest. St. Simon was one of the earliest of those Utopian socialists who were to some extent the forerunners of the present Marxian Socialism. It is curious that Mrs. Opie should be interested in the St. Simoniennes only as a Friend. Surely in the long years of the Reaction she must have very completely forgotten the spirit of Holcroft, of Godwin, and the rest of the London circle who were her friends in the early nineties, or she would have recognized the old social idealism under the new form. She seems to have had no premonition that this primarily economic, collectivistic Revolutionism might be in some sense the successor to the older, primarily political, individualistic Revolutionism of her youth.[2]

Mrs. Opie was the author of ten works of fiction, five of which were novels, the rest collections of short stories. All contain some expression of her liberal political belief (one can hardly call anything so gentle Revolutionism). As it is obviously not

---

[1] Brightwell, *Amelia Opie*, p. 263.
[2] It will be remembered that Lucas classifies the Illuminati as one of the sects of Revolutionary philosophers. (Chapter IV.) St. Simon was, according to George Sand, high in the councils of the eighteenth-century secret society of that name.

worth our while to discuss all of these in detail, we may confine ourselves to the two in which Revolutionism plays the most important *rôle*, and consider these as typical of the rest.

Adelina Mowbray, or Mother and Daughter (1804) borrows its general idea from the life of Mary Wollstonecraft,[1] but the plot as a whole is entirely fictitious. Adelina Mowbray is the only daughter of a wealthy widow, who poses as being very intellectual. Mrs. Mowbray is especially fond of the new and radical philosophies. Adelina, however, accepts in all earnestness the theories which are merely pose with her mother. Mother and daughter make the acquaintance of the young philosopher, Glenmurray, whose book against marriage has greatly influenced Adelina. Glenmurray, in love with Adelina, wishes to renounce his theories and marry her; but she, enthusiastic and ready for martyrdom, insists that they shall scorn prejudice and dispense with the marriage ceremony. Her mother, horrified, disowns her, saying:

Little did I think you were so romantic, as to see no difference between amusing one's imagination with new theories and new systems, and acting upon them in defiance of common custom and the received usages of society. . . . The poetical philosophy which I have so much delighted to study, has served me to ornament my conversation, and make persons less enlightened than myself wonder at the superior boldness of my

[1] *Cf.* Chapter VIII., Section 2, of this thesis.

fancy and the acuteness of my reasoning powers; but I should as soon have thought of making this little gold chain around my neck fasten the hall door, as act upon the precepts laid down in those delightful books.[1]

Not a bad satire, this, on a certain type of lady Revolutionist. Mrs. Opie is quite capable of appreciating intellectual honesty.

For a number of years Adelina is happy with Glenmurray, in spite of the occasional insults and inconveniences to which her position subjects her. But Glenmurray, always an invalid, goes into consumption. As he is dying he repents of his destructive philosophy. "As those opinions militated against the experience and custom of ages, ought I not to have paused before I published, and kept them back until they received the sanction of my maturer judgment?"[2] He makes Adelina promise that after his death she will marry his cousin Berrendale, who will understand and protect her and her child. But in a few years Berrendale tires of her and deserts her. Left without resources, she appeals to her mother, but receives no answer. After a few years of struggle against illness and poverty, she returns to her old home. Her mother, she finds, had long ago forgiven her, but had been prevented from receiving her letters. Adelina dies, leaving her little daughter to her mother's care, with the pathetic injunction:

[1] *Works of Mrs. Opie*, vol. i., p. 127.
[2] *Ibid.*, vol. i., p. 177.

Oh! Teach my Editha to be humble, teach her to be slow to call the wisdom of ages contemptible prejudices; teach her no opinions that can destroy her sympathies with general society, and make her an alien to the hearts of those among whom she lives.[1]

As a bit of gentle good sense opposed to Pure Reason absurdities, *Adelina Mowbray* is certainly beyond criticism. As an interpretation of Mary Wollstonecraft, if such were intended, it is not unjust, but merely absurdly inadequate. Amelia Opie was one of those simple, kindly souls to whom the real power and originality of a mind like that of Mary Wollstonecraft must remain forever a closed book. Mrs. Opie did not misjudge her friend; she merely did not see quite all that she amounted to. What was to Mary only one side of life, and that not the most important, seems to Mrs. Opie to blot out all the rest. If Godwin sat for Glenmurray, the portrait is a flattering one.

Valentine's Eve (1816) is the only other one of Mrs. Opie's in which Revolutionism is more than incidental. General Shirley has disowned his son for marrying beneath him. When the son is killed in battle, the General relents and adopts his granddaughter, Catherine Shirley, who has grown to womanhood without his seeing her. Catherine is visited in her new home by her foster-sister, Lucy Merle. Mrs. Opie uses the girls to illustrate two somewhat different ideals. Cather-

---

[1] *Mrs. Opie's Works*, vol. i., p. 223.

ine is a girl of enthusiastic religious principles. Lucy represents the Revolutionary philosophy. Her father was "one of the many republicans, or democrats, some twenty years ago, whom profligacy and poverty led to rally round that respectable standard, which was originally erected from the purest love of civil and religious liberty."[1] But Lucy herself represents a finer type; she had "imbibed the purest flame of liberty and the purest love of republicanism." The conclusion at which the author is aiming is the superiority of the religious basis of morals and manners to the philosophical basis even at its best. A speech of Catherine's may be taken as stating the point of the whole novel:

Her standards and mine are different; with her, everything is republican virtue, amongst which virtues she reckons freedom of speech, vehemence to defend opinions which she thinks right at all risks and before all persons. . . . But my standard is Christianity, which teaches forbearance on all occasions as one of the first of duties. . . . Miss Merle has real republican virtues. She is temperate, frugal, industrious, and self-denying. But then these are Christian virtues also; and though I admire moral virtues as much as she can do, I think them durable and precious only as they are derived from religious belief and the consequence of it. Without that, all morals appear built upon a sandy foundation, and are liable to be swept away by the flood of strong temptation. Here Lucy and I differ;—

[1] *Mrs. Opie's Works*, vol. ii., p. 152.

she thinks morality can stand alone, without the aid of religion; nay, she even fancies republican firmness sufficient to enable us to bear affliction. But if she is ever seriously afflicted, I am sure she will find her error.[1]

From all of which it is clear that Mrs. Opie insists on judging a great movement of social idealism by somewhat limited and personal standards. One might even argue that her Christianity is as limited as her Revolutionism.

The rest of the novel is perfectly commonplace. Catherine marries an Earl, and affords an edifying picture of an insistently religious woman in society, which might almost be regarded as a variation of the "Child of Nature" device for criticizing the morals and manners of the world in general. She quotes Scripture in season and out, revels in a martyrdom of singularity, and lives up to the standards of the Sunday School Library—a congenial atmosphere in which, I am told, the works of Mrs. Opie still survive.

Such was Mrs. Opie's Revolutionism. Her early life was passed in an atmosphere of radicalism and dissent. Hence she was, in a gentle feminine fashion, a Republican. But she did not begin to write novels until the age of Reaction had set in. By that time whatever Revolutionary ardour she may have had has faded to an affectionate and respectful memory. Her real interest is in a purely

[1] *Mrs. Opie's Works*, vol. ii., pp. 186, 187.

personal form of religion, and the domestic virtues, like the typical Lady Novelist she is.

SECTION 3: MRS. CHARLOTTE SMITH

Another literary lady who has left in her novels some expression of her liberal political convictions is Mrs. Charlotte Turner Smith (1749–1806). As eldest daughter of a landed gentleman of Sussex, she received an elaborate and expensive education devoted entirely to accomplishments. At the Kensington Seminary where she was sent for a final polish, a schoolmate records:

> She was considered romantic by her young companions; she had read more than any one else in the school, was continually composing verse, and was thought too great a genius for study.[1]

At the age of fifteen she was persuaded by her family into a marriage which did not prove altogether happy. Her young husband seems to have been extravagant, deficient in good sense, and in continual financial difficulties. Under the pressure of necessity Charlotte developed decided business ability. Her stern old father-in-law declared "she could do more from his directions in one hour than any of his clerks in a day."

Besides being the business head of the house, home-maker, and mother of twelve children, Charlotte added to the family income by writing. She finally obtained a legal separation from her worth-

[1] Brightwell, *Literary Ladies*, vol. i., p. 285.

less husband and supported herself almost entirely by her pen. Her published works amounted to nearly fifty volumes.

There are certain circumstances in her life which may have influenced her political opinions: a residence of some years in France, made necessary by her husband's financial difficulties, and the marriage of one of her daughters to a French *émigré*. Her connexion with the little circle of Radicals in London probably did not extend beyond a mere acquaintance with one or two of them.

The first and fullest expression of Charlotte Smith's Revolutionary politics was her novel *Desmond* (1792). The preface gives interesting evidence as to the source of Mrs. Smith's Revolutionism.

As to the political passages dispersed through the work, they are, for the most part, drawn from conversations to which I have been a witness, in England and France, during the last twelve months. In carrying on my story in those countries, and at a period when their political situation (but particularly that of the latter) is the general topic of discourse in both; I have given to my imaginary characters the arguments I have heard on both sides; and if those in favor of one party have evidently the advantage, it is not owing to my partial representation, but to the predominant power of truth and reason, which can neither be altered nor concealed.[1]

[1] *Desmond*, vol. i., p. ii.

The plot is simpler than is usual in novels in letter form. Desmond, a young man of virtue and sensibility, has a Werther-like platonic passion for an unhappily married lady, Mrs. Geraldine Verney. He goes to France to endeavour to forget her, attracted thither by his interest in the Revolution. He visits a young French nobleman of republican sympathies, Count Montfleuri, and his uncle, of intense aristocratic prejudices, Count d'Hauteville. His observations on the actual conditions of the country, as contrasted with the lurid reports that reach England, are detailed in his letters to his friends.

Meanwhile, Mrs. Verney's husband has ruined himself at cards and gone to France, leaving her unprotected with three children to care for. Desmond, returning to England, manages to help her secretly. Her husband sends for her to meet him in France, and she dutifully obeys. She falls into the hands of one of the wild bands of royalist marauders. Desmond rescues her. She learns that her husband was among these bandits, but had been mortally wounded some time before. She and Desmond find him and care for him. He dies, leaving Desmond the guardian of his children. Desmond, of course, marries his Geraldine, and his friend Montfleuri marries her younger sister Fanny.

The letters devoted to the actual narrative would scarcely fill more than one of the three volumes. The rest is devoted to conversations and arguments about the Revolution. One feels that the author is really giving a pretty fair representation of the political conversations afloat in English society at the time. It all has a very natural sound. The young enthusiast Desmond, sure that the Revolution is really ushering in a new era, that all discouraging reports from France are merely misrepresentations by parties interested in preserving despotism; his friend Bethel, older and less sanguine, republican in his sympathies but not so sure of the successful outcome of the present struggle; and the young French nobleman, Montfleuri, with his accurate knowledge of the old régime to balance the mistakes of the new: these represent the radical side. Opposing them, there are all shades of opinion: General Wallingford, irascible, vituperative, who regards the French as the natural enemies of England; Lord Newminster, a young fop, who "wishes the King and Lords may smash them all—and be cursed to them"; a Bishop who defends order, the Establishment, and Church properties; a London merchant, who "wishes the whole race were extirpated, and we were in possession of their country, as in justice it is certain we ought to be,"[1] and a host of others. There is a narrative of a (supposedly typical) French farmer whose life is made intolerable by the game laws and special privileges of his overlord. Montfleuri gives an interesting analysis of the historical causes leading up to the Revolution, and of its philosophies, concluding:

[1] *Desmond*, vol. i., p. 86.

Montesquieu had done as much as a writer, under a despot, dared to do, towards developing the spirit of the laws, and the true principles of government; and, though the multitude heeded not, or understood not his abstract reasoning, he taught those to think, who gradually disseminated his opinions. Voltaire attacked despotism in all its holds, with the powers of resistless wit. . . . Rousseau with matchless eloquence: . . . and, as these were authors who, to the force of reason, added the charms of fancy, they were universally read, and their sentiments were adopted by all classes of men.

The political maxims and economical systems of Turgot, and the application of these principles by Mirabeau, excited a spirit of inquiry, the result of which could not fail of being favourable to the liberties of mankind; and such was the disposition of the people of France, when the ambitious policy of our ministry sent our soldiers into America to support the English colonists in their resistance to the parent state.[1]

Desmond has long discussions with various opponents of Revolutionism, in which he answers the characteristic conservative arguments. The ultra aristocratic Count d'Hauteville advances an argument which (the author says in a footnote) "has been called unanswerable." "You consider your footman on an equality with yourself,—Why then is he your footman?" Desmond answers very concisely that abolishing an aristocracy of birth does not necessarily mean introducing social

Desmond, vol. i., pp. 150–51.

or economic equality. This is a crucial point in Revolutionism. It is to be observed that Charlotte Smith's answer is the answer of early commonsense Revolutionism, not of later philosophic and religious Revolutionism. Bage might have answered so; Holcroft and Shelley never.

The general conclusions of the book are something like the following: "A revolution in the government of France was absolutely necessary; and, that it has been accomplished at less expense of blood, than any other event."[1] English opposition to the French Revolution is due to three principal causes: (1) The ancient hatred to France, as England's natural enemy; (2) misunderstandings, party prejudice, and "the apathy of people who, at ease themselves, indolently acquiesce in evils that do not affect them"; and finally, (3) the vast numbers of people "whose interest, which is what wholly decides their opinions, is diametrically opposite to all reform, and of course, to the reception of those truths which may promote it."[2] Desmond and his friends agree in criticizing the English government. The counts against it are three: (1) Inequality of representation and corrupt elections; (2) penal laws, with capital punishment for slight offences, and unspeakable prison conditions; (3) slow, uncertain and inefficient legal procedure, especially in the

[1] *Desmond*, vol. ii., p. 52. This illustrates the general opinion in 1792.
[2] *Ibid.*, vol. ii., p. 54.

Courts of Equity and Chancery. But the immediate establishment of a republic in England is considered neither necessary nor desirable. Conditions are radically different from those in France.

Charlotte Smith's next novel, *The Old Manor House* (1793), contains no direct references to the French Revolution, and few distinctively doctrinary passages. Nevertheless, it has a certain interest for us. The first part is a satire on pride of birth. Mrs. Rayland, an eccentric old lady of noble family and great wealth, disowns her humble cousin. She is induced, however, to allow his young son Orlando to visit her, and gradually becomes attached to the boy. The plot concerns itself chiefly with the manoeuvrings of Mrs. Rayland to keep Orlando in her power without definitely promising to make him her heir, and with Orlando's love for the housekeeper's gentle niece. Orlando obtains an ensign's commission, and is sent to the war in America. Here follow scathing satires on governmental bad policy, corrupt motives, and general mismanagement in the war with the colonies. Of course, on Orlando's return he finds that Mrs. Rayland has died and left a will in his favour after all.

The last of Mrs. Smith's novels which has any significance for us is *The Young Philosopher, Nature his Law and God his Guide* (1798). At this stage of events Charlotte Smith's Revolutionism has lost some of its optimism and complacent belief in the efficacy of reforms. There is a new note of bitterness in her satire of existing conditions. At the same time, she is much more interested in the philosophic aspect of Revolutionism than she was at the beginning. Evidently she feels the need of an intellectual justification for her liberal principles, now that practical justification in the form of a successful republican government in France has failed.

The preface says with some bitterness that the author is well qualified to describe the "evils arising from oppression, fraud, and chicanery." She refutes a recent charge of plagiarism from *The Wrongs of Woman*,[1] a work "by an author whose talents I greatly honor and whose untimely death I deeply regret."[2] In closing she disclaims any personal responsibility for the sentiments of her characters and declares that her only moral is "to show the ill consequences of detraction and the sad effects of parental resentment." The year 1798 was not so propitious as the year 1792 had been for the frank avowal of radical political views.

The plot centres in the misfortunes of a young man of Rousseauistic education and principles, in a state of society where he is regarded as being, at best, harmlessly insane. He wishes to settle

---

[1] Probably refers to certain similarities in plot between *Desmond* and *The Wrongs of Woman*, by Mary Wollstonecraft. For a summary of the latter see Chapter VII., Section 2, of this thesis.

[2] *The Young Philosopher*, vol. i., p. iii.

down as a contented farmer but finds that the abuses of the world fairly force themselves upon him in his retreat, and demand that he do his best to spread the truths which are their only remedy. From the time he is a boy at Eton he is forced into a Shelley-like rebellion against cruelty and oppression.

From detestation against individuals, such as justices and overseers, he began to reflect on the laws that put it thus in their power to drive the poor forth to nakedness and famine. . . . And he was led to inquire if the complicated misery he every day saw could be the fruits of the very best laws that could be formed in a state of society said to be the most perfect among what are called the civilized nations of the world.[1]

He began to read the writings of the French philosophers, "who have been supposed to have contributed to the production of the great and awful changes that were approaching."[2] Finally, prejudice and persecution, together with his own too keen perception of the miseries under the surface of society, make England intolerable to the young philosopher; he departs for the wilds of America.

These three novels represent distinct stages in English Revolutionism. *Desmond* was written when, in spite of decided opposition in high places, the tide of popular opinion had not yet fully

[1] *The Young Philosopher*, vol. i., p. 54.
[2] *Ibid.*, vol. i., p. 60.

turned against France. Revolutionary sympathizers, of whom there were many, hoped that the worst was passed and that the progress of reform in England might suffer no check from the example of a neighbouring conflict. In 1793 the Reaction set in in full force, war was declared, and the situation looked black for Radicals of all sorts. In her novel of this year, Charlotte Smith drops the question of the French Revolution altogether, and goes back to safe Whig ground. In 1798 she ventures again upon the subject, with renewed fervour. But the emphasis is changed. She has lost faith in reform, and is now a philosophic Revolutionist.

SECTION 4: SOME OTHER LADY NOVELISTS

Elizabeth Inchbald, Amelia Opie, and Charlotte Smith were the most important Lady Novelists of Revolutionary sympathies. There remain, however, several names of less prominence to be discussed; ladies who wrote only one novel that is of interest to us, and some with a less direct claim upon our attention.

Elinor, or The World As It Is, by Mary J. Hanaway (1798), has a typical Revolutionary sub-title. There are traces of the influence of Bage in the style and in occasional references. There is an eccentric old lady, a champion of the Rights of Women, who is mildly satirized, but is nevertheless quite a favourite with the author. Beyond this, there is little trace of Revolutionism in the novel.

In 1802 appeared a novel by Mary Hays, *The Memoirs of Emma Courtney*, which was obviously written under the influence of Godwin. The author says in her preface that:

> The most interesting and the most useful fictions are such as delineate one strong indulged passion or prejudice, affording material by which the philosopher may calculate the power of the human mind.[1]

Caleb Williams is frequently referred to, and there is a striking resemblance to Godwin's later novel, *Mandeville* (1817). The central figure is the same: a morbid individualist seized with a ruling passion amounting to mania, which no reasoning can overcome. Only, instead of a man obsessed with an insane hatred, we have here a woman obsessed with an insane love.

Emma Courtney becomes infatuated with a man who cares nothing for her. In spite of her own reason and the warnings of her friends, she gradually loses all pride and dignity and writes him hysterical letters describing the extent of her devotion, and her utter inability to control it. It would appear to a casual observer that all this was in the nature of an argument against the Pure Reason philosophies. But a Godwinian friend gives the author's intended moral in his admonitions to Emma. "You have nursed in yourself a passion which, taken in the degree in which you have

[1] *Memoirs of Emma Courtney*, vol. i., p. i.

experienced it, is the unnatural and odious result of a distempered and unnatural civilization."[1]

Miss Hays's method is as Godwinian as her moral. She begins with an idea that: "The science of mind is not less demonstrable and far more important than the science of Newton."[1] Whereupon she proceeds to a minute introspective analysis of a mind which, supposedly owing to the present faulty environment, is under the influence of passion instead of reason. The result is the usual one in psychological novels; instead of any real insight into the normal mind, she merely gives us an unpleasant study of the abnormal without apparently realizing the pathological nature of her subject.

Miss Hays leaves us in no doubt as to the sources of her philosophy. Godwin, Holcroft, Paine, Wollstonecraft, Rousseau, and Holbach are quoted frequently. She is a necessitarian, a perfectibilian, a "Pure Reasoner," and, above all, an individualist.

> Individual happiness [she says], constitutes the general good. All systems of morals founded on any other principle involve themselves in contradictions and must be erroneous.[2] Man does right when pursuing interest and pleasure; it argues no depravity—this is the fable of superstition; he ought only to be

[1] *Memoirs of Emma Courtney*, vol. i., p. 2.
[2] It was the Godwinian fallacy to make the self-consistency of any system the test of its truth.

careful that in seeking his own good he does not render it incompatible with the good of others.[1]

In the following year was published *What Has Been* (1803), by a Mrs. Mathews, who was evidently as much influenced by Holcroft as Miss Hays had been by Godwin; and a great deal more wholesome influence it appears to have been. She quotes Holcroft frequently; one of her characters, a benevolent old lady, is actually named Mrs. Ann St. Ives.[2] Emily, the heroine, thrown upon her own resources, has at first too much pride to become a governess: "Her reason was not yet sufficiently matured to correct this error."[3] But in the end she marries a young Revolutionist without income or prospects, learning contentment in poverty through a truer scale of values. The moral with which the novel concludes is that: "Civilization has introduced luxury, from which originate an innumerable throng of vices which spread their destructive influence to the lowest ranks of society."[4]

One of the devoted friends of Mary Wollstonecraft, who was with her at the time of her death, was Mrs. Eliza Fenwick. Her best-known novel, *Secrecy*,[5] is not in its main outlines Revolutionary.

[1] *Memoirs of Emma Courtney*, vol. ii., p. 35.
[2] This is, however, not intended to be the same person as Holcroft's *Anna St. Ives*. (*Cf.* Chapter III., of this thesis.)
[3] *What Has Been*, vol. i., p. 24.
[4] *Ibid.*, vol. i., p. 304.
[5] Not dated. Probably not earlier than 1792 or later than 1796.

But it frequently attacks the evils of unquestioning obedience to any authority whose only sanction is custom.

The perpetual hue and cry after obedience has almost driven virtue out of the world [says Mrs. Fenwick], for be it unlimited obedience to a sovereign, to a parent, or a husband the mind yielding itself so, loses its individual dignity.[1]

Another Lady Novelist who was an enthusiastic Revolutionist was Miss Ann Plumptre (1760–1818). One of her contemporaries says of her:

She was well known as a democrat and an extravagant worshipper of Napoleon. In 1810 she declared she would welcome him if he invaded England, because he would do away with aristocracy and give the country a better government.[2]

But strange to say, her novels show almost no traces of her political opinions. Possibly this may be accounted for by the fact that Miss Plumptre did not begin to write until popular prejudice against Radicals was at its height, and she may not have cared to antagonize her public.[3]

One Lady Novelist of a slightly later period who

[1] *Secrecy*, vol. i., p. 237. This novel is dedicated to "A personal friend, Eliza B." Could this be Eliza Bishop, Mary Wollstonecraft's sister?

[2] Crabbe Robinson, *Diary*, vol. i., p. 156.

[3] Her first novel, *The Rector's Son*, was published in 1798, her other three in 1801, 1812, and 1818.

certainly deserves to be mentioned here from her connexions, if not for her own work, is Mary Shelley, daughter of Mary Wollstonecraft and Godwin, and wife of the poet Shelley. Mary Shelley was the author of several novels which show traces of the influences by which she was surrounded; but their connexion with Revolutionism is so indirect as scarcely to warrant us in discussing them.

The latest, perhaps, of the Lady Novelists whose connexion with the Revolution is distinctly traceable was that spoiled child of the age of Reaction, Lady Caroline Ponsonby Lamb, Viscountess of Melbourne (1785-1828). The records of her contemporaries show her to us as a woman of delicate and appealing beauty, and rare charm of manner. But it is also apparent that she was a bundle of nerves and absolutely undisciplined temper, with an insatiable craving for excitement of every sort. She was apparently happily married to a man who came as near to managing her successfully as any one could, when Lord Byron first appeared in London society and became the craze of the hour. Lady Caroline was fascinated by him. In 1816, when their affair came to an end, she rushed into print with her account of it, thinly disguised as a novel. The title *rôle* in *Glenarvon* is a travesty of Lord Byron; the heroine is the writer herself, under the name Lady Calantha. Byron's friends were exasperated. Byron himself coolly remarked that if the lady had told the truth it would really have made a better story. A recent description of a certain type of modern novel fits *Glenarvon* admirably; it is "neurotic, erotic, and tommy-rotic." A more incoherent mass of Rousseauism, Revolutionism, and sheer nonsense it would be hard to find. Lady Caroline's literary style is a part of all that she has met. Romantic titanism, Ossianic interludes with wild Irish priestesses, and a truly Godwinian treatment of the ruling passion idea are mingled in nightmarish confusion with society wit in the Restoration manner and incongruous bits of typical Lady-Novelist didacticism. The plot is hopelessly incoherent, but one gathers that Glenarvon was a desperately, alluringly wicked serpent, and the lady an innocent little bird whom he had fascinated. In the end, Calantha is deserted by Glenarvon, cast off by her husband, dies penitent, and returns to haunt Glenarvon in the most approved manner. In real life, one regrets to say, the lady did nothing so sensible as to take her useless self out of the world at an early age. Her husband did actually institute divorce proceedings against her at one time, but it was principally on account of her intolerable temper.

It would be interesting to know how many other portraits appear in *Glenarvon*. One of the characters, for instance, is a certain Irish seeress, Elinor St. Clare, who calls herself Saint Clara. In her brunette beauty one may, perhaps, trace a resemblance to Jane Clairmont, who called herself Clare.

Jane Clairmont was the stepdaughter of Godwin, and must have been well known to Lady Caroline. Her affair with Byron was not unlike that of Saint Clara with Glenarvon.

With all its absurdities, one person at least seems to have taken *Glenarvon* seriously enough to consider it a menace to public morals. In the following year appeared *Purity of Heart, or Woman As She Should Be. Addressed to the Author of Glenarvon by an Old Wife of Twenty Years.* The preface inveighs against the "horrible tendency of the dangerous and perverting sophistry of this work." The novel is occupied mainly with the ravings of "Lady Calantha Limb" about her De Lyra of the "rattlesnake eyes," and her intention to publish a book in which she will "sacrifice decency to revenge."[1] By way of contrast there is a virtuous matron of the Griselda type whose adventures give the novel its slight semblance of plot. One cannot help feeling that "An Old Wife" was rather wasting her time in parodying a book which effectively parodies itself.

Lady Caroline Lamb wrote two other novels. *Graham Hamilton* (1822) is in striking contrast to her earlier attempt. This is an entirely commonplace moral tale. There are echoes of Rousseau and Godwin, and the humanitarian and "victim of society" motifs appear frequently; but there is little in the novel for which the most orthodox of Lady Novelists need apologize. Its purpose,

[1] *Purity of Heart*, vol. i., p. 125.

apparently, is to point out the suffering among tradespeople caused by society women who live beyond their incomes and refuse to pay their debts.

Her last novel, *Ada Reis* (1823), is, if not Revolutionary, at least distinctly Byronic in the type of imagination displayed. Ada Reis is an Oriental pirate who aspires to be a king. He enters into treaty with a Spirit of Evil who haunts him in the guise of a mysterious stranger. Ada Reis's daughter, Fiormonda, is loved by a Spirit of Good, the brother of the Evil One. These represent rival forces in the universe, in a manner very suggestive of the Manichean theology of *Cain*. Fiormonda forgets her first love and turns to the Evil Spirit. After death, Fiormonda and Ada Reis reign, proud and unhappy, in a vague Kingdom of Darkness.

Lady Caroline Lamb's relation to Revolutionism and to the titanism of the age of Reaction is that of a child who repeats incoherently half-understood phrases. She was an admirer of Godwin, and corresponded with him for some time.[1] But it is quite evident that her knowledge of Revolutionism was very superficial, and her use of its catchwords was little more than a fad.

[1] Several of her letters to Godwin are preserved in Paul's *William Godwin, His Friends and Contemporaries*.

CHAPTER VII

THE FRENCH REVOLUTION AND THE RIGHTS OF WOMAN

SECTION I: INTRODUCTION AND BACKGROUND

AMONG the novels which we are considering there are a number which concern themselves with various aspects of what our grandmothers called "the Rights of Woman." These deal with a special aspect of eighteenth-century radicalism. Their significance can hardly be made clear without some preliminary discussion of the earlier literature of the subject by way of background.

There is a popular tendency to date the entire modern feminist movement from the period of the French Revolution. Mary Wollstonecraft has frequently been referred to as the "first champion of the Rights of Women." This is a half-truth, not to be accepted without explanation and comment. There was a steadily increasing literature dealing with every aspect of the woman question for centuries before the time of Mary Wollstonecraft.

Dr. Alexander tells us that "Boccaccio was the

first who started the idea of writing anything better than a song or a sonnet to woman."[1] But it was in the sixteenth century in England that discussions of the equality of the sexes began in good earnest. This was precisely the kind of subject to appeal to that discussion-loving age; offering infinite scope for the display of intellectual adroitness with no danger of reaching any conclusion. It combined the gallantry of the mediaeval courts of love with the semi-theological hair-splitting of the schoolmen as to whether women were or were not to be considered human beings. However extreme the position on either side, these pleasant polemics were never intended to be taken seriously. They indicate no social maladjustment, hardly even individual discontent; and with the possible exception of the grim diatribes of John Knox, aim at no practical result.

English feminist literature of the sixteenth and seventeenth centuries falls into three general classifications: (1) panegyrics of woman in the abstract, and lives of distinguished women; (2) discussions of the relative merits of the sexes, and defences of women's logical right to enter various professions; and (3) rules of conduct for ladies.

At the close of the seventeenth century comes a *Serious Proposal to Ladies*, by the gentle and

[1] Alexander, *History of Women*, quoted in *Westminster Review*, vol. clviii., p. 312.

scholarly Mary Astell.[1] She feels a real inadequacy in the educational opportunities open to women. Her "Proposal" is for the establishment of a studious retreat, something between a nunnery and a seminary; a plan which was actually tried during the following century.

The year 1739 is an important one in the history of feminist literature. It is marked by a number of articles appearing almost simultaneously in various periodicals. The first is a very significant article in the *Craftsman's Magazine* pointing out the waste involved in keeping single women of the middle class untrained and unemployed. The writer advocates "making women as useful and capable of maintaining themselves as men, and preventing them from becoming old maids."

This economic feminism in the *Craftsman's Magazine* finds its idealistic counterpart in the *Gentleman's Magazine* for July of the same year, in a little essay praising women of civic virtue, "who preferred public safety to private conquest."

An unidentified sentimentalist, writing in a periodical called *Common Sense* on "The Province of Women," denies them everything but "love."[2] This called forth a spirited little volume entitled *Woman Not Inferior to Man* (etc.). The writer,

---

[1] The authorship of the *Serious Proposal to Ladies* has been called in question in a recent publication of the Modern Language Association. Until the point is settled, however, I think we may continue to assume that Mary Astell is the author.

[2] *Westminster Review*, vol. cl., p. 536.

who signs herself "Sophia, a Gentlewoman," has been not inaptly called "the first of the militants." Her somewhat irritating assertiveness was not allowed to pass unchallenged. "A Gentleman" answers promptly, in a book with the equally uncompromising title: *Man Superior to Woman: or A Vindication of Man's Natural Right of Authority Over the Woman.* The nature of his reply makes his *nom de plume* seem a touch of irony; he disdains even the obvious arguments, and resorts to ribald vituperation. "Sophia" retorts at once, in a treatise, *Woman's Superior Excellence Over Man: A Reply to the Author of a Late Treatise—In Which the Excessive Weakness of that Gentleman's Answer is Exposed.* "Sophia," one feels has rather lost her temper, but it must be admitted that she "exposes" her opponent with entire success.

Several attempts have been made to identify the participants in this interesting little literary skirmish. A suggestion has even been hazarded, plausible but without foundation, that this is an anonymous continuation of hostilities between Pope and Lady Mary Wortley Montagu.

In the same year, the *Gentleman's Magazine* contains a correspondence on the abstract right of women to be represented in any professedly representative government. It was at about this time also that an episode occurred which Lady Mary Wortley Montagu records in her *Letters*. An attempt was made to exclude ladies from hearing the debates in the House of Lords. Rather than lose this privilege, the ladies resorted to methods rather suggestive of the twentieth century. For seven hours, "they stood at the door without bite or sup, and carried their point."

Within these two years (1739 and 1740), we find in embryo most of the elements of subsequent feminist literature: dreary wastes of fanaticism *versus* prejudice, absurd sentimentalism and equally absurd appeals to abstract rights, but withal, two elements of permanent value: a perception of the economic factor, and a sound ideal of the social duties and responsibilities of women.

During the next fifty years the only significant additions to feminist literature were a number of sentimental theories on the education of girls, all more or less directly influenced by Rousseau's *Émile*. Mary Wollstonecraft discusses the most noteworthy of these; Dr. Gregory's *Legacy to His Daughters*, Fordyce's *Sermons*, and Hester Chapone's *Letters*.

It should be observed that between the feminism of Rousseau and that of Mary Wollstonecraft there is no connexion whatever. They hold exactly opposite views of the chief end of woman. "Sophie" exists purely for "Émile." Rousseau cannot conceive of her as being of any value to herself or to society as a whole. Her one aim in life is to be attractive; her one happiness is in being loved. She reflects, "that a thinking man may not yawn in her society." Instead of an education,[1]

[1] Rousseau, *Émile*, Book V.

she has "accomplishments." Her very modesty exists only to give zest to the wooing of her. It is against this conception that Mary Wollstonecraft protests. The basis of all her writings is the assumption that women are before all else human beings, with all human dignity and responsibilities. Her ideal is one of self-respect and service to society, whether that service be the writing of books or the rearing of future citizens. To the objection that seems to Rousseau conclusive: "Educate women like men, and the more they resemble our sex the less power will they have over us," she replies finely: "This is the very point I aim at; I do not wish them to have power over men, but over themselves."[1]

Unquestionably the outbreak of the French Revolution marks a distinct epoch in the feminist movement. "Since when have women occupied themselves with politics?" Napoleon is said to have asked Madame de Staël. "Since they have been guillotined," was the reply. Perhaps the first serious demand ever made by women for political representation and equal suffrage was the Cahier presented to the king at the meeting of the States General in 1789. A similar petition was addressed to the National Assembly in the same year, and endorsed by the philosopher Condorcet. It was rejected, "with scorn and derision." But many of the leaders of the Revolution were in favour of it, among them Talleyrand-Périgord,

[1] *A Vindication of the Rights of Woman*, ed. Boston, 1792, p. 112.

Bishop of Autun, to whom *A Vindication of the Rights of Woman* is dedicated.

Miss McIlquham says: "Three valuable pleas for justice to womanhood were undoubtedly the outcome of the French Revolution, viz., Condorcet's *Sur l'Admission des Femmes au Droit de Cité*, Mary Wollstonecraft's *Vindication of the Rights of Woman*, and Count Ségur's *Women, Their Condition and Influence in Society.*"[1] It is not quite accurate, however, to call *A Vindication of the Rights of Woman* an outcome of the French Revolution, in spite of the stimulus it unquestionably received from that source. During the latter half of the eighteenth century there were other forces at work in England, forces dimly foreshadowed by that unknown writer in the *Craftsman's Magazine*. Not least of the social maladjustments arising from the Industrial Revolution were those affecting women. As factories developed, the home became less and less a centre of industry. The spinning and weaving of cloth, for example, lacemaking, and all manner of handicrafts were no longer carried on in each individual family for use or sale. The woman in the home found her range of occupation rapidly diminished. Below a certain social scale she followed her work into the factories. But the self-supporting middle-class woman found herself facing an economic situation that was fast becoming intolerable. Without a "fortune" she could not marry advantageously; the superfluous

[1] *Westminster Review*, vol. clx., p. 541.

daughter or sister in the home was no longer a valuable asset; and outside the home the wretchedly paid and almost menial occupations of governess, "companion," and seamstress were the only ones open to her. It is the consequent somewhat vague and uncomprehending social unrest that finds expression in Mary Wollstonecraft, rather than a desire for political rights. She was undoubtedly much influenced, as we shall see, by Godwin and his circle. But leaving aside the extraneous matter borrowed from the Pure Reason philosophies, *A Vindication of the Rights of Woman* reduces itself to a clear-headed and surprisingly modern demand for a truer ideal, a sound education, and the right to work.

> Is not that government very defective [she writes], and very unmindful of the happiness of its members, that does not provide for honest independent women by encouraging them to fill respectable stations? How many women waste life away, the prey of discontent, who might have practised as physicians, regulated a farm, managed a shop, and stood erect, supported by their own industry![1]

Perhaps no other single book cut so deep into the mind of the time as this. Everywhere it was hailed as the beginning of a new movement and greeted with a storm of protest. On its publication, criticism was divided. The *Analytical Review* endorsed it unhesitatingly. The *Critical Review* writes in a tone of patronizing disapproval:

[1] Wollstonecraft, *Vindication of the Rights of Woman*, chapter i.

We are infinitely better pleased with the present system. In truth, dear young lady, endeavour to attain the elegancy of mind, and sweet docility of manners, the ornaments of your sex; we are certain you will be more pleasing, and we dare pronounce that you will be infinitely happier.

Other commentators are less courteous: instead of discussing the book they resort to irrelevant and often scurrilous attacks upon the character of the author.

For at least a quarter of a century after its publication, all the ideas of the woman movement were practically identified with the *Vindication*. It was one of those inevitable books that crystallize a tendency in their time. Mary Wollstonecraft became the symbol of a certain form of unrest. The general trend of discussion we shall find fully illustrated in the novels which we are about to consider.

With this brief sketch of early feminist literature as a background we may turn to our subject proper, —Mary Wollstonecraft as a novelist, and some other novels of the Revolutionary period dealing with the position of women.

SECTION 2: MARY WOLLSTONECRAFT

It can hardly have failed to occur to us how few of the novelists we have considered so far are living figures in the world of literature. A few volumes gathering dust on the shelves of libraries and special collections, occasional perfunctory notices in histories of the novel; these are all that remain of the little group who echoed in the fiction of their time the splendid audacities that so inspired the poets of the Revolution.

But there is one figure in the group about whom controversy has never ceased to rage. Throughout the century that has elapsed since her death, Mary Wollstonecraft has been honoured and bitterly attacked, but never treated with indifference; loved and hated, but never forgotten. The spirit of controversy is as strong in her twentieth-century commentators as it was in her contemporaries.

We are concerned here primarily with the novels, which formed a very insignificant part of her work. Two were early attempts; the most important, *The Wrongs of Woman*, was left unfinished at her death. As novels, her critics agree, none of the three are very valuable. If it be objected that these form but a very small excuse for a somewhat lengthy discussion of the author, we can only plead that in order to arrive at any just estimate of *The Wrongs of Woman* we must know something of the "Rights of Woman" movement, and, most of all, something of the rights and wrongs of the woman of whose life and personality these novels are so largely a record. It is to Mary Wollstonecraft herself that we must turn for the explanation of her works. She knew life at first hand, thought for herself with vigour and directness, and managed somehow to see so far below the surface of her time that the conclusions she reached have not yet become commonplaces.

Biographical details are usually rather dull reading; but how, in every record that she touches, Mary Wollstonecraft lives! Our own contemporaries are not more real to us than this woman of a hundred years ago. One has an odd feeling of having known and talked with her somewhere—the girl of Opie's portraits, with her sweet, wistful face under the soft waves of dark auburn hair, the expressive brown eyes that Southey praised so, the sensitive, almost childlike mouth.

The first eighteen years of her life were passed in an atmosphere of poverty and family squabbles in which she usually acted as buffer. Her father, a combination of brute and sentimentalist, aroused his daughter's fierce contempt. One gets strange glimpses of the child interfering to protect her mother and the four younger children from actual cruelty. This intolerable family life Mary left to become a paid companion to a widow of uncertain temper, but after a few months was called home by her mother's illness. After the death of her mother Mary left home definitely, and went to live with her friend Fanny Blood, a girl whose home was almost the duplicate of Mary's own. Mrs. Blood joined them, and for two years the three women eked out a precarious living by needlework. Meanwhile Mary's younger sister Eliza had married a Mr. Bishop, fancying that matrimony offered a better means of escape from an intolerable home than Mary's plan of self-support. It did not. By 1783 the Bishops had reached a domestic crisis, and the task of rescuing her sister fell upon Mary. She persuaded Fanny Blood to join her in starting a school at Islington, where her sister might find a refuge; in January, 1784, Eliza was smuggled away from her husband's house, half-insane, "biting her wedding ring to pieces in the coach." Mary wrote to her sister Everina: "I hope B. will not discover us; for I could sooner face a lion. . . . Bess is determined not to return. Can he force her?" He could, legally, as she very well knew; but fortunately he did not. Meanwhile Mary felt the full force of popular opinion, and writes bitterly:

I knew I should be the shameful incendiary in the shocking affair of a woman's leaving her bedfellow. They thought the strong affection of a sister *might* apologize for my conduct, but that the scheme was by no means a good one. In short, quite contrary to all the rules of conduct that are published for new-married ladies, by whose advice Mrs. Brook was actuated when she with great grief of heart gave up my friendship.[1]

The school struggled along for several years on the verge of failure. Fanny Blood married, and died soon after. Eliza and Everina Wollstonecraft took positions as governesses. Mary continued to

[1] Taylor, *Mary Wollstonecraft*, p. 50.

make a bare living with the pupils that remained, by doing all the work of the cottage herself. She decided to try her hand at writing. In 1785 her *Thoughts on the Education of Daughters* was published by Joseph Johnson. It is characterized by her usual good sense and independence of thought, and contains many of the very modern ideas which she afterward expressed more fully in the *Vindication of the Rights of Woman*. Johnson paid her ten pounds for it, which she promptly handed over to the Bloods, who certainly did not need it any more than she did.

In 1787, Mary gave up the hopeless task of trying to run a school with neither capital nor patronage, and took a position as governess to Lady Kingsborough. Here she had her first taste of aristocratic and fashionable life. Her reaction is vigorous and characteristic. "There is such a solemn kind of stupidity about this place as froze my very soul," she wrote to her sister. After a year as a governess she could endure it no longer, and came to London, boldly determined to support herself by her pen. Her letters at this time show the courage of desperation. "I am, then, to be the first of a new genius. I tremble at the attempt. But I *must* be independent."

For the next four years Mary Wollstonecraft lived in London, a shabby, overworked young hackwriter. She was successful from the first, but she had an incurable habit of giving away almost all she earned. During this time she kept in school three of her brothers and sisters, sent Eliza to France to learn the language, and virtually supported her father in addition. Mary's family were all stupid, disagreeable people, not in the least worth the trouble she took with them; her sisters afterward showed themselves thoroughly spiteful and ungrateful. But Mary never expected sympathy or appreciation from those she helped. She took care of them as a matter of course, because it was plain that they would not take care of themselves.

During these years however, there was another side to Mary Wollstonecraft's life. Through her friendship with Joseph Johnson, the publisher of most of the radical literature of the time, she came in touch with a group of men and women of intellect and originality who were thinking in terms of the French Revolutionary philosophies. Johnson treated her like a daughter; Paine, Horne Tooke, Fordyce, Godwin, Fuseli, Holcroft, and all their brilliant circle welcomed her as an equal. In that congenial fellowship her powers of intellect and personality reached their full development. She was a woman whom men of genius always admired. Dr. Price had long been her devoted friend, and as a young girl she had even succeeded in attracting the attention of the great Dr. Johnson. It is obvious that her ideas were profoundly influenced by the extreme Revolutionary doctrines of the group in which she now found herself. Rather, it is needful to point out wherein she differed from them; and how it is that in some respects this obscure girl teacher saw her time with clearer eyes than any of its professional philosophers.

In 1790, Burke's *Reflections on the Revolution in France* appeared, attacking Dr. Price's sermon before the Revolution Society. Mary Wollstonecraft was the first in the field with an answer. *A Vindication of the Rights of Man, in a Letter to the Right Honourable Edmund Burke* is as clever a bit of rough and ready argument as any in the language. Its defects in style and structure are numerous; it was written over night, almost, and Mary never could be induced to take any interest in questions of mere literary craftsmanship. But it has a more serious fault. It is not fair to the great statesman against whom it is directed. Humility was never Mary's strong point. The tone which she adopts towards her distinguished opponent is almost insolent in its audacity. Burke had undeniably scored against the Revolutionists when he insisted that political systems are of slow growth, built on practical needs and expediencies, not on abstract reasonings. But Mary Wollstonecraft meeting Burke on his own ground of practical consideration of facts, convicts him in turn of building air castles, and saying "all is well" where all is far from well. She brushes aside all his rhapsodies on the sacredness of the past and the glories of England, and goes straight to the heart of his whole concern for the maintenance of the established order. "Security of property! Behold in a few words the definition of English liberty. But softly,—it is only the property of the rich that is secure." She sees perfectly clearly the economic basis for the conservatism of the property holders; but, belonging herself to the earning rather than to the owning classes, she does not feel quite so forcibly as Burke the extreme sanctity of capital. Furthermore, his eloquent tears over the sufferings of the Queen of France were a little too much for the patience of the woman who knew by experience how much chivalry his world had for women on the wrong side of the economic situation. If there was one thing Mary hated it was sentimental cant. She meets Burke's condemnation of the French Revolution on the basis of its early acts by pointing out conditions existing under that British government Burke so admired; closing with a burst of indignation more forcible than courteous. "What were the outrages of a day to these continual miseries? Such misery demands more than tears. I pause to recollect myself and smother the contempt I feel for your rhetorical flourishes and infantine sensibility."[1]

Two years later came the publication of Mary Wollstonecraft's best-known book, *A Vindication of the Rights of Woman*, the significance of which we have discussed elsewhere. This may to some

[1] Wollstonecraft, *Rights of Man*, ed., London, 1790, pp. 23 and 144.

extent be taken as the text of which her semi-autobiographical novels are the illustration.

The last four years of Mary Wollstonecraft's life show another side of her very complex character. She was a woman who could not only think clearly and act resolutely, but feel greatly. There are many unprofitable ways of considering the love affairs of Mary Wollstonecraft; her well-meaning commentators have done their best to furnish us with examples of all of them. It is a subject fatally easy to preach about or sentimentalize over. One fancies how intensely annoyed Mary herself would be with either attitude. It may be well to point out that society settled its score with her something over a hundred years ago. There was little enough of happiness in her short life. One would think the most incurably ethical might be satisfied with the moral to be drawn from her conduct and its consequences to herself.

Briefly, in 1792 or thereabouts, Mary Wollstonecraft, having forgotten her own very wise remarks on the dangers of platonic friendships, found herself too much interested in the painter Fuseli for either her own peace of mind or that of his wife. Whereupon she very sensibly ran away to France. There she witnessed some stirring scenes in the great drama of the time, and wrote her conclusions upon them in *A Historical and Moral View of the French Revolution*. It is to be observed that Mary's emotional crises never affected her remarkable insight into the economic causes underlying political phenomena. She was perhaps the only one of the English Radicals who was never misled as to the real significance of the French Revolution.

I wish I could inform you [she wrote], that out of the chaos of vices and follies, prejudices and virtues, rudely jumbled together, I saw the fair form of liberty slowly rising and virtue expanding her wings to shelter all her children. . . . But if the aristocracy of birth is levelled to the ground only to make room for that of riches, I am afraid the moral of the people will not be much improved by the change. . . . Everything whispers to me that names, not principles, are changed.[1]

While in Paris, Mary met Captain Gilbert Imlay, an American, with whom she formed the connexion that has caused such acute embarrassment to her apologists. It has been pointed out that conditions in Paris were such as to make a formal marriage with its accompanying declaration of nationality extremely dangerous. Mary was certainly registered at the American Embassy as Imlay's wife, and acknowledged as such by him in documents which would be accepted in many countries as conclusive evidence of marriage. But later, when Imlay's fickle conduct forced Mary most unwillingly to give him up, society was shocked to discover that there was no legal constraint to prevent their separation.

Imlay was himself the author of a tendenz novel, *The Emigrants*, attacking "The sacrilege which

[1] Wollstonecraft, *Posthumous Works*, vol. iv., p. 43.

the present practices of matrimonial engagement necessarily produce." J. Stirling Taylor says of it:

It would be interesting to know—which we do not—whether these heterodox views came from Mary, or whether it was the other way round and Imlay the teacher. Since the book was almost certainly finished in Paris, either theory may be true; the influences may have been mutual.[1]

In the Pure Reason philosophies of Godwin and his circle, marriage was often referred to as a form of tyranny. But Mary was not of the type of mind that seeks martyrdom for metaphysical abstractions. She usually drew her own conclusions from actual observation. When one remembers the homes Mary had known best—her own and the Bloods'—and her experiences in rescuing her sister from the old English marriage law which regarded the wife as "property," it is not incomprehensible that Mary developed a certain lack of appreciation of the desirability of having her own marriage legally binding.

However that may be, she received drastic demonstration of the extreme unwisdom of her course. The Imlay letters, published after her death, are a pathetic record of her brief happiness, Imlay's unfaithfulness, her desperate efforts to regain his affection, growing estrangement, and the final parting: "I go to find peace. May you never

[1] Taylor, *Mary Wollstonecraft*, p. 137.

know by experience what you have made me endure."

She returned to London. That haunting tendency to melancholia, the result of nerves shattered in her early struggles, overwhelmed her; and for the second time in her life Mary Wollstonecraft attempted suicide. She was rescued from the Thames, however, and took up her work again, gradually regaining her lost peace of mind through the necessity of caring for herself and her child, Fanny Imlay. Mary cared little for social position or for wealth; the two things she could not live without were her own self-respect and her economic independence. There is a flash of the old spirit when Imlay offers to support her and his child.

I never wanted but your heart—that gone, you have nothing more to give. Forgive me then if I say that I shall consider any direct or indirect attempt to supply my necessities as an insult which I have not merited, and as done rather out of tenderness for your own reputation than for me.

But Mary Wollstonecraft was too fully developed a human being to brood long over the sentimentalized memory of an emotional experience, however intense it had been. Her friendship with William Godwin ripened gradually into love, and those two strangely contrasted temperaments found happiness together in a married life the eccentricity of which was equalled only by its beauty. Godwin says of Mary: "She was a worshipper of domestic life, and possessed in an unparalleled degree the art of communicating happiness." It seemed that she had at last "found peace." She was still a young woman—thirty-seven, to be exact,—and the best of her life was yet before her. But within the year she died in giving birth to the daughter who bore her name—Shelley's Mary Wollstonecraft Godwin.

So ends the life of which the novels we are about to consider are little more than faint, distorted reflections. She, who saw so clearly, has left us a summing up of herself in one sentence, the full force of which it has taken us a century to realize:

All the world is a stage, thought I, and few there are in it who do not play the part they have learned by rote; and those who do not, seem marks set up to be pelted at by fortune; or rather sign posts, which point out the road to others, whilst forced to stand still themselves amidst the mud and dust.

The fiction Mary Wollstonecraft wrote is not large in amount; two frankly tendenz novels, a fantastic tale called *The Cave of Fancy*, and a book of children's stories, moral lessons connected by a very slight thread of narrative, with which we need not concern ourselves in the present discussion.

The first of her novels was written during her life as a governess, in 1782. *Mary, A Fiction* is not remarkable as a literary achievement, although there are fine passages in it, and some spirited satire. The preface is interesting as an expression of the author's ideals of novel writing. She practically admits the strong personal, almost autobiographical element in her work.

> Those compositions only [she writes], have power to delight and carry us willing captives where the soul of the author is exhibited. . . . These chosen few wish to speak for themselves and not be an echo—even of the sweetest sounds. The paradise they ramble in must be of their own creating.

She adds a demure footnote: "I here give the reviewers an opportunity of being very witty about the Paradise of Fools."[1]

G. R. Stirling Taylor says of this novel:

> There is little doubt that *Mary* is autobiographical. That she should make the sick friend die in Lisbon is an obvious reference to the death of Fanny Blood. But these resemblances are of trivial importance. The chief interest lies in the fact that the "Mary" of the tale speaks the mind of Mary the author. This close link between the story and the author's individuality is marked by a mass of cumulative evidence; the life explains the story and the story the life. The author says of her heroine, "Her mind was strong and clear, when not clouded by her feelings, but she was too much the creature of impulse and the slave of pity."[2]

The Cave of Fancy, A Tale, was planned at the

[1] Mary Wollstonecraft, *Mary*, preface, p. ii.
[2] Taylor, *Mary Wollstonecraft*, p. 88.

same time as *Mary, A Fiction*, but it was never finished, appearing only among her posthumous works. It is far inferior to the two novels based upon Mary's own life, which in spite of all their faults in literary craftsmanship are not without power. The facts of her experience and the conclusions she drew from them she could express with vigour and directness. But when she relies upon her imagination for plot and incident her weakness becomes apparent. Short as *The Cave of Fancy* is, the action drags and the didacticism is wearisome.

Even so, it is not without interest. Mary Wollstonecraft never could keep her own personality out of anything she wrote; and she herself has been called everything from an "angel" to "a hyena in petticoats" (Horace Walpole's little tribute), but never a bore.

The plan, never completed, was of the *Arabian Nights* type; a narrative framework for a group of stories. In an enchanted cavern dwells a very unplausible sage named Sagestus. A shipwreck at his doors devolves upon him the responsibility of caring for and educating a little girl, the sole survivor. The inference is that the child is very fortunate in the prospect of an education so directed, for her mother was of the type of woman Mary Wollstonecraft particularly disliked: "Not having courage to form an opinion of her own, she adhered with blind partiality to those she adopted."[1]

[1] Mary Wollstonecraft, *Posthumous Works*, vol. iv., p. 123.

Sagestus conducts the education of the child by the aid of spirits summoned to the cave, who tell her the stories of their past lives. Only one of these stories was written; that of a woman in whose experiences one traces the inevitable resemblance to those of the author.

The last and unquestionably the best of Mary Wollstonecraft's novels exists only in the rough draft left unfinished at her death. It is for our purpose the most interesting on account of its doctrinary character.

It is hardly fair to criticize the technique of an unfinished work. Certainly in its present form the whole seems badly constructed. The story begins in the middle, in an insane asylum, leaves us for several chapters in utter bewilderment, and then resorts to the expedient of the heroine's diary to explain the events of what should have been the first two volumes. Horrors are piled on with Gothic lavishness, and there is a nightmarish incoherence due to continual digressions.

Nevertheless, it is safe to say that Mary Wollstonecraft had grasped certain principles of tendenz novel writing more fully than any of the other novelists we have considered so far. With most of them the "purpose" appears to be incidental. The method is to construct a plot at random, and then allow the characters to indulge in an occasional political or philosophical discussion. The story would go on just as well with the doctrinary passages omitted. Sometimes a preface announces the purpose; and one feels that such guidance is not superfluous. In *Caleb Williams*, for instance, the subject announced is "Man the enemy of man." But since there is considerable disagreement among commentators as to how the novel illustrates the moral, and even as to what the moral is, it is clear that Godwin has not made his point very forcibly.

Mary Wollstonecraft, on the contrary, having decided to make society aware by means of a novel, of its injustice to women, goes about it with her characteristic directness. The wrongs she has in mind are no mere violations of abstract principles of political justice. She confines herself to such social maladjustments as have come under her personal observation. She takes Maria — any woman—places her in a perfectly possible situation, and brings down upon her a series of calamities which are the natural consequences of the social, legal, and economic disabilities which society of that time placed upon women. There are passages that preach, of course; there are whole chapters of special pleading introduced; but always the plot is the main argument.

Maria is the eldest daughter in a home similar to the Wollstonecrafts'. But she is the favourite of a wealthy uncle who intends to leave her a fortune. Seeing that her home life is intolerable, and thinking matrimony the only refuge for a woman, he persuades her to marry a young man who on short acquaintance has impressed her favourably. The young couple go to London, where George proceeds to use up Maria's dowry in a life of dissipation. In a few years his gambling has reduced them to poverty, and his character has so far degenerated that he alternately neglects and abuses the forlorn young wife, whom the death of her uncle has left without a friend to protect her. When her husband actually attempts to sell her to a lover in payment of a gambling debt, she leaves him. Whereupon she discovers that she and everything she owns are legally the property of her husband. He hunts her from one hiding-place to another, with the aid of the law. Finally he captures her, takes her child from her, and imprisons her in a private asylum. There she meets a man whom she learns to love. He helps her to escape, and persuades her that she is no longer morally bound to her husband, although she cannot obtain a divorce. With this man she is happy, until her husband discovers them, institutes divorce proceedings against her, and secures the imprisonment and trial of her lover. Here the story breaks off, leaving only a few scattered notes to indicate the tragic ending intended by the author.

There is a second plot, in the form of a long digression, to illustrate the wrongs of a woman of a lower social order. It is the story of the woman attendant at the asylum who helps Maria and her lover to escape. Jemima was a foundling. A wretchedly abused little servant maid, she was literally forced when scarcely more than a child to become a social outcast. Every attempt to gain an honest living being thwarted she becomes a hardened, determined criminal.

> How often have I heard [she says], that every person willing to work may find employment? It is the vague assertion, I believe, of insensible ignorance when it relates to men; but with respect to women I am sure of its fallacy, unless they will submit to the most menial bodily labour; and even to be employed at hard labour is out of the reach of many, whose reputation misfortune or folly has tainted.[1]

Such, in Mary Wollstonecraft's opinion, were the "wrongs of woman." The book has behind it the force of conviction growing out of a knowledge of facts. Mary Wollstonecraft had no illusions left about the opportunities life offered to the average middle-class woman of her time. She had had intimate knowledge of several marriages where the good home bargained for was by no means secured. She had furthermore learned by drastic experience the impossible economic conditions confronting the self-supporting single woman. Seamstress, governess, "companion"; these practically exhausted the list of gainful occupations open to a young woman without any special talent. Even Elizabeth Inchbald, for all her ability, found marriage a necessity. It required the indomitable courage of a Mary Wollstonecraft to gain even the

---

[1] Mary Wollstonecraft, *Posthumous Works*, vol. i., p. 112.

most modest economic independence, a century ago.

There are two novels written by her friends in which under a thin disguise Mary figures as the heroine: Godwin's *St. Leon* and Mrs. Opie's *Adelina Mowbray*. Both we shall consider in detail elsewhere. There is little likeness to the Mary we know in St. Leon's Margaret excepting a certain strength and dignity under misfortune. But Mrs. Opie has virtually written a biography of Mary Wollstonecraft during certain years of her life, with details changed. In Adelina she has caught some of the charm of Mary's personality, and does full justice to the essential purity and nobility of her character, while pointing out the fallacy of some of her opinions. Mary's deep and sincere religious belief is emphasized with great effectiveness. But Mrs. Opie's zeal for drawing a moral makes her Adelina a much more limited personality than the original. Mary was never crushed by the verdict of society, and her marriage with Godwin was hardly a recantation. She never attacked marriage in theory; only the intolerable marriage laws of her time. In any case, Mary Wollstonecraft's views on marriage were a very unimportant part of her contention for the right of women to human dignity and economic independence, and the emphasis given to this phase of her life is justified only in a work of pure fiction like *Adelina Mowbray*.

SECTION 3: SOME OTHER "RIGHTS OF WOMEN" NOVELS

Perhaps the earliest novel in our period dealing with the woman question is a rather stupid narrative sermon by "Prudentia Homespun" (Mrs. West), entitled *The Advantages of Education, or, The History of Maria Williams* (1793). This is merely a plea for fewer "accomplishments" and more solid domestic virtues in young ladies of the day, and has little connection with the new tendencies.

In the closing years of the century appeared a curious book by James Lawrence, *The Empire of the Nairs, or The Rights of Women. An Utopian Romance.* This was suppressed in England, but immediately appeared in France. The plot is fully outlined in the *Revue des Romans*, and a number of quotations from it are available.[1] It is difficult, of course, to determine without reading the book the nature of the author's purpose. It is incredible that this Utopia should be the expression of a serious opinion. Possibly it may be a satire on the theories of Godwin and Rousseau, after the manner of Swift. But the extreme indecorum of the method employed casts suspicion upon the sincerity of any "purpose" the author may have professed, other than that of gaining a certain notoriety. There is a curious note on the Nairs

[1] Gerauld de Saint-Fargeau, *Revue des Romans* (1839), vol. ii., p. 42.

in *Robert and Adela* which seems to indicate that this was mistaken for a serious account of a real nation.[1]

To counteract the dangerous vogue of *A Vindication of the Rights of Woman*, there was published, in 1795, *Robert and Adela, or, The Rights of Women best Maintained by the Sentiments of Nature*. Although it is anonymous, one is quite sure from the style that the writer was a woman. Like most novels in letter form it has a variety of sub-plots, but we need concern ourselves only with the main narrative. The principal characters are young Lord Landsford and his two sisters. Lady Sabina is happily married; her function in the novel is obviously to represent the ideal of feminine virtue and wifely docility. The younger sister, Lady Susan, is a young woman of great beauty and intelligence; but she has been educated by her grandmother, who was one of the regrettably increasing number of women corrupted by the new ideas of independence and equality with men. However, since this eccentric old lady has left Susan a considerable fortune as well as a stock of detrimental ideas, Lord Landsford is not without hopes of finding a good match for her. He has in mind a friend of his, Count Robert de Montfort, an *émigré*. Susan is pleased with the Count, but is in no hurry to marry and give up her cherished independence. From this point the novel is an account of Susan's outrageous opinions and con-

[1] *Robert and Adela*, vol. ii., p. 95.

duct and the remonstrances of her brother and sister. Sometimes the effect is a little lost upon a modern reader; one forgets to be shocked when a young woman says, for instance, that she wishes she could play cricket. Susan's most serious escapade, however, is not without interest. She visits the House of Commons (from which women were excluded), disguised as a young officer; a footnote explains that this was actually done by Lady Wallace and "some other spirited ladies who had a mind to gratify their curiosity."

Lady Susan has many admirers besides the Count, all of whom she teases unmercifully. But she obstinately refuses to marry.

To sit down tamely and own a master—Oh the horrid idea! [she writes, and adds, lest there be any doubt as to the source of her theories], That dear Mrs. What-do-ye-call-her, who has asserted the rights of our sex! How I adore her! Would she ever suffer herself to be sunk into a tame domestic animal? No! No! She knows and will maintain the dignity of the sex, which she has raised to the level with that of man! She hardly allows the men to take the lead in anything![1]

Lord Landsford warns her:

Believe me, masculine manners are not calculated to attract our sex, which I cannot but think, after all your declarations, is your intention. 'Tis singularity you aim at, and that affectation, of all others is most

[1] *Robert and Adela*, vol. i., p. 118.

pernicious and dangerous to women. Your rights are established when you properly perform the duties of a wife and mother.[1]

The letters of Lady Sabina are of especial interest as giving the author's own opinion on the whole question, in the person of the ideal woman.

I know that you can easily foil me in argument on any subject. I have little more to urge than the sentiments of a female heart against that lofty way of thinking, in which I suspect, from your frequent use of certain phrases and sentiments, you have been confirmed by Mrs. Woolstone Croft's *Vindication of the Rights of Woman*. You insist on an equality of rights and privileges—I cannot understand, perfectly, what you mean; for to be in all respects on a footing of equality with the men seems to me to be impossible. How can the infirmities and tender cares to which women are doomed, by the constitution of their nature, accord with the agitation of public assemblies? . . . I am persuaded Mrs. Woolstone Croft would never have dreamed of writing such a book about the rights of women if she had been a happy wife and mother; . . . the true glory as well as the true happiness of women consists in the exercise, not of the heroic, but of the amiable virtues. [Praise of meekness and patience.] Patience, as Rousseau observes, even under a husband's injustice. Such gentleness of manners is in fact the best armour in which the delicacy of the female frame can be clothed; for women are committed by Providence to the care of fathers, brothers, husbands,

[1] *Robert and Adela*, vol. ii., p. 182.

and other relatives. Usually an amiable woman has her full share of sway, and in politics, too, it is well known that women have power without the formality of constitutional votes. . . . We should always comply with the prevailing system, to deviate may incur censure, which every female should studiously avoid.[1]

Lady Susan is quite unaffected by all this admonition. Her brother in despair pronounces her "unworthy the serious attention of any man of sense." The Count accordingly turns his attention to her younger sister, who very opportunely emerges from a convent school because the exigencies of the plot require an unmarried Sabina. Susan, in a pique, marries the next man who offers himself, giving as her reason "that she may have something to torment." As she neglected to secure a settlement, her husband makes away with her property, and beats her. She finally leaves him, recants her errors, and devotes the remainder of her life to philanthropy, "on all occasions inculcating the maxim that *an amiable female gains everything by assuming nothing: and that the rights of women are best maintained by the sentiments of nature.*"[2]

So ends the career of Susan as an awful warning. The Rousseauistic moral is quite clear; although one is tempted to observe that Susan's troubles begin only when she gives up her principles by

[1] *Robert and Adela*, vol. i., pp. 179–85.
[2] *Ibid.*, vol. ii., p. 310.

marrying. There is an obvious effort at fairness. The heroine is made very attractive, and at times is allowed to express her theories with considerable eloquence. The author has caught Mary Wollstonecraft's favourite phrases (even though she could not spell the name), and uses them in very clever satire. But one cannot feel that there is much real connexion between the type of ideas represented by this wealthy and aristocratic coquette, to whom social independence is a caprice, and those of the struggling girl hack-writer, to whom economic independence was a grim necessity.

There are some interesting discussions of political matters in the course of the novel. Writing from an orthodox Whig point of view the author contrasts France, "that land of anarchy," with "this happy island of regulated liberty; for so it is, whatever men may preach against it. From the abuses which, in the course of years, have crept into all states, Britain is not exempt. But I cannot conceive, because a few repairs are necessary, that the building should be razed to the ground."[1] The landed gentry are regarded as the mainstay of the nation. Landsford says:

> To live at home as our ancestors used to, should be the aim of our nobility. It was crowding to the court and neglecting everything for the smile of a prince that brought France into that horrid anarchy and convulsion in which it now labours.

[1] *Robert and Adela*, vol. i., p. 9.

He refuses to follow the general tendency to raise the rents of his tenantry.[1]

On the other hand, the author is no blind defender of the principle of hereditary aristocracy. She writes with what was, for that time, considerable boldness:

> The high pride of families I begin to think somewhat absurd, having witnessed so many virtues and such a fund of genius in the lower orders of society that more than make up for the mere adventitious circumstance of birth. Superior intellect surely is more than equal to any title that is dependent on the breath of kings.[2]

A later novel, distinctly Tory in its political point of view, offers a fair sample of what were considered really advanced ideas on the woman question during the period of conservative Reaction. *Blue Stocking Hall* (1827)[3] is written to defend the thesis that a young lady need not be entirely uneducated in order to be attractive. The author in his preface avows himself a recent convert to this radical doctrine. The plot is simple. Mrs. Douglas and her three daughters live quietly on their country estate in Ireland, devoted to philanthropy, religion, and studious pursuits under the guidance of a tutor of remarkable attainments.

---

[1] Cf. *The Magic of Wealth.*
[2] *Robert and Adela*, vol. i., p. 24.
[3] *Blue Stocking Hall* is attributed to William Scargill, and also to Mrs. Jane Webb, in the Boston Public Library catalogue; but no author is given in the book itself.

The girls study Latin, Greek, modern literature, mathematics, and a little botany. Young Frank Howard, Mrs. Douglas's nephew, visits them. He has heard that his cousins are "learned ladies" and intends to give his aunt a warning of the error of her course.

> Men of the present day dread a "blue" more than a scorpion; which argument I believe, never fails with a mama. To be sure, they cannot unlearn all that old dominie has crammed into their noddles, but if they are frightened into careful concealment there is not much harm done.[1]

Of course he finds his cousins charming girls, not at all inclined to pose. His prejudices are shaken. The second and third volumes are devoted to the progress of his conversion, and the long arguments of Mrs. Douglas in favour of the education of young ladies. She hastens to admit that: "The great object to which a girl's prospects should tend from infancy to maturity is marriage," and that she "prizes one unselfish movement of the heart above all the intellect that ever adorned the greatest philosophers." But the prejudice against learned ladies is, she thinks, without foundation. It is only a little learning that is dangerous to feminine docility. Real learning tends to humility. Social intercourse and marriage will gain equally when ladies are permitted to acquire more culture. Finally, she enters into an elaborate

[1] *Blue Stocking Hall*, vol. i., p. 30.

argument to prove that the education of women is neither explicitly nor implicitly forbidden in the Scriptures.[1]

Mrs. Douglas carefully disavows any sympathy with the *Vindication of the Rights of Woman*.

A book [she says], which long ago found its resting place amidst dust and cobwebs. The French Revolution set many heads distracted and loosened the whole framework of our morals, but we are sobered, and have consigned to oblivion the grosser absurdities of that disjointed period.[2]

There is a secondary discussion running through the book which is very significant. Education, the author insists, is only for the upper classes. "The accomplishment of reading, considered without reference to religious instruction, is about as necessary and suitable to a poor labouring man as a gold snuff box would be."[3] Reading of the Bible might be allowed, but: "The ethics of Mr. Cobbett and the religion of Mr. Carlile are better kept from the poor."[4] "The will of God has made inequality the very essence of every social system. No spread

---

[1] *Blue Stocking Hall*, vol. i., p. 218. Contrast Mary Wollstonecraft's vigorous treatment of this time-worn argument, in chapter v. of the *Vindication of the Rights of Woman*. "Were an angel from heaven to tell me that the account of the Fall of Man were literally true, I could not believe what my reason told me was derogatory to the character of the Supreme Being."
[2] *Blue Stocking Hall*, vol. i., p. 222.
[3] *Ibid.*, vol. i., p. 138.
[4] *Ibid.*, vol. i., p. 150.

of knowledge can improve the lot of him who must till the soil by the sweat of his brow."[1]

It is interesting to note the author's antipathy to the poems of Byron. Mrs. Douglas will not allow a copy of *Don Juan* in her library; she declares "Byron, like Milton's Satan, stands pre-eminent at the head of all mischief makers of the present time."[2][3]

Such were three typical novels of the "Rights of Women." *The Wrongs of Woman* expresses the spirit of the Industrial Revolution, in terms coloured by the philosophies of the French Revolution. It speaks for the women the Sentimentalists ignored; the women not provided with comfortable fortunes or affectionate male relatives eager to support them in idleness. These were the women who, finding that the old ideals had no cognizance of them or of the economic conditions that produced them, were demanding a new and nobler ideal.

The Rights of Woman Best Maintained by the Sentiments of Nature is a contemporary protest of the older Sentimentalists, re-enforced by Rousseauism, against these grimly iconoclastic women of the great Revolutions. Not unfair in its criticism, not unkindly in its satire, but not quite comprehend-

[1] *Blue Stocking Hall*, vol. i., p. 154.
[2] *Ibid.*, p. 279.
[3] *Zeluca: or, Educated and Uneducated Women* (1815) may be an earlier treatment of the same subject, but it is unfortunately not accessible.

ing because aware only of the comfortably wealthy classes,—this is the generous and dignified comment of the older ideal upon the newer.

Last of all, in an age when the idealisms of the Revolution are dead, *Blue Stocking Hall* is the contribution of the Reaction at its worst. Mary Wollstonecraft's noble and eloquent demand for a higher ideal and the right to work has dwindled into a simpering plea that "young ladies," forsooth, be no longer forbidden to dabble in Latin and Greek. Mary Astell had asked as much a hundred years before. But an age so complacent in accepting poverty and ignorance as the divinely ordained lot of the working-man, is not an age to err through over-enthusiastic advocacy of fantastic "Rights of Woman."

CHAPTER VIII

SOME OTHER FORMS OF LITERATURE AFFECTED BY THE FRENCH REVOLUTION

SECTION I: THE POETS

The French Revolution and the English Poets. The influence of the French Revolution upon the poetry of the time has been fully discussed in at least three most admirable books devoted primarily to that subject.[1] It would be out of place here to attempt to do more than recall briefly some of the conclusions reached in these comprehensive treatments.

The poets whose works reflect the ideals of the Revolution fall into three distinct groups, in order of time. 1. There are the precursors of Revolution: certain poets whose works, considered in the light of later developments, seem to foreshadow the

[1] Dr. A. E. Hancock, *The French Revolution and the English Poets;* Professor Edward Dowden, *The French Revolution and English Literature;* and Dr. Charles Cestre, *La Révolution et les Poètes Anglais* (1709-1809). To which may be added the first two chapters of Professor Dowden's *Studies in Literature from 1789 to 1877.*

coming philosophies, although in truth they are little more than humanitarians and Sentimentalists, with the correct Whig principles in politics. Of these poets Cowper and Crabbe are representative. 2. During the actual period of the Revolution, the currents of popular feeling were reflected in the minds of the so-called Lake Poets, Wordsworth, Coleridge, and Southey. To these may be added two independent writers, Burns and Blake. 3. Finally, after the close of the true Revolutionary period, during the later Napoleonic wars and the period of Reaction, come the poets of the afterglow; Byron and Shelley, and their lesser contemporaries, Moore, Leigh Hunt, and Landor.[1]

William Cowper was, according to Professor Dowden, "undesignedly and unawares, the chief representative of Revolutionary sentiment in the days before the Revolution."[2] Cowper was an orthodox Whig in politics and an ardent Evangelical in his religion.[3] Although the denunciation of

---

[1] Professor Dowden discusses the work of all these poets, in the order given, adding various other works (many of which we have already considered in Chapter II). Dr. Cestre confines himself to the poets of the Revolution proper, considering the work of Wordsworth, Coleridge, and Southey in great detail, and adding an excellent chapter on Burns and Blake. Dr. Hancock selects four poets as representative; Shelley, Byron, Wordsworth, and Coleridge. These he discusses in the order named, with the addition of a chapter on Godwin and another on the French philosophers.

[2] Dowden, *French Revolution and English Literature*, p. 30.

[3] On this point Professor Dowden makes an observation significant in connection with the relation which we have traced

luxury and certain other markedly Rousseauistic elements find place in his verse, "it was less by virtue of his ardour in behalf of political liberty, genuine as it was, than by his feeling for simplification and his humanitarian sentiment that Cowper belongs to the Revolution."[1] When the Bastile fell, Cowper was an old man; his period of original writing was over; and the new hopes of the time found him apparently apathetic.

Cowper's younger contemporary, Crabbe, touches the theories of the Revolution only on its humanitarian side. But of the facts that lay below the surface of the movement, the terrible by-products of the Industrial Revolution, he wrote with a grim realism unrelieved by any Utopian visionings for the future.

The earliest of the true Revolutionists was Burns, the poet of Equality. Remote from the sphere of Pure Reason philosophies and of Sentimentalism, from the very life of the time his poetry "sounds the note for the revolt of the proletariat."[2] Professor Dowden adds:

So long as the Revolution retained a philosophic and doctrinaire aspect, it left Burns almost untouched.

---

between the Revolutionists and certain forms of dissent: "The gospel of Rousseau is translated by Cowper into the gospel according to St. Paul. The combination is a curious and interesting one for literary study, of the sentiment of the Revolution with the faith and fervor of the Evangelical revival" (p. 41).

[1] Dowden, *French Revolution*, etc., p. 30.
[2] *Ibid.*, etc., p. 140.

It is only when the Revolution became violent, tragic, and essentially a movement of the popular masses, when it ceased to be a declaration of abstract principles and passed into a conflict of the passions that Burns was deeply moved.[1]

His Revolutionism expressed itself in songs passionate and satiric, and in several escapades which sorely endangered his livelihood as an exciseman. For Burns was a true proletarian in this also, that he was often forced into submission for bread and butter reasons when below his surface docility the fires of revolt still burned.

Another poet somewhat out of the main current of Revolutionary philosophy was William Blake. In 1791, Blake was employed by Joseph Johnson to illustrate Mary Wollstonecraft's *Original Stories*. This brought him in contact with the little group of radical writers that gathered at Johnson's weekly dinners: Paine, Horne Tooke, Godwin, Holcroft, and the rest. Under this stimulus Blake published a poem on the Revolution, now lost. But it is not to be supposed that either the philosophies of the Johnson circle or the social unrests of the time ever really penetrated the consciousness of Blake. Reason and sense of fact were alike subordinated to his glorious but undisciplined imagination. It is the Revolution as a spiritual entity, an eternal, archetypal Revolution quite distinct from the actual political phenomena, that

[1] Dowden, *French Revolution*, etc., p. 146.

lives in the *Marriage of Heaven and Hell* and the *Song of Liberty*, and whose failure cast a shadow over the *Songs of Experience*. Dr. Cestre says of him:

> Dans l'isolement moral où il se complaît, entouré de belles fictions et de douces émotions, la Révolution française ne l'atteint que sous une forme, pour ainsi dire, généralisée. Il ne connait ni ses doctrines philosophiques, ni ses revendications politiques. Il comprend seulement qu'une souffle puissant d'espérance et de justice traverse la terre. Il croit à une rénovation prochaine et complète de cette société, pour laquelle il a une répulsion instinctive. Il voit, dans la Révolution, un événement voulu par Dieu pour ramener ici-bas la vertu et le bonheur. Le monde idéal des *Songs of Innocence* va se réaliser.[1]

Wordsworth's Revolutionism resembles that of Blake in one respect at least; he had little or no grasp of the real social and economic forces at work, and his mind was ill at ease in an atmosphere of pure reason. An account of his relation to the Revolutionary movement must concern itself primarily with his subjective experiences. To summarize briefly Dr. Hancock's chapters: the French Revolution served to humanize Wordsworth. In his early life the love of nature was his absorbing interest. His mind was extraordinarily sensitive and receptive; possessing, moreover, a "clairvoyant quality," a sense of "plastic power" informing the visible world.

[1] Cestre, *La Révolution et les Poètes Anglais*, p. 210.

He acquired a faith in the existence of the things of the spirit, and in a Supreme Being who revealed by gleams the highest truths, and further, a faith in the mind itself as an active and creative thing, adding to experience contributions of its own.[1]

In 1790 and again in 1791, Wordsworth went to France, but felt only a perfunctory interest in the political drama that was acting there. His friendship with the enthusiastic young republican Beaupuis awakened in him a like Revolutionary ardour, based, however, upon sympathy rather than understanding. On his return to England Wordsworth avowed himself a Revolutionist, remaining unshaken by England's declaration of war in 1793, and even extenuating the violence of the Terror.[2]
This emotional enthusiasm lasted until 1796, when it became apparent that France had entered upon a campaign of conquest. At this point, "bereft of the support of his feelings, he began to rationalize," under the influence of Godwin.[3] The result was disastrous to his earlier transcendentalism.

Hume showed that if there was no more in experience than Locke's view permitted it to contain, then the hope of any transcendent knowledge or faith for humanity was indeed gone.[4]

[1] Hancock, *The French Revolution and the English Poets*, p. 129.
[2] *Ibid.*, p. 136.
[3] In his *Letter to the Bishop of Llandaff*.
[4] Professor Royce, quoted by Hancock, p. 139.

To a mind like Wordsworth's the loss of a super-rational belief was agony. *The Borderers* marks the point at which he rebels against the tyranny of Pure Reason.[1] "It is a reductio ad absurdum of the doctrine that the individual intellect should be the sole guide of conduct."[2] Wordsworth returned to the lake country that he loved, and there found peace once more in communion with nature, building up for himself an almost mystical interpretation of life; that "the sensitive, receptive, and creative mind obtains through nature's manifold forms the intimation of transcendent truths." Dr. Hancock concludes:

The French Revolution as a reform humanized Wordsworth, but its philosophy threatened to invalidate his earlier experiences; it served, through his reaction against it, to stimulate his constructive power, and it was the indirect cause of his latter conservatism and faith.[3]

Like Wordsworth, Coleridge was temperamentally antipathetic to the materialistic and atheistic elements in Revolutionism. His individualism was transcendental rather than sceptical. Never-

---

[1] *The Borderers*, written in 1797.
[2] Hancock, *French Revolution*, etc., p. 141.
[3] *Ibid.*, etc., p. 122. Professor Dowden, in his *Studies in Literature* (chapter i.), gives a very illuminating discussion of Wordworth's relation to the nineteenth-century Transcendental movement. This, however, hardly falls within the scope of our subject, excepting as it illustrates the subsequent metamorphoses of Revolutionary Sentimental Individualism.

theless, he too was attracted for a time by the finer significances of the Revolution. He greeted the fall of the Bastile with an ode. In 1793, he denounced the coalition against France and satirized the use of Christianity as a pretext for violence. In 1794, he contributed to the radical *Morning Chronicle* a series of sonnets in praise of the Revolutionary leaders. The *Religious Musings*, in the same year, show strong influences of Rousseau and Godwin. But Coleridge was always discriminating in his acceptance of Godwin. In 1794, he wrote of him:

> Godwin appeared to me to possess neither the strength of intellect that discovers truth nor the powers of imagination that decorate falsehood. He talked sophisms in jejune language. I like Holcroft a thousand times better, and consider him a man of much greater ability.[1]

By 1795 Coleridge was bitterly opposed to Godwin, attacking his philosophy in the *Bristol Lectures* and in the *Watchman*, and withdrawing all his former praises. In the *Bristol Lectures*[2] Coleridge distinguishes clearly between Revolution in the abstract and the concrete political phenomena in France. He divides the "opponents of things as they are" into four classes:

[1] Hancock, *French Revolution*, etc., p. 169. This estimate is of interest, in connection with the pre-eminence we have given to Holcroft in our discussion of the novel.
[2] Delivered in 1795. Afterward printed under the title *Conciones ad Populum*.

First, men unaccustomed to thorough investigation, whose minds are excited by flagrant evils, and who give an indolent vote in favour of reform. Second, men who hate priest and oppressor, who listen readily to the demagogues, and whose hearts are thereby inflamed to revenge. Third, those who, without wavering sympathies or ferocity, desire reforms from motives of self-interest. They desire the abolition of privileged orders and the removal of restrictions only for their own benefit.[1]

The fourth class, in which Coleridge includes himself, are "the glorious band of disinterested patriots." Certainly at the time these lectures were written there was no foundation for the charge that Coleridge was a Jacobin. He shows a very undemocratic tendency to distrust the people as a whole and a distinctly hostile attitude towards the main body of the new doctrines.

The Pantisocracy scheme, which Coleridge proposed to Southey in 1794, was Sentimental, Rousseauistic, but not essentially Revolutionary. There is the greatest possible difference between desiring to change the entire structure of society, and being content to escape from society to an artificially perfected environment. Such colonizing schemes are often resorted to by Revolutionists who have lost hope; but this by no means identifies them with Revolution. Coleridge himself says of Pantisocracy: "What I dared not expect from

[1] Hancock, *French Revolution*, etc., p. 172. *Cf.* other analyses of Revolutionism by its opponents, in Chapter V.

constitutions of government and whole nations, I hoped from religion and a few chosen individuals."[1]

The course of events gradually concentrated Coleridge's love for humanity into the more conventional channels of patriotism; he became a decided Nationalist. In 1797 was published the *Ode to France*, also called *Recantation*, which appears, says Professor Dowden, "hazardously near to political despair."[2] This marks the final break between Coleridge and the Revolutionists. But in truth he had never been genuinely in accord with the movement as a whole, however much he may have sympathized with certain phases of it.

Southey, like Wordsworth and Coleridge, was captivated in his youth by the fine idealism and optimism of the Revolution. Under the impulse of this early enthusiasm he wrote a tragedy, *Wat Tyler*, which, as Professor Dowden very justly observes: "May serve to warn any young poet of the dangers of making his art a direct vehicle for political doctrine."[3] Later, his Girondist sympathies led him into writing another political drama, *The Fall of Robespierre*, in which Coleridge collaborated. Southey's third Revolutionary effort was an epic, *Joan of Arc*, sound Revolutionism, but very indifferent literature. Coleridge, examining

[1] Hancock, *French Revolution*, etc., p. 180.
[2] Dowden, *The French Revolution*, etc., p. 210
[3] *Ibid.*, etc., p. 162.

it years afterward, "was astonished at the transmogrification of the fanatic virago into a modern novel-pawing proselyte of the Age of Reason, a Tom Paine in petticoats, but so lovely!"[1]

In the volume of *Minor Poems*, published in 1797, the humanitarian note predominates.[2] Humanitarian sentiment was, after all, the strongest element in Southey's Revolutionism, and this remained when, like the other Lake Poets, he lost faith in the power of the Revolution to bring about a happier state of society. It is not quite fair to call Wordsworth, Coleridge, and Southey lost leaders. Their defection was inevitable. In any case, leaders of Revolutionary thought they never were.

The opponents of the Revolution were not without their representation in the verse of the time. In November, 1797, appeared the *Anti-Jacobin, a Weekly Review*, under the direction of Gifford and a brilliant group of young Tories. This periodical continued for nearly five years to bombard the new philosophies with shafts of pointed ridicule. Satires and parodies without number were directed against the solemn absurdities of Pure Reason and Sentimentalism. This was the criticism, not merely of political prejudice, but of wit and sound sense, an echo from the age of Pope. One cannot but feel that it was heartily deserved.

[1] Dowden, *French Revolution*, etc., p. 167.
[2] This contains a poem called *The Triumph of Woman*, dedicated to Mary Wollstonecraft.

So ends, in a note of triumphant satire, the poetry of the Revolutionary period. The age of generous hopes and of lawless individual enthusiasm is dead. The forces of conservatism and expediency reign undisturbed. There remain for idealism only a small group, the poets of the afterglow; these, and one bright spirit like an evening star. Of that one we have spoken already, in a more fitting place. Not Shelley, but Byron is the true representative of this latter age; a judgment which the popular verdict of the time confirms.

The forces of conservatism had conquered, but they paid dear for their victory. Byron casts up the score, and finds that the bargain was not altogether a good one. The apotheosis of expediency was but a poor substitute for social idealism. The curse of Sentimentalism was in no wise lifted by the repudiation of democracy. The real aristocracy of intellect, the fine deferences and disciplines of the Age of Authority, were not so easily restored. Southey as poet laureate might recant his Revolutionism, but there was found no Dryden to replace him.

Of such an age is Byron at once the representative and the critic. Hating his time, both for what it was and for what it had made of him, he lacked the power to rise above it. He is the poet of Revolt, not of Revolution. The intense sentimental individualism of Rousseau, alternates in his verses with the mocking iconoclasm of the

Anti-Jacobin. Only Byron's love of liberty remained unspoiled for him; and this was in the end his salvation from a life of half-sincerities.

Three lesser poets must be mentioned who spoke for liberty and social idealism under the Holy Alliance: Landor, natural aristocrat and follower of Milton; Leigh Hunt, with his "bright chivalry for whatever assumed to itself the cherished name and aspect of liberty"[1]; and Moore, whose *Fudge Family in Paris*[2] and his *Fables for the Holy Alliance*[3] are second only to *Don Juan* in satiric cleverness. These escaped to some extent from the false conservatism of the age, but their songs and satires are altogether a less serious indictment of it than the mocking titanism of Byron.

Such was the reflection of the Revolution in the poetry. Of the poets of its earlier periods we may say that a study of the Revolution adds more to the interpretation of their work than their work adds to an understanding of Revolutionism. They were merely caught for a time in the fierce eddy of popular feeling, returning afterwards, somewhat disillusioned, to the serene course of their own meditations. It was only as a lost cause that the Revolution found its full poetical expression, and the Reaction its satiric criticism.

[1] Dowden, *French Revolution*, etc., p. 249.
[2] *Fudge Family in Paris*, published in 1818.
[3] *Fables for the Holy Alliance*, published in 1823.

SECTION 2: THE DRAMA

The French Revolution and the English Drama.[1] The period of French Revolutionary influence in England was not one of the great ages in the history of the drama. It was a time of deep-seated changes and profound unrests. There was a continuous war taxing the country heavily in lives and in money. In such a time men go to the theatre to be amused, to get away from the problems of the time, not to gain a deeper insight into them. Nevertheless, the theatres reflected to some extent the principles of the Revolution and the reaction against them.

Dates have an especial significance here. It will be remembered that in England those genuinely understanding the new theories were a comparatively small group, composed largely of young writers and thinkers. When word came from France of the summoning of the States General and the fall of the Bastile, the country was on the whole pleased. It seemed at first merely an affirmation of generally accepted Whig principles. But later events in France cast discredit upon the principles of the Revolution. In 1793, Pitt saw a chance to profit by the disturbances in the English struggle for a world market for her increased manufactures, and accordingly he forced England into a war with France to defend the sacred principles of religion

[1] This section is intended to be little more than a brief explanation of the material gathered in the Appendix.

and monarchy. These conditions operated together to produce a complete revulsion in popular feeling. A war always deluges a country with a certain type of unthinking jingo patriotism. The small body of real Revolutionary thinkers came to be regarded as a menace to society. The country at large became hypersensitive to any taint of Revolutionary philosophy or propaganda. The government was almost hysterical in its zeal for suppression.

All these changes in feeling were reflected in the acting drama of the time. From 1789 to 1793 a play was all the more favourably received for containing sympathetic allusions to the Revolution in France. In 1793, France declares war and a censor stops a play of Cumberland's for a fancied political reference. From that date direct allusions to the French Revolution are barred. Instead, there is a continued deluge of plays abusing France and celebrating the war, Royalty, Britannia, and so forth, all written in a fine frenzy of patriotism and imbecility and finding favour with a public full of the same sentiments. Verily, St. Jingo was the patron of the time.

Meanwhile the Revolutionist-baiting goes merrily on. The censor and a majority of the public are cordially agreed that the theatre is no place in which to illustrate new and possibly dangerous theories. But the doctrines of the so-called Revolutionists bear such a curious resemblance to mere ethical generalizations and moral commonplaces that they are not always easy to identify. Hence the public becomes capricious and is apt to attach to almost any passage a political significance never dreamed of by the author. A few plays with real implications of Liberty, Equality, and Fraternity slipped by unobserved. But poor Holcroft had the misfortune to get himself effectually identified in the public mind with the detested party, and audiences became very subtle in finding dangerous tendencies in his plays.

In the drama as well as in the novel, Holcroft may be taken as our representative Revolutionist. His position as a dramatist was a prominent one. Besides being the author of fifteen or more plays, and himself a fairly successful actor, he was for two years the editor of a periodical called the *Theatrical Recorder*.[1]

Yet comparatively few of Holcroft's plays are sufficiently doctrinary to be of importance in this discussion. Even those few are of interest chiefly as they show how sensitive were the prejudices that could take offence at them. Holcroft himself complains that "present and local applications are so liable to be made where none are intended."

His only play with a frankly avowed doctrinary purpose is the *School for Arrogance* (1791). This is a satire on pride of rank and pride of wealth. A French count of illustrious ancestry falls in love

[1] 1805, 1806.

with the daughter of a London alderman and is soundly snubbed by her vulgar mama, who knows of no country but England and thinks herself the greatest lady in that. His lady-love points out to him that after all his own intense consciousness of rank has in it not much more true nobility of mind than the absurd pretences of her ignorant mother. Hazlitt says of this:

The School for Arrogance is the first of the author's pieces in which there appeared a marked tendency to political or philosophical speculation. Sentiments of this kind, however, and at that time, would rather have intended to increase than diminish the popularity of the piece. A proof of this is that the very epilogue (which is seldom designed to give offence) glances that way.

> Such is the modern man of high-flown fashion?
> Such are the scions sprung from Runny-Mead!
> The richest soil bears oft the rankest weed!
> Potato-like, the sprouts are worthless found;
> And all that's good of them is underground.[1]

In 1793, *Love's Frailties* was acted at the Haymarket. A considerable disturbance was caused by the following speech: "I was bred to the most useless and often the most worthless of all professions—that of a gentleman." Genest says: "Considering the political ferment of the time, the manager was imprudent in allowing this short

---

[1] Hazlitt, *Memoirs of Holcroft*, vol. ii., p. 86.

speech to be spoken." Holcroft says in his preface: "The persons offended, though violent, were few. Their intention doubtless was good. The same cannot be said for their intellect."

Holcroft's next play, *The Deserted Daughter*, was published under another name, because, as Genest says, "Holcroft in 1795 laboured under violent political prejudices." In 1798, *Knave Or Not* met with a cool reception for the same reason. Holcroft says in his preface that the acting version was cut, "particularly the passage where Morose inquires into his qualifications for being a lord."

Like Mrs. Inchbald, Holcroft did some of his best work in a play of humanitarian sentiment. He treats dramatically the life of De L'Épée, the famous French teacher of the deaf. The play is entitled *Deaf and Dumb*.

A priori, one would expect the plays of William Godwin to hold a position of considerable importance in this discussion. Such is not the case however. Godwin is the author of two plays, *Antonio*[1] and *Faulkner*.[2] But we need not seek for political prejudice to explain their unpopularity. Like the novels of Godwin they exhibit a sombre, oppressive kind of power and a strong tendency toward the Gothic Romance type. But as plays they have little value and of Revolutionary doctrines they exhibit no trace.

Another play in which we might reasonably

[1] Acted December 13, 1800, at Drury Lane.
[2] Acted December 10, 1807, at the Haymarket.

expect to find the influence of the author of *Political Justice* is the younger Colman's popular dramatization of Godwin's frankly doctrinary novel, *Caleb Williams*. *The Iron Chest* was first acted at Drury Lane March 12, 1796. The novel on which it was based, *Caleb Williams or Things As They Are*, was intended, it will be remembered, to illustrate how completely the machinery of justice may be perverted by the rich and powerful to their own ends. The novel contains one chapter in which the author discusses with genuine feeling the evils of the English prison system; in the play all this is carefully omitted, only the story remaining.

Godwin's arraignment of the prison system does however find a place in the drama, in the work of his friend Mrs. Inchbald. The title of her play, *Such Things Are*, immediately suggests the subtitle of Godwin's novel. The play was, the preface tells us, written in 1786, some time before the publication of *Caleb Williams*. But the connexion is none the less traceable. The authors were early identified with the same school of thought and an intimate personal friendship, if nothing more, existed between them. Both works are inspired by that spirit of humanitarianism which went hand in hand with the spirit of the French Revolution in England; the pointing out of individual abuses was only a corollary to a denunciation of the existing social order.

Such Things Are is founded on the character of John Howard whose noble work of prison investigation earned him the thanks of the House of Commons in 1774. It is interesting to note here that Howard's book on lazarettos was published in the eventful year 1789. "Haswell," his representative in the play, is drawn with rare dignity and sincerity of feeling. The main plot is as follows: Scene: an island in the East Indies. The leader of a rebellion loses his wife in the struggle. He becomes Sultan and, embittered by grief, adopts harsh measures against political prisoners. Haswell visits the prisons (good descriptive scene), and pleads in vain with the Sultan for reforms. Eventually, however, he gains the confidence of the Sultan and persuades him to visit the prisons for himself. In the worst of them the Sultan finds his lost wife. Haswell's speech to the Sultan at this point is striking:

Your wife you will behold, whom you have kept in want, in wretchedness, in a damp dungeon for these fourteen years, because you would not listen to the voice of pity. Dread her look, her frown— Not on her account alone, but for hundreds of her fellow sufferers; for while your selfish fancy was searching with wild anxiety for her *you* loved—unpitying, you forgot— others might love like you.[1]

Mrs. Inchbald rarely forgets the larger significance of the individual case. She is arraigning that stupidity of the imagination which, so long as the

[1] Mrs. Inchbald, *Such Things Are*, Act V., Sc. 3.

evils of the system do not touch one's self, is content with things as they are.

In connexion with that defiance of creeds, miscalled "irreligion," that characterized the Revolutionary thinkers, it is significant that "Haswell" says the full statement of his humanitarian principles is found in "a book called *The Christian Doctrine.*"[1]

The sub-plot of this remarkable play is a clever satire on Lord Chesterfield's advice to his son, the cynical worldly wisdom of which was abhorrent to the Revolutionists.

Mrs. Inchbald's other plays show traces of the same point of view, but none decidedly enough to entitle them to a place in the present discussion.

There is one play of the opposing party which merits attention: Sheridan's *Pizarro* (May 24, 1798). Sheridan was a figure of some importance in the political as well as in the literary world; a prominent M.P. attached to the party of Fox. This gives the play an almost official significance. Genest says of the speech of Rolla to the soldiers:

Its primary object was to reprobate the principles of the French Revolution. Such was the popularity of this T. that the king could not resist his desire to see it.[2]

It is of interest to note some extracts from this much-applauded semi-official discussion of the French Revolution:

[1] Mrs. Inchbald, *Such Things Are*, Act III., Sc. 2.
[2] Genest, *English Stage*, note to May 27, 1798.

They by strange frenzy driven fight for power, for plunder, and extended rule; we for our country, our altars, and our homes. They follow an adventurer whom they fear and obey a power which they hate; we serve a monarch whom we love—a God whom we adore. . . . They call on us to barter all the goods we have inherited and proved for the desperate chance of something better which they promise. The throne we honour is the people's choice: the laws we reverence are our brave fathers' legacy.[1]

It seemed to young thinkers of the next few decades that all fine idealisms were shattered; barred forever from attempting a practical part in the progress of social development. But the spirit of the French Revolution was not destroyed, only forced to remain underground and to find expression in less direct ways. In this latent period of Revolutionism there appear with increasing frequency plays built about the type-figure of the Benevolent Outlaw, the man who feels a fundamental wrong in the social system against which he must forever rebel without having the power to change it, and who is forced outside the social order by all that is strong or noble in his own nature. This is the type which finds expression in much of Byron's work. But the Benevolent Outlaw manifested a tendency of the time, as these plays indicate. It is a mistaken criticism that gives Byron credit for originating

[1] Sheridan, *Pizaro*, Act II., Sc. 2.

the type of which he was the most popular exponent.[1]

[1] The closet dramas of Wordsworth, Coleridge, Southey, Byron, and Shelley do not properly belong in a discussion of the popular acting drama. They have been mentioned already in the preceding section, as poetry.

CHAPTER IX

CONCLUSIONS

PERHAPS it may be well to summarize the material which has been presented before we attempt to formulate our general conclusions.

The true Revolutionists—the writers who had the ability to distinguish the real conflict of ideas below the surface of events and form a consistent conviction more or less independent of the changes in popular feeling—these were necessarily a very limited group. Only three of them were among our novelists. Of these the earliest and in every way the most truly representative was Thomas Holcroft. His Revolutionism was no lightly adopted surface philosophy, but was created from within by the intensity of his social idealism. The vital principle of his ethical and political system was the subordination of individual rights and ambitions to the service of the social whole. Holcroft had reached that high plane of ethical thought where the ideals of service and self-development are no longer in conflict. Furthermore, his idealism is modified by a considerable knowledge of the world, and a sense of humour that enabled him to laugh even at himself without bitterness.

William Godwin was influenced by Holcroft, but his Revolutionism was dominated by his metaphysical studies and by his intensely introspective temperament. Being quite devoid of any saving sense of fact, he formulated a political system that was a *reductio ad absurdum* of the rationalistic tendencies of his age. His novels are curiously illustrative of the morbid egoism which is the result of an over-individualistic philosophy. They are, however, redeemed by some rather fine passages of humanitarian feeling.

Shelley's three novels belong to his early and little known prose period. Although valueless in themselves, they serve to mark distinct stages in the development of the author. Shelley's other prose writings are more significant. These express certain phases of his Revolutionism which find no place in his poems, and without which it is impossible to form a correct estimate of his political wisdom.

So far, we have observed two distinct elements in the Revolutionary philosophy: democratic individualism and social idealism. In Godwin individualism dominates. In Holcroft and Shelley it is completely subordinated to social idealism.

The opponents of Revolutionism wrote a number of novels, two of which at least show a remarkably clear insight into the weak points of democratic individualism. The argument most frequently advanced against it is its inadequacy as a system of social or even of personal ethics.

Followed to its logical conclusion it would result in anarchy and insanity. The second objection is of a somewhat more theoretical nature. This involves a classification of the various heterodox tendencies of the time; arriving at the conclusion that these all have their basis in a revolt from the principle of authority, and a substitution of individual reason or individual feeling for all general standards, religious as well as political. Another conservative protest against the new tendencies is in the form of an attack on the financial methods of the new capitalist classes and a lament for the passing of the older land-owning gentry.[1]

These attacks are, it will be observed, directed mainly against democratic individualism. Social idealism is dismissed with a rather superficial charge of inexpediency. The representatives of conservatism seem quite unaware of the rather fine idealisms implicit in the old order. Their criticism is purely destructive and quite fails to distinguish the elements of permanent value either in the old or in the new ideals.

Revolutionism was not a ready-made hypothesis which one either accepted or rejected. It was a movement by which one was more or less influenced. It is not sufficiently accurate to classify our novelists merely as "Revolutionists" and "opponents of Revolutionism." Between the conscious democratic individualist accepting the

[1] *Cf.* Chapter IV., especially novels of Lucas, Walker, and E. T. Sun.

philosophy with a full understanding of its implications and the equally intelligent defender of the principle of authority, there was a much larger number of writers whose opinions ranged through all possible degrees of sympathy and disapproval.

The finest representative of these Revolutionary sympathizers was Robert Bage. Bage was a man entirely capable of perceiving the full implications of both philosophies, but he was also capable of a fine moderation in his enthusiasms. He was free from Sentimentalism, and his Revolutionism was held in check by a large fund of common sense. It was apparent to him that the Conservatives and Reactionaries were a little more wrong than any one else at that time; hence he was a Revolutionist, with important reservations.

Probably all the other semi-Revolutionists fancied themselves actuated by a fine discrimination like that of Bage. But it is only too apparent that in nine cases out of ten their eclecticism was sheer muddle-headedness. They were well-intentioned people whose attention had been attracted by some crying evil of the time—the prison system, the slave trade, rotten boroughs or the like—or who had discovered that an aristocracy of birth was illogical; and who thereupon proceeded to dabble in Revolutionary philosophy. They were for the most part entirely unaware of any fundamental principles involved in the movement which they regarded with such patronizing favour.

It is in this group that we must classify the lady novelists. Their Revolutionism was in every case traceable to the influence of some man of their acquaintance who was a Revolutionist, from whom they received their political opinions with exemplary feminine docility. But they in no wise allowed their philosophic radicalism to interfere with their religious orthodoxy; to which they clung with gentle firmness, as a substitute for thinking.

The new impetus which the feminist movement received at this time was connected with Revolutionism only indirectly. Its real source was to be found in the changes arising from the Industrial Revolution, rather than in the political philosophies of the day, however glibly some of its later exponents may have used phrases borrowed from the French Revolution. The principle involved was not individualism *versus* authority, but simply the question of whether a woman was to be regarded as a human being with all that that implies of dignity and responsibility, or whether she was a sort of secondary creation, valuable only through her sex attributes. Mary Wollstonecraft's clear-headed perception of the point at issue and of the economic situation which had precipitated the whole discussion constituted the only real contribution of the Revolutionists to the feminist question.

With this summary of the material presented, we may perhaps venture a few generalizations upon special aspects of Revolutionism.

In our discussion of the background of ideas,[1] we observed certain parallelisms in the progress and development of political and theological concepts. The seventeenth-century movement of democratic individualism was closely identified with certain forms of Dissent. The novels which we have considered indicate that the same connexion existed between eighteenth-century Revolutionism and the later theologies of Dissent.

It may be well to summarize our observations on this point.

Holcroft, like most sensible men, was rather chary of defining his beliefs. His religion was a force rather than a formula. But from his criticisms on churchmen, and on the absurdity of any attempt to secure uniformity of belief, we may conclude that he was pretty well out of sympathy with the Establishment. It is probable that in his youth he was attracted for a time by some of the finer spiritual values of the new Methodist movement. But he was soon repelled by the superficial enthusiasm to which it was rapidly tending.

There is no difficulty in classifying the religious opinions of Godwin. The son of a dissenting minister, educated in a dissenting theological seminary on a mental diet of metaphysics and Calvinism, he represents theological individualism in its most extreme form.

Shelley's atheism has always proved a trap to the unwary critic. The efforts that have been

[1] *Cf.* Chapter I., Section 2.

made to prove that he was really only a deist, or that he was on the point of changing his opinions at the time of his death are distinctly amusing. Shelley himself, in answer to the question: "Why do you call yourself an atheist?" said:

It is a word of abuse to stop discussion, a painted devil to frighten the foolish, a threat to intimidate the wise and good. I used it to express my abhorrence of superstition; I took up the word as a knight took up a gauntlet, in defiance of injustice.[1]

From which it is clear that Shelley was quite aware of the meaninglessness of the word. But so far as the term has an accepted meaning, Shelley was quite correct in calling himself an atheist. It is naturally rather confusing to persons of a literal mind to find the one profoundly religious personality in an orthodox but unspiritual age manifesting his fervour by a wholesale denunciation of the very foundations of the creeds. The orthodox have no cause to be alarmed over his influence, however, for it is only too apparent that the majority of people are quite incapable of understanding the Shelleyan type of atheism.

Whether Robert Bage was a Friend or not, we have Scott's opinion that he was "a sectary—and could be a friend neither to the Church of England nor to the doctrines she teaches." Probably his theological opinions were much the same as those of Holcroft. Amelia Opie was brought up a Unitarian and later became a Friend. Mrs. Inchbald

[1] Trelawney, *Records*, p. 62.

was a Roman Catholic with occasional fits of scepticism. Concerning the other novelists of our group no record remains on this point. So far as we know, not one of the Revolutionary novelists was a member of the Established Church.

The opponents of Revolutionism were very decidedly aware of the connexion between Dissent and political radicalism. Lucas and Walker virtually identify the two as phases of the same spirit of individualistic revolt against authority.

The intimate connexion between religious and political theory is no new observation. It is at least as old as Machiavelli's *Prince*, although it seems to have been pretty well overlooked in recent discussions of Revolutionism. The opposition of Dissenters to the government has been attributed to discontent arising from their legal disabilities. That was doubtless a contributory cause. But if we are interested in the more general principle involved, we shall have little difficulty in perceiving an affinity between democratic and theological individualism that need not go for its explanation to accidental circumstances like test acts.

Besides the philosophy of Revolutionism, there is an economic element which has been somewhat neglected in discussing the literature of the movement.[1] We have already observed in our dis-

---

[1] In fact, Dr. Cestre is the only critic, so far as I am aware, who treats this aspect of the time in relation to the literature of Revolutionism. He touches upon it in his *Révolution et Les Poètes Anglais*, and also in his *Life of Thelwall*.

cussion of the background of events how seriously the entire social structure had recently been affected by the changes and maladjustments arising from the Industrial Revolution. The whole nation was pervaded by social unrests which influenced the thought of the time to a degree which it is hard to overestimate.

Our little group of novelists were somewhat divided in their attitude toward the economic implications of their philosophy. Those whom we have called the true Revolutionists were willing to follow social idealism and democratic individualism wherever they might lead. They saw clearly that political equality was valueless as an ideal if its attainment was to be merely the prelude to increased economic inequality.

Holcroft was himself of the "lower" class by birth and early environment. Consequently his attitude on industrial questions is quite free from Sentimentalism and also from indifference. He saw clearly that it was not for the good of the social whole that any considerable group should be prevented from maintaining a decent standard of living. He felt that the complaints of the wage-workers were not without foundation. But the spirit of class hatred seemed to him entirely stupid and harmful. Instead of preaching a doctrine of violent Revolutionism among the dispossessed classes, Holcroft addresses the property holders in a tone of stern and sorrowful admonition. Repent, and institute reforms of your own accord, lest a worse thing befall you, is his message. The possession of wealth he regards not as an absolute right, but as an obligation to service. This is the extent of Holcroft's communism.

Godwin, as we might expect, has all manner of economic whimsies. Property, he says, belongs to him who needs it most. This is the only property right that is valid according to political justice. But Godwin's extreme communism is modified by some recognition of the inexpediency of its immediate introduction. The result is, that between the boldness of his theory and the timidity of his immediate programme, Godwin contributes just nothing to the economic wisdom of his time.

Shelley, like Holcroft, is interested primarily in the moral and intellectual improvement of mankind. But being no Sentimentalist, he perceives that economic questions must be dealt with as a means to that end. As a true social idealist, he demands a more equable distribution of wealth, not on the ground of abstract right, but as a matter of a higher expediency, because the extremes of wealth and poverty are alike destructive to the finer values in life. "Every man has a right to a certain degree of leisure and liberty because it is his duty to attain a certain degree of knowledge. He may before he ought," says Shelley.

Robert Bage was himself a factory owner; but his opinions on economic questions are as free from any class bias as those of the proletarian Holcroft. If he has rather less to say about the anti-social effect of extreme poverty, his denunciations of wealth and luxury are none the less vigorous.

But most of the general sympathizers with the Revolution were either unaware of any economic question at all, or took a firm stand for the sacred rights of property. Mrs. Inchbald is the only one of the lady novelists who has anything to say on the matter. She is aware of the intense social unrests which were threatening a violent outbreak of Revolutionism among the industrial workers, and she ironically admonishes the benevolent rich to "give a little, lest the poor, driven to despair, should take all."

The writer who saw most clearly the economic basis of the conflicts over political theory in France and in England, was Mary Wollstonecraft. Her charge, that the extreme solicitude of the dominant bourgeoisie for the preservation of law and order was in reality merely a concern for the security of their own property rights, is amply borne out by the testimony of her opponents as well as by various significant events. It is quite clear that Walker and Lucas, for instance, see in Revolutionism only a threatened insurrection of the ignorant and irresponsible masses against their natural superiors the capitalist classes; an effort on the part of the lazy and inefficient to overthrow society for their own gain. Ownership of capital is to them an absolute right, the protection of which constitutes the chief function of government. It carries with it no responsibility or obligation.

The function of the poorer classes is to produce as much as possible. That of the rich is to consume, and thereby stimulate production. Walker actually declares that "the rich would do better without the poor than the poor without them."[1] These writers draw no moral inference from the economic maladjustments, as did Holcroft and Shelley.

It may be said that a writer's attitude on this question of property right is the crucial test of his Revolutionism. Bourgeois capitalism had much in common with democracy in its opposition to the hereditary aristocracy. But capitalism soon perceived that the democratic ideal was a dangerous ally. We have observed how quickly popular feeling in England was changed when the bourgeois Constituent Assembly with its property qualifications for suffrage gave place to the violent democracy of the Paris mob.

There were two antagonistic forces in England during the Revolution. The force in control of the government was the new aristocracy of wealth, inspired not so much perhaps by greed as by the desire for power, to whom the national prosperity consisted in the rapid accumulation of capital at all costs and the securing of commercial supremacy over other nations. Opposed to them were the industrial workers and the small property owners, dispossessed by the Industrial Revolution. These perceived only the hopeless wretchedness of their

[1] *Cf.* Chapter V.

own condition, and regarded the dominant class with a bitter unreasoning resentment.

The issue between these two forces was in no way a moral or intellectual one: it was a blind elemental struggle for existence and power. Class hatred was about equally strong on both sides. Of course each was quite willing to use moral argument as a weapon to turn public opinion against the other. The proletariat clearly perceived the sin of greed and luxury, and the bourgeoisie were fully aware of the evils of laziness and inefficiency and lawlessness. The rights of man on the one side, and the sanctity of law, order, and respect for superiors on the other, were catch phrases frequently heard in connexion with riots and harsh repressive measures. But excepting for a sentimental bourgeois humanitarianism and an equally sentimental proletarian regard for the "republican virtues," neither side was willing to apply moral judgment and discipline to its own case.

Between these two opposing forces stood the little group of Revolutionists,—democratic individualists in their philosophy, but pure social idealists in their ethical and economic programme. These writers insist boldly and uncompromisingly that the issue is in the last resort a moral one, and that both sides are in the wrong. They refuse to regard wealth and poverty, individual or national, as facts of supreme importance in themselves, excepting in so far as they help or hinder human development. The right of the individual to do as he will with his own property they regard as entirely subordinate to his duty and to the rights of the social whole. If the social idealists seemed unduly to favour the proletarian side, it was because at the time of the Revolution that was distinctly the oppressed party. But nothing was farther from their desire than to substitute a reign of uneducated lawlessness and indolence for a reign of semi-educated selfishness and greed. Their doctrine furnished as severe a moral discipline for the one as for the other.

The principle of social idealism was the true and abiding contribution of the Revolutionary philosophy to political wisdom. The belief that a high and conscious purpose transcending petty expediencies is not merely a factor in sound government but its guiding principle, has never been more courageously maintained. There was sore need of such a doctrine in the eighteenth century; the principle of authority was outgrown, and social idealism was the only thing that could supply its place as a political faith and discipline.

Social idealism made many mistakes at first; partly, perhaps, because of its temporary alliance with democratic individualism. The points of Burke were well taken; expediency, the wisdom of the past, and the organic nature of society had all been disregarded in an insistence on abstract principles. But in a right conception of government the function of a regard for expediency and tradition is critical and corrective, not initiative. When practical considerations succeed in obscuring the real purpose of government evil is sure to follow. For social idealism is, after all, only a higher form of expediency, a perception of what makes for the highest good of the social whole rather than for the temporary advantage of some part.

APPENDIX TO CHAPTER VIII, SECTION 2

Lists of Plays Showing Tendencies Influenced by the French Revolution

The method of presenting the material here collected was chosen, after considerable deliberation, in the hope of thus giving a more complete view of the subject than is possible in a treatment, necessarily limited, of separate writers. This Appendix is intended to supplement Chapter IX, Section 2: the conclusions of the chapter are based upon both.

The writer is endeavouring to present here the results of an examination of Genest, covering the period from 1789 to 1812 inclusive,[1] with a view to throwing light upon such questions as these: To what extent was the stage of that period sensitive to current political tendencies? How far did the government censorship act as a check on the theatres in this respect? What was the prevailing political sentiment of the theatre-going public, and especially, what was their

---

[1] These dates are chosen rather arbitrarily. The first is the date of the summoning of the States General, the actual beginning of the French Revolution. The second is chosen as being late enough in the Napoleonic era to show fully the reaction against the principles of the French Revolution.

The quotations are all from Genest. Page references are omitted, as the date is sufficient to locate the passage.

attitude towards the French Revolution? Did the point of view of the "Revolutionary School" find a minority representation in the theatre? The answers might have a decided value in showing us the tendencies of the time in their true proportion. The adherents of the Revolutionary principles bulk so large in the literature of the time, that we are sometimes prone to forget how insignificant and despicable a minority they must have seemed to their contemporaries.

The list, based upon Genest, the *Theatrical Recorder*, and an examination of the plays themselves whenever available, includes as nearly as possible all plays appearing for the first time in the period considered which seem to have a particular bearing upon the political tendencies of the time. They are arranged, in the hope of making apparent certain tendencies, as follows: 1. Plays which, in general, express the reaction against the French Revolution; which are inspired by the violent patriotism of war times, and support the policy of those in power. 2. Plays which have a more direct bearing upon the principles of the French Revolution in England; especially, those which caused popular demonstrations or had difficulties with the censor and licenser.

In such an examination as the present a number of subordinate tendencies stand out very clearly. One finds the dramatic representatives of the Gothic Romance, the Byronic Hero, the Noble Savage, etc. Most of these topics have but an indirect bearing upon the subject of this chapter. But there are two types which seem to me so closely allied to the spirit of the French Revolution in England that I have added them to the list, in separate groups. These are

(1) the Benevolent Outlaw or Brigand, of the type of Schiller's *Raüber*, and (2) plays built around certain humanitarian movements, such as prison reform, care of defectives, abolition of chattel slavery, etc. I have further noted a few significant revivals of old plays.

PLAYS OF GENERAL PATRIOTIC AND ANTI-FRENCH SENTIMENT. PLAYS SUPPORTING THE PARTY IN POWER AND CELEBRATING CURRENT EVENTS

1789, May 19. *Lacedemonos;* or, *A People Made Happy.*
"A loyal effusion, on the King's recovery."
1793, May 3. *To Arms;* or, *The British Recruit*
1793, May 11. *The Rival Soldiers.*
1793, Sept. 12. *Caernarvon Castle;* or, *The Birth of the Prince of Wales.*
"An extravagant compliment to royalty."
1794, Feb. 29. *British Fortitude.*
1794, March 9. *Siege of Meaux.* (PYE.)
Plot: Rescue of nobility from attacks of peasants after the siege of Poitiers. Exaltation of England.
1794, March 24. *Fall of Martinico,* or, *Britannia Triumphant.*
1794, July 18. *Rule Britannia.* (ROBERTS.)
1794, July 20. *Britain's Glory,* or, *A Trip to Portsmouth.*
1794, May 6. *Temple of Hymen.*
"A masque in honor of the nuptials of the Prince and Princess of Wales."
1794, Sept. 23. *The Rage.*
"Said to be full of allusions to the Duke of Q."
1794, Dec. 6. *Town Before You.* (Mrs. COWLEY.)
(G.) "Ostentatious display of patriotic sentiments."
1795, Feb. 21. *England Preserved.*
(G.) "The subject was doubtless chosen for the sake of introducing patriotic sentiments and invectives against the French."

1795, April   6. *Windsor Castle.* (PEARCE.
                    "In honor of the marriage of the Prince and Princess of Wales."
1795, May   6. *Death of Captain Faulkener;* or, *British Heroism.*
                    "English and French frigates appear at back of stage in act of engagement."
1795, June   3. *Secret Tribunal.*
                    "In the last scene of the second act, a compliment to the 'Isle of Glory' (England) is introduced with much propriety."
1796, July   11. *Siege of Quebec.*
1797, Feb.   20. *Bantry Bay.*
                    "Founded on the attempt of the French to land in Bantry Bay. Has nothing to recommend it but its loyalty."
1797, May   11. *Surrender of Trinidad.*
1797, Nov.   9. *Trip to the Nore.*
                    "Temporary piece to celebrate Lord Duncan's victory. Franklin says he wrote it in ess than a day."
1798, May   21. *Escape.*
                    "A Pantomime Interlude, founded on a recent fortunate event."
1797, Feb.   27. "Toward the voluntary contribution now open at the Bank for the defence of our Country."
1797, Sept.   20. *England's Glory,* or, *The Defeat of the Dutch Fleet by the Gallant Admiral Duncan.*
1798, March   31. *Raft;* or, *Both Sides of the Water.*
                    "A temporary trifle by Cross; it was written at the time when Bonaparte threatened to invade England with an army who were to cross the channel on rafts."
1798, July   21. *Cambro-Britons.*
                    "It would seem from the preface that Boaden's chief object in writing this was to show his patriotism and loyalty."
1798, Nov.   6. *Rama Droog.*
                    In the last scene British troops take a fort.

1799, Oct.	7.	*Naval Pillar.* (T. DIBDIN.)
1800, Sept.	2.	*Review;* or, *Wags at Windsor.*
		"Review represented at the end by figures in perspective."
1801, Jan.	29.	*Veteran Tar.*
		"At the conclusion, French and English vessels seen engaging."
1803, March	5.	*John Bulls;* or, *An Englishman's Fireside.* (COLMAN.)
1803, May	20.	*King John,* as altered by Dr. Valpy.
		"The allusions to the state of France in 1800 which he has thrown in are contemptible."
1803, Oct.	24.	*Maid of Bristol.*
		"The Epilog was written by the Younger Colman. It contains some most bitter sarcasms on Bonaparte, all expressed in very neat and pointed terms."
1803, Dec.	13.	*English Fleet in 1342.*
		"Dibdin heaps compliment on the English, upon compliment, in a way that can hardly fail of being nauseous to any person of good sense."
1805, Sept.	12.	*Who's Afraid? Ha! Ha! Ha!*
		"A patriotic effusion, founded on the intended invasion."
1805, Nov.	11.	"A Melo-Drama piece, by Cumberland, to commemorate the victory and death of Lord Viscount Nelson."
1808, Nov.	10.	*Siege of St. Quentin;* or, *Spanish Heroism.*
		"By Hooke; merely written with a view to introducing some popular sentiments about the modern Spanish Patriots."
1809, Feb.	16.	*Monody on the Death of Sir John Moore.*
1809, July	4.	*Soldier's Daughter.*
1809, Oct.	25.	*Britain's Jubilee.*
		"Written to celebrate the entrance of the king on the fiftieth year of his reign."
1811, June	10.	*Royal Oak.*
		"Based on the escape of Charles II." King appears as a noble and generous character.

PLAYS HAVING A MORE DIRECT BEARING UPON THE THEORIES OF THE FRENCH REVOLUTION IN ENGLAND. ESPECIALLY, PLAYS WHICH WERE INTERFERED WITH BY THE CENSOR, OR WHICH CAUSED ANY POPULAR DEMONSTRATION

1789, Nov. 7. *National Prejudice.*
1789, Nov. 13. *Island of St. Margaret.* (Hon. JOHN ST. JOHN.)
"Founded on Voltaire's account of the Man in the Iron Mask. Iron Mask is confined in a castle. The mob arise and restore him to his liberty. The great success with which this was acted was due to the references to what was passing in France, and in particular to the taking of the Bastile. At the conclusion of this Opera the Temple of Liberty arises from among the ruins of the castle."

1791, Dec. 3. *A Day in Turkey.* (Mrs. COWLEY.)
"The political allusions would have been better omitted. Death is said to be an Aristocrat. If Death be not a complete leveller the devil is in it."

1793. *The Armorer.* (CUMBERLAND.)
"Cumberland wrote a Comic Opera on the story of Wat Tyler, which being objected to by the Licenser, he was obliged to remodel it, and produce it under the title of the *Armorer*. As the piece was not printed, it is impossible to say positively that there was nothing objectionable in it. . . . But certainly no one but a dog in office could suspect Cumberland of writing anything of a bad political tendency."

1793, Jan. 20. "On this evening there was no play performed, from respect to Louis XVI., who was murdered in Paris on that day."

1793, June 7. *Fontainebleau.*
1793, Sept. 22. *Box Holly Challenge.*
"Jack Crotchet says to Sir Toby, who has been reproaching him with being the son of a

printer: 'We that cannot count up our generations have oftentimes the sense to outwit you whose ancestors hang by the wall from King Arthur's time to the present day. . . . What are they but a catalogue of insignificants? One printer, one compositor, one poor corrector of the press, is worth them all and his country gains more credit by his labors.'"

1794, Feb. 22. *Travellers in Switzerland.* (BATE DUDLEY.)
Lady satirized for pride of ancestry. Has taken a dislike to hero merely because he was without a coat-of-arms. He disguises himself as a valet, and wins her nevertheless.

1795, March 7. *France As It Was.* (Altered from *Fontainebleau.*)

1799, May 24. *Pizarro.* (SHERIDAN.)

1799, Aug. 21. *Red Cross Knights.* (HOLMAN.)
"Holman says in his preface he had adapted *The Robbers* to the English stage—and that it was refused a licence—he acknowledged that on dispassionate investigation he found much to justify the licenser's decision." Appears in this form altered, and with omissions. "But unfortunately the spirit has in a great degree evaporated."

1800, May 12. *School for Prejudice;* or, *Liberal Opinions.*
Farce, by T. DIBDIN. Satirizes pride of rank, and haughty manner to social inferiors.

1802, Jan. 15. *Alfonso, King of Castile.*
Plot deals with conspiracy against king, and counter conspiracy to save him. Hero stabs his friend to save the king.

1803, Dec. *Caravan Driver and his Dog.*
Scene, in Spain under a cruel king who forms the villain of the piece.

1803, Dec. *Wallace;* or *The Patriot.*
In Scotch theatre, first.

1808, Jan. 12. *Wanderer;* or, *Rites of Hospitality.*
Originally founded on the escape of the Pretender. "The licenser refused his sanction

to the English play, and Kemble was obliged to change the scene from Scotland to Sweden."

1808, Dec. 1. *Venoni;* or, *The Novice of St. Mark's.* (LEWIS.) Strongly anti-clerical.

1809, July 1. *Killing No Murder.*
Suppressed by a Methodist censor because of some references to the Methodists. Author inserts a passage ridiculing censor, "Which, as it touched not politics nor religion, he could not expunge." Little bearing upon the Revolution, but illustrated folly and power of the censor.

1809, Sept. Prices raised in Covent Garden. Rioting, violent and long continued. "Cobbett observed that the demand for old prices was unreasonable, being *a violation of the rights of property*, and an attempt to compel people to sell entertainment at the price pointed out by the purchaser."

By the final agreement, "The proportion which had always subsisted between the boxes and the pit was now done away, the boxes being for the first time double the price of the pit." Very significant in the light of the social changes resulting from the Industrial Revolution.

1811, Nov. 29. *Gustavus Vasa.*
"The piece had been announced for representation under the title *Gustavus of Sweden*. . . . forbidden by Mr. Larpent (the censor). The only reason that could be conjectured for this absurd and arbitrary conduct of these petty tyrants was, that the Ex-king of Sweden being in England at this time, and the ministers being determined not to acknowledge him, they were afraid that people should imagine, that a play called *Gustavus of Sweden* had some reference to him."

1812, May 15. *Day After the Wedding.*
"The original title of this piece (*John Bull*),

is said to have been objected to by the Lord Chamberlain. It was however restored on the twentieth."

"To O'Keefe's works must be added *Le Grenadier,* meant for presentation at Covent Garden in 1789—but it was merely the foundation of a play which was never finished. O'Keefe meant to have exhibited the taking of the Bastile, and other recent events at Paris. See his *Recollections,* vol. ii., p. 143." (Genest, vol. vii., p. 403.)

A FEW PLAYS WHICH, ALTHOUGH NOT "REVOLUTIONARY" IN A STRICT SENSE, EXHIBIT STRONGLY THE ALLIED HUMANITARIAN TENDENCIES OF THE TIME

1789, Aug. 5. *The Benevolent Planters.* (BELLAMY.)
 Plot: Lovers reduced to slavery. The Planters restore them to liberty and to each other.

1790, Aug. 11. *The Basket Maker.* (O'KEEFE.)
 Plot: A master and servant carried off by Indians. Servant can weave baskets, master can do nothing. So Indians force him to serve his servant.
 (This belongs properly in the preceding group.)

1793, Aug. 24. *The Female Prisoner.*
1793, Aug. 25. *Inkle and Yarico.* (COLMAN.)
 Anti-slavery. "The only excuse for buying our fellow-creatures is to rescue them from the hands of those who are unfeeling enough to bring them to the market." Plot: Inkle, an Englishman, is tempted to sell a savage girl, who has saved his life, and thinks herself his wife.

1799 *Negro Slaves.* (On the Scotch stage first.)
1800, Sept. 6. *The Indian.*

1808, May   3.   *The Jew of Mogadore.*
                  Nabob in the habit of purchasing slaves and giving them their liberty.

PLAYS OF THE "PHILANTHROPIC BRIGAND" TYPE.

1789, Aug.   11. *Battle of Hexam.*
1793, Aug.   3.   *The Mountaineers.* (COLMAN.)
                  Hero driven by his wrongs to flee from society.
1794, Feb.   25. *Fontainville Forest.*
1797, May   19. *Honest Thieves.*
1797   *The Borderers.* (WORDSWORTH.)
1799, Aug.   21. *Red Cross Knights.*
                  Based on Schiller's *Die Raüber.*
1801, May   4.   *Adelmorn, the Outlaw.*
1805, Aug.   26. *Venetian Outlaw.*
                  Holcroft says the plot is from the same source as that of *Venice Preserved.*
1805, Oct.   18. *Rugantino;* or, *The Bravo of Venice.*
                  Much the same plot as the preceding play.
1806, April 10. *White Plume;* or, *The Border Chieftain.* (DIBDIN.)
1807, Feb.   19. *Curfew.*
                  Rayner. (JOANNA BAILLIE.)
                  Sir Francis Drake and Iron Arm. (CROSS.)

SOME SIGNIFICANT REVIVALS OF OLD PLAYS DURING THIS PERIOD.

1789, Oct.   31. *Oronooko.* (Not acted in five years.)
1795, Oct.   21. *Venice Preserved.*
                  "After the third night this play was obliged to be laid aside on account of some of the political passages. When Pierre said: 'Cursed be your Senate, cursed your Constitution!' he was rapturously applauded."
                  It appears from Genest that this play was not performed again for a number of years. But after 1800 it appears as frequently as ever.

1809, Feb. 1. *Cato.* (Not acted in twenty years.)
1809, March 18. *Alexander the Great.* (Not acted in twenty years.)
1809, Dec. 27. *Tamerlaine.*

BIBLIOGRAPHY

NOTE

The following lists are in no way intended to present a complete bibliography of the subject, although they indicate the principal sources from which such a bibliography might be obtained. They are intended merely to indicate the principal works used in the preparation of this study, and to offer a classified bibliography of the works generally available on the subject under consideration.

SOURCES FOR LISTS OF NOVELS[1]

E. A. BAKER.
   Descriptive Guide to the Best Fiction. (1903.)
ZELLA A. DIXON.
   Comprehensive Index to Universal Prose Fiction.
JOHN COLLINS DUNLOP.
   History of Prose Fiction.
EUSÈBE GÉRAULT DE SAINT-FARGEAU.
   Revue des Romans. (Paris, 1839.)
A. L. GOODRICH.
   Prose Fiction. A Bibliography.

Catalogues of the following libraries:
   Harvard University Library.
   Radcliffe Library.
   Boston Public Library.
   Boston Athenaeum.

---

[1] I wish to acknowledge an especial indebtedness to a manuscript card list of prose fiction by Professor C. N. Greenough, which formed the basis for my working list of Revolutionary fiction.

Columbia University Library.
Hammond Collection of Old Novels in the *New York Society Library.*
Library of the University of Chicago.
British Museum Catalogue.
Yale University Library.
Library of Congress, Washington, D. C.

BIBLIOGRAPHY TO CHAPTER I

SECTION I.
General References:
    CHARLES CESTRE.
        John Thelwall, a Pioneer of Democracy. (1906.)
    JOHN RICHARD GREEN.
        Short History of the English People.
    WILLIAM THOMAS LAPRADE.
        England and the French Revolution, 1789–1797.
        (In Johns Hopkins University Pamphlets, 1909.)
    FREDERIC AUSTIN OGG.
        Social Progress in Contemporary Europe. (1912.)
    J. H. ROSE.
        The Revolutionary and Napoleonic Era. (1895.)
    H. MORSE STEPHENS.
        European History from 1789 to 1815. (1893.)
    H. D. TRAIL.
        Social England. (1899.)

On Industrial History:
    W. CUNNINGHAM.
        Outlines of English Industrial History. (1895.)
    H. DE B. GIBBINS.
        Industrial History of England. (1908.)
    G. T. WARNER.
        Landmarks in English Industrial History. (1899.)
    H. T. WOOD.
        Industrial England in the Middle of the Eighteenth Century. (1910.)

On the Revolution in France:
  F. M. ANDERSON.
    The Constitutions and Other Documents of the French Revolution. (1904.)
  ERNEST BELFORT BAX.
    The Last Epoch of the French Revolution. Being a History of Gracchus Babeuf and the Conspiracy of the Equals. (1911.)
  CHARLES CHASSIN.
    Les Élections et les Cahiers de Paris en 1789. (In Translations and Reprints.)
    Cahier of the Nobility, Baillage of Blois.
    Cahier of the Clergy, Baillage of Blois.
    Cahier of the Third Estate, Baillage of Versailles.
  P. A. KROPOTKIN.
    The Great French Revolution, 1789–1793. (Translation by F. F. Dryhurst, 1909.)
  SHAILER MATHEWS.
    The French Revolution. A Sketch. (1906.)
  H. MORSE STEPHENS.
    History of the French Revolution. (1902.)
  ARTHUR GUY TERRY.
    The Spirit of Propaganda in the French Revolution, 1789–1793. (Abstract of a Ph.D. thesis presented at the University of Pennsylvania in 1906.)

SECTION 2.

Background of Ideas:
    A Comparative Display of the Different Opinions of the Most Distinguished British Writers on the Subject of the French Revolution. (1793.)
  JAMES BONAR.
    Philosophy and Political Economy. (1903.)
  EDMUND BURKE.
    Complete Works.
  WILLIAM ARCHIBALD DUNNING.
    A History of Political Theories from Luther to Montesquieu. (1905.)
  ROBERT FLINT.
    A History of the Philosophy of History. (1843.)

WILLIAM HAZLITT.
    Memoirs of Thomas Holcroft. (1816.)
ARTHUR CUSHMAN M'GIFFERT.
    Protestant Thought Before Kant. (1911.)
JOHN MORLEY.
    Rousseau. (1891.)
    Burke. (In the English Men of Letters series.)
J. H. OVERTON.
    The Evangelical Revival in the Eighteenth Century.
BENJAMIN RAND.
    Classical Moralists. (1909.)
    Modern Classical Philosophers. (1908.)
JEAN JACQUES ROUSSEAU.
    Complete Works.
LESLIE STEPHEN.
    A History of English Thought in the Eighteenth Century. (1878.)

THOMAS HOLCROFT

Works of Holcroft.[1]

Novels:
    1780. *Alwyn;* or, *The Gentleman Comedian.*
    1792. *Anna St. Ives.*
    1794. (Latter part in 1797), *Hugh Trevor.*
    1805. *Memoirs of Brian Perdue.*

Some other works, mentioned in this discussion:
    1795. *A Narrative of Facts Relating to a Prosecution for High Treason: Including an Address to the Jury which the Court Refused to Hear.*
    1795. *A Letter to the Right Hon. William Wyndham on the Intemperance and Dangerous Tendency of his Public Conduct.*
    1804. *Travels from Hamburg, through Westphalia, Holland, and the Netherlands, to Paris.*

[1] The list of Holcroft's writings is too long to give in complete form.

1805–1806. *The Theatrical Recorder.*
1810. *Memoirs of Thomas Holcroft written by himself and Continued to the Time of his Death by William Hazlitt.*

Works on Holcroft.
"A friend of a Manufacturer."
A Letter, not in Answer to, but Induced by a Late Publication of Thomas Holcroft, on the Subject of Political Intemperance, Endeavouring to Illustrate its Dangerous Effects on the Commercial Part of the Kingdom; and the Material Difference Between Theory and Practise. Addressed to Every Workman in England and Every Man who Keeps One. (1795.)
C. KEGAN PAUL.
William Godwin, His Friends and Contemporaries.
LETTERS OF CHARLES LAMB.
(*Ed. A. Aenger*, 1888.)
Miss MITFORD.
Recollections of a Literary Life. (1852.)
GENEST.
Account of the English Stage.
(ANON.)
The Georgian Era. (1834.)
Article on Holcroft in the Dict. Nat. Biog.

WILLIAM GODWIN

Works considered in this discussion:
1793. *Political Justice.*
1794. *Caleb Williams,* or *Things As They Are.*
1799. *St. Leon.*
1805. *Fleetwood,* or, *The New Man of Feeling.*
1817. *Mandeville.*
1830. *Cloudesley.*
1833. *Deloraine.*

Works of Reference:
William Godwin, His Friends and Contemporaries. C. KEGAN PAUL. (Pub. London, 1876.)

William Godwin's Romance. Inaugural Dissertation zur Erlangung der Doktorwurde, Leizig, 1906. JOHANNES MEYER.
On the English Novel. WILLIAM HAZLITT.
William Godwin. (In *Biographical and Historical Essays.*) THOMAS DE QUINCEY.
William Godwin's Novels. (In *Studies of a Biographer.*) LESLIE STEPHEN.
On St. Leon and Mandeville. PERCY BYSSHE SHELLEY.

SHELLEY

Complete Works of Shelley. Edited by BUXTON FORMAN, London, 1880.
List of Shelley's works giving his political opinions.

Poems (including prefaces):
    Queen Mab.
    The Revolt of Islam.
    Prometheus Unbound.
    Masque of Anarchy.
    Swellfoot the Tyrant.
    Ode to the Assertors of Liberty, and other short poems.

Prose Works:
    An Address to the Irish People. (1812.)
    Proposals for an Association. (1812.)
    Declaration of Rights. (1812.)
    A Letter to Lord Ellenborough. (1812.)
    An Address to the People on the Death of the Princess Charlotte. (1817.)
    A Proposal for Putting Reform to the Vote. (1817.)
    A System of Government by Juries.
    Fragment on Reform.

Works on Shelley:
    EDWARD JOHN TRELAWNEY.
        Records of Shelley, Byron, and the Author. (1887.)
    EDWARD DOWDEN.
        The Life of Percy Bysshe Shelley. (1886.)
    ALBERT ELMER HANCOCK.
        English Poets and the French Revolution. (1899.)

ROBERT BAGE

Dictionary of National Biography.
Prof. WALTER RALEIGH, *The English Novel.*
Prof. WILBUR L. CROSS, *Development of the English Novel.*
CHARLES KEGAN PAUL, *William Godwin, His Friends and Contemporaries.* (1876.)
Sir WALTER SCOTT, *Life of Bage,* prefaced to *Ballantyne's Novelists Library.*
HUTTON. *History of Derby.*

Robert Bage's Works:
    Mount Henneth. (1781.)
    Barham Downs. (1784.)
    The Fair Syrian. (1787.)
    James Wallace. (1788.)
    Man As He Is. (1792.)
    Man As He Is Not. (1796.)

MRS. INCHBALD

Mrs. Inchbald's novels:
    A Simple Story.
    Nature and Art.
    (Edited 1880, with prefatory memoir by WILLIAM BELL SCOTT.)
JAMES BOADEN.
    Memoirs of Mrs. Inchbald. (1833.)
CECILIA LUCY BRIGHTWELL.
    Memoirs of the Life of Amelia Opie. (1843.)
ANNE KATHERINE ELWOOD.
    Memoirs of the Literary Ladies of England. (1843.)
FRANCES ANNE KEMBLE.
    Record of a Girlhood. (1878.)
GENEST.
    Account of the English Stage from 1660 to 1830.
CLARA TOBLER.
    Mrs. Elizabeth Inchbald, eine Vergessene Englische Buhnendichterin und Romanschriftstellerin. Berlin, 1910. (Gives exhaustive bibliography.)

Accounts of Mrs. Inchbald in the *Dictionary of National Biography, Chambers's Encyclopedia,* and Walter Raleigh, *The English Novel.*

MRS. OPIE

Novels by Amelia Opie:
- *The Father and Daughter.* (1801.)
- *Simple Tales.* (1806.)
- *Temper.* (1812.)
- *Tales of Real Life.* (1813.)
- *Valentine's Eve.* (1816.)
- *New Tales.* (1818.)
- *Tales of the Heart.* (1820.)
- *Madeline.* (1822.)
- *Illustrations of Lying.* (1845.)

Works of Reference:
CECILIA LUCY BRIGHTWELL.
  Memorials of the Life of Amelia Opie. (1854.)
Lady A. I. T. RITCHIE (Miss THACKERAY).
  Book of Sibyls. (1883.)
Mrs. JOHN TAYLOR.
  Account of Mrs. Opie, in *The Cabinet.* (1807.)
Accounts of Mrs. Opie, in the *Dictionary of National Biography, Chambers's Encyclopedia,* and Raleigh, *The English Novel.*

CHARLOTTE SMITH

Charlotte Smith's Novels:
- *Emmeline,* or, *The Orphan of the Castle.* (1788.)
- *Celestine.* (1792.)
- *Desmond.* (1792.)
- *The Old Manor House.* (1793.)
- *Ethelinde,* or, *The Recluse of the Lake.* (1789.)
- *The Banished Man.* (1794.)
- *Montalbert.* (1795.)
- *Marchmont.* (1795.)
- *The Young Philosopher, Nature his Law and God His Guide.* (1798.)
- *The Solitary Wanderer.* (1799.)

Bibliography

Reference Works:
  Anna Katherine Elwood.
    Memoirs of the Literary Ladies of England. (1843.)
  Sir Egerton Brydges.
    Censuria Literaria. (1815.)
  Sir Walter Scott.
    Biography of Charlotte Smith. (In his *Miscellaneous Prose Works*, vol. i.)

LADY CAROLINE LAMB

Novels by Lady Caroline Lamb:
  Glenarvon. (1816.)
  Graham Hamilton. (1822.)
  Ada Reis. (1823.)

Reference Works:
  Mrs. K. B. Thompson.
    Queens of Society.
  Anon.
    Biographical Sketch, in *New Monthly Magazine*, July, 1819.
  Accounts in *Chambers's Encyclopedia*, and the *Dictionary of National Biography*.

MARY WOLLSTONECRAFT

William Godwin.
  Memoirs of the Author of "A Vindication of the Rights of Woman." (1798.)
  A Defence of the Character and Conduct of the Late Mary Wollstonecraft Godwin, in a Series of Letters to a Lady. (1803.)
Knowles.
  Life of Fuseli.
Anna Katherine Elwood.
  Memoirs of the Literary Ladies in England from the Commencement of the Last Century. (1843.)

CHARLES KEGAN PAUL.
> *William Godwin, His Friends and Contemporaries.* (1876.)
> *Mary Wollstonecraft: A Prefatory Memoir.* (1879.)

CHARLES MORICE.
> *Le Féminisme au XVIIIme Siècle.* (Grand Revue. Paris, 1899.)

EMMA RAUSCHENBUSCH CLOUGH.
> *Mary Wollstonecraft and the Rights of Woman.*

G. R. STIRLING TAYLOR.
> *Mary Wollstonecraft: A Study in Economics and Romance.* (1911.)
> Articles on Mary Wollstonecraft in the *Dictionary of National Biography* and in *Chambers's Encyclopedia of English Literature*.

Works of Mary Wollstonecraft:
> *Thoughts on the Education of Daughters. With Reflections on Female Conduct. Added, Fénelon, Archbishop of Cambrai's "Instructions to Governesses and an Address to Mothers."* (1787.)
> *Original Stories from Real Life, with Considerations Calculated to Regulate the Affections.* (1788, 1791, and third edition illustrated by BLAKE, 1796.)
> *Mary, A Fiction.* (1790.)
> Translation of Salzmann's *Elementarbuch*, illustrated by BLAKE. (1790.)
> *A Vindication of the Rights of Men, in a Letter to the Right Honourable Edmund Burke.* (1790.)
> *A Vindication of the Rights of Woman.* (1792.)
> *A Historical and Moral View of the Origin and Progress of the French Revolution, and the Effect it has Produced in Europe.* (1794.)
> *Letters Written in Norway, Sweden, and Denmark.* (1796.)
> *Posthumous Works.* (1798.)
> > CONTENTS:
> > *Maria*, or, *The Wrongs of Woman.*
> > *First Book of a Series of Lessons for Children.*
> > *Letters on the French Nation.*
> > *Letters on the Management of Infants.*
> > *Letters to Mr. Johnson.*

The Cave of Fancy: A Tale.
On Poetry and our Relish for the Beauties of Nature.
Hints, chiefly Designed to have been Incorporated in the Second Part of "A Vindication of the Rights of Woman."
Letters to Gilbert Imlay. (1879.)

BIBLIOGRAPHY TO CHAPTER IX

Section 1. Poetry.

Charles Cestre.
   La Révolution Française et les Poètes Anglais, 1789–1809. (Paris, 1906.)

Edward Dowden.
   Studies in Literature, 1789–1877. (Ninth ed., 1906.)
   The French Revolution and English Literature. (N. Y., 1897.)

Albert Elmer Hancock.
   The French Revolution and the English Poets. (N. Y., 1899.)

Section 2. The Drama.

Genest.
   The English Stage from 1660 to 1830. (Volumes 6, 7, and 9.)

William Hazlitt.
   Memoirs of the Late Thomas Holcroft. (1816.)

Thomas Holcroft.
   The Theatrical Recorder. (1805–1806.)

INDEX

	PAGES
Adelaide de Narbonne.	184
Amicable Quixote.	183
Analytical Review.	238
Anti-Jacobin.	280
Asmodeus.	185

Astell, Mary:
    Serious Proposal. 233

Bage, Robert. . . . . v, 161–180, 296, 299, 302
    Barham Downs. 165
    Fair Syrian. . . . . 165 n.
    Hermsprong, or Man As He Is Not. 168–172, 202
    James Wallace. 165
    Man As He Is. . . . . 167 f.
Baxter. 52
Blake. 59, 271–274
Blue Stocking Hall. 265–269
Brown, Charles Brocken. 108, 185
    Arthur Mervin. 185
Bulwer:
    Strange Story. 100
    Zanoni. 100
Bunyan. 52, 87
Burke. 27, 43, 44, 157, 187
    Reflections on the Revolution in France. 28, 44, 245–246
Burns. 272
Byron. 123, 227–230, 268, 281, 291

Chapone, Hester. 235
Clarke. 182
Coleridge. 58, 88, 165, 276–280

334 Index

	PAGE
Colman, the Younger	94
Iron Chest	94, 288
Condorcet	236, 237
Cowper	271–272
Crabbe	271
Craftsman's Magazine	233, 237
Critical Review	238
Cypher	156
Declaration of Rights	17, 18
Defoe	23
Deism	40, 41, 89, 196
De Quincey	98
Diderot	145, 146
Edward and Sophia	156
Encyclopaedists	30, 40
Fair Methodist	154
Fawcett, Joseph	88, 93
Fenwick, Eliza	225
Secrecy	225
Fordyce	235, 244
Fox, Charles James	73 n., 88, 181, 204
Fuseli	244, 247
Gentleman's Magazine	233, 234
Gifford	280

Godwin, William, 43, 49, 50, 58, 59, 68, 86–119, 122, 125, 137, 140, 177, 180, 185–186, 195–198, 207, 210, 223, 227, 230, 244, 273, 287, 294, 298, 302,

Antonio	287

Caleb Williams, 82, 92–99, 103, 104, 110, 113, 116, 202, 223, 288

Cloudesley	110
Deloraine	112–113, 122, 125, 133
Faulkner	287
Fleetwood	103
Life of Mary Wollstonecraft	140, 145
Political Justice	v, 43, 84, 89, 90, 91, 114, 116, 119
St. Leon	99–103, 122, 125, 258

Index

Gregory, Dr.:
   Legacy to his Daughters............................ 235

Hanaway, Mary....................................... 222
   Elinor, or The World As It Is....................... 222
Hardy, Thomas.............................. 55, 57, 203
Hayes, Mary... 223
   Memoirs of Emma Courtney....................... 223
Hazlitt....................................... 50, 60, 69, 98
   Memoirs of Holcroft....................... 45 ff., 54, 71
Helvetius... 175
Henrietta, Princess Royal of England.................. 189
Hobbes...................................... 34, 35, 146
Holbach.. 175, 224
Holcroft, v, 29, 49–85, 88–91, 102, 177, 194, 195, 197, 224, 225,
   244, 273, 285–287, 293, 297, 301
   Alwyn... 60
   Anna St. Ives................. 49, 59, 61–70, 84, 137, 225
   Dramas..................................... 285–287
   Hugh Trevor................... 58, 59, 70–81, 139, 202
   Memoirs of Brian Perdue....................... 82–84
Howard... 204, 289
Hume.................... 37, 38, 137, 146, 148, 155, 156, 185
Hunt, Leigh..................................... 271, 282
Hutton.................................... 161, 163, 166

I'll Consider of It.................................... 157
Illuminati...................................... 151, 186
Imlay... 248
Inchbald.................... 98, 191–202, 257, 288, 299, 303
   A Simple Story............................. 198–199
   Dramas.. 288 f.
   Nature and Art............................. 199–202
Interesting Memoirs of Marie Antoinette.................. 188
Itanoko... 188

Johnson, Joseph....................... 203, 243, 244, 273

Kramer:
   Hermon of Unna................................ 183

Index

	PAGE
Lamb, Lady Caroline	227–230
Ada Reis	230
Glenarvon	227–228
Landor	271
Last Man	156
Lawrence, James:	
Empire of the Nairs	259
Levellers	33, 36, 42
Locke	36, 41, 43, 45, 137
Lucas	300, 303
Infernal Quixote	73, 144–154
Mackenzie:	
Slavery, or The Times	187
Magic of Wealth	157
Malthus	44
Man in the Moon	181, 182
Man Superior to Woman	234
Marx	8
Mathews:	
What Has Been	225
Memoirs of a Female Philosopher	155
Memoirs of a Old Wig	155
Methodism	39, 40, 71, 73, 87 n., 149, 149, 154, 155, 186, 205
Negro Equalled by Few Europeans	188
Opie, Mrs. Amelia Alderson,	195, 196, 203–213, 222, 299
Adelina Mowbray	208–210, 285
Valentine's Eve	210–212
Oronooko	169, 186, 187
Paine	43, 59, 89, 132, 136, 137, 180, 224, 244, 273
Peacock	189
Plumptre	204, 226
Price	43, 182, 244
Priestley	43, 90, 155
Purity of Heart, or Woman As She Should Be	229
Quakers	151, 167, 172 n., 204, 205, 206

Index 337

Robert and Adela............................260–265
Rousseau, 18, 30, 40, 41, 84, 104, 117, 137, 148, 180, 186, 217, 224, 230, 236, 262, 281

Scott, Sir Walter................161, 172, 175, 176, 179, 204
Shaftesbury................................... 146
Shelley, Mary Wollstonecraft....................227, 251
Shelley, Percy Bysshe, 11, 12, 91, 120–133, 134, 177, 227, 294, 298, 302
    Assassins................................... 124
    Declaration of Rights.........................128–129
    Marlow Pamphlets...........................130–131
    St. Irvyne........................100, 121, 122, 125
    Zastrozzi...................................121, 125
Sheridan.......................................88, 290
Smith, Charlotte Turner.........................213–222
Society for Constitutional Information........28, 54, 55, 89, 147
Sophia, a Gentlewoman............................ 234
Southey..............................59, 204, 279–280
Spirit of the Book................................ 189
St. Simon...................................... 206
Système de la Nature...........................89, 163

Took, Horne................................55, 57, 203

Voltaire........................137, 145, 146, 169, 217

Walker, George...............................300, 303
    The Vagabond..............................135–144
West:
    Advantages of Education....................... 259
Wollaston..................................... 182
Wollstonecraft, Mary, 90, 100, 105, 114, 140, 141, 142, 145, 162, 172, 186, 197, 208–210, 224–227, 231–258, 264, 273, 297, 303
    Vindication of the Rights of Women, 145, 183, 237–239, 260, 262, 267, 268
    Maria, or the Wrongs of Women.......202, 220, 240, 254–258
    Cave of Fancy..............................251–254
    Mary, A Fiction............................251–253
Wordsworth..................59, 104, 204, 271, 274–276